TOBACCO WIFE

TOBACCO WIFE

Ghana to Coromandel India

A rural life - 1960 to 1986

Natalie Wheatley

First published/designed by Natalie Wheatley, 2008

ISBN 978-0-9544680-1-9

1st and 2nd printing 2003 and 2008 in Great Britain by
The Lavenham Press Limited, CO10 9RN

3rd printing 2012 by
MPG Biddles Limited, King's Lynn, Norfolk PE30 4LS

By the same author

The Swaffs from the Shires, published by Natalie Wheatley 2003
No Bananas 2011
Cadbury-Brown – The Family behind the Modernist Architect 2011

Author's summary
This is my story, a real story about real people. No attempt has been made to change names or hide identities. Offence has not been intended but sincere apologies are offered if offence has occurred. There are bound to be inaccuracies, misquotes and anomalies and for these I am sorry. At times the unreliability of the spoken word is proved when sifting through memories.

Photos
Front cover: Hassan 1967 – The Wheatley children with their ayah, Sarpinamma
Back cover: Huhunya, Ghana1960 - Mike Wheatley with PTC field staff

This is a book for Mike and our children, Susina, Simon, Andrea and David, their wives and husbands and our grandchildren, Laurence, Nicholas, William, Jackson, Fay and Tom. Each one is precious and I thank them all for their love and support.

Acknowledgements

Rebecca for sending me a card in 2006, *Time & Tide Waiteth for No Man,* and for constantly egging me on.

Andrea for her sensible advice and total support.

Susina for her enthusiasm, an expatriate wife of the 21st century - and Amy for quiet encouragement.

My boys - Simon for drumming up catchy titles, David for reading chapters, and Laurence – this is your own *Memoir of a Granny*.

Dr Rosie Llewellyn-Jones for her careful reading of the final draft followed by wise and professional suggestions.

Mike for re-living his career and painstakingly checking through the manuscript.

Vanessa Wiseman for her spirited and encouraging emails winging their way from Venice.

Contents

Introduction – London and America

“Ah Natalie! Sir Hugh Casson is coming this morning," my architect employer, Jim Cadbury-Brown, was in his usual hurry and never listened, "Just pirouette on your navel. Oh, and make some coffee." He was gone leaving me speechless and horrified at such an unbecoming suggestion. As a plump teenager fresh from the provinces, coffee was easy but definitely no pirouetting.

Architects were a new breed to me, but an interest in late 1950s modernism made me realise that flat roofs and clean lines were very different from my one chimney, four windows doll's house. It was a small office with three architectural assistants in the airy design room and me, the secretary, in a tiny book lined room at the rear with an ancient gas fire to keep me cosy. Everybody warmed their bottoms on my fire and visitors were numerous. Eager to learn, the job was more exciting than previous experiences of retailing in Harrods and deadly filing at Regent Oil. A year in London had prepared me for new challenges and more money. There was a chaotic filing system but, with a talent for order and chronology, it was fairly easy to sort out. The boys in the office were impressed and quickly invented affectionate and outlandish nicknames for me; *Colander Lugs* was dreamed up following a bad bout of perforated eardrums.

We were all busy with the administration of the design of the new Royal College of Art, next to the Albert Hall. This was just one of the exciting projects that came up the steep stairway of the Clarges Street office.

Also coming up the stairs were Jim's nephews, the identical Wheatley twins. They joined British American Tobacco Company as pupils in the early 50s. Before that they did their National Service in Nyasaland with the Kings African Rifles, coinciding with the Mau Mau rebellion. On demob they sailed home and, as ensigns, carried the rain sodden colours of the KAR at the Queen’s Coronation in June 1953. They worked on the leaf-growing side of BAT in Africa, Gerald in the east and Michael in the west.

At 18 I was an easy catch, sitting primly behind a big wooden desk with a clickety clack Olympia typewriter. There was a black Bakelite telephone (Mayfair 6296) attached to a two line wooden boxed exchange with a handle. Enamel eyelids blinked as a call came through and stayed down when the line was engaged. Gerald returned from Uganda and took me out for dinner with friends. A year later his lookalike, Michael, on leave from Ghana, came into my office with his little black book. He seemed the same as Gerald, but was different with an obvious sincerity, a lovely smile, an impish attitude, very blue eyes, blonde wavy hair and a golden tan. He looked like a stocky rugby player, and he was.

"Can you phone some of these girls please?" he handed me his little black book and sat smoking on the big leather chair, "They're mostly nurses," he added. His face became disappointed as no one, it seemed, was free that evening and he was looking embarrassed. In desperation he said, "Well, will you come out then?"

"Err," I was blushing and mumbly at such a sudden invitation; he didn't know me at all.

"We'll go for dinner," he was smiling, "And we can take a spin to Heathrow for a drink."

"Heathrow!" It had only just opened.

"Thank you," it was an awkward moment and immediately was the problem of what to wear.

Promising to collect me at 7-30 he smiled and left the room. Work was finished for the day and it was time to catch the tube and go home to my digs in Earls Court.

Michael Wheatley with his King's African Rifles Askari

Home was Clydesdale, in Nevern Place, an unusual mixed hostel where residents were entrusted with a front door key and no curfew hours. There was a permanent smell of stewing cabbage, loud cockney voices from the kitchen beneath stairs, stiff lino, an unfriendly and cold sitting room and a cavernous basement laundry. Mrs Hart, the daily from the North End Road, rattled around with a bucket and a tin of Harpic, her hair neatly bundled into a Mrs Mop turban. Four large houses mingled into one, fronted by pillared porticoes, high steps, and bay windows. They were managed by a porky, white overalled matriarch called Ma Williams and her creepy, cadaverous husband, Pa. To her favoured male guests she was *a mother indeed* but to the girls she was a doubting tyrant.

"Those girls! Those girls!" she cried up the stairways "Snoggling on the beds again, can't trust them I can't."

Ma hailed from the slag heaps of the Welsh valleys and, a few years earlier, wisely purchased the houses from a Mrs Keeble who was more classy but less firm, interviewing potential tenants from her bed wearing a hat. Some of the elderly original inmates remembered her, she was Oscar Wilde in manner and enquired, "Do you play chess or bridge, perhaps sing a little?" Ma was less interested in such refinements, apart from opera which was her love, but as keen as mustard on morals. No racist she, the incumbents included Persians, Sinhalese, South Africans, Norwegians, Swiss, South Americans; youngsters from all over the globe sheltered under her roof.

This was my home for two years and a place to make long lasting friends. Clothes were washed in the cellar in huge butler sinks, dried on rope and pulley racks and pressed using hissing gas irons. Damp and gloomy it was often the only place to find someone to talk to, and many a tryst was made over the turn of a collar or the crease of tomorrow's trousers.

Clydesdale produced a handful of talented people; John Stobart, a millionaire British marine artist domiciled in Boston, still lusts after Adrienne Gilmour, music student, last seen in Heals with a plump Jew buying a double bed. Glyn Jones sang with the D'Oyley Carte Opera Company, Peter and Don Friston from a railway carriage in Norfolk braved the smog and trained at the London School of Printing, and Jens Jahnke was sent by his father from Hamburg to learn English and the intricacies of freight forwarding. Sal from South Africa met Narve from Oslo and lived happily ever after, Dick Woods trapped in a world of solicitors broke free and was ordained, and little Johnny from Wales believed he was Frank Sinatra and owned every record the crooner made. Dark eyed Sonia, a doctor from Nicaragua, struggled with language and Nydia, her quiet sister, married blonde, pink and very English Peter, while Corsican Rosaly sunned herself on the front steps and was pronounced *trollop* by moral Ma.

In the late 50s Earls Court was incredibly lively and known as Kangaroo Valley. Many Australians disembarked at Northolt and made a beeline to the Earls Court Road. The hungry ate in the Express Dairy cafeteria, the thirsty drank in the Tavern, and everyone rushed off to work from the tube station with its creaking lifts monotonously intoning *Mind the doors please.* A delicatessen opened up near Golly's Garage and was soon swamped with customers wanting pasta, cheesecake and large fat Greek olives. In the Overseas Club you could drink a pint of Fosters and jive on Wednesday nights to mad jazz bands. Italians arrived in black and white tweed coats singing *Volare* and Earls Court became cosmopolitan, coffee bars and spaghetti houses overtaking fish and chips. It was a fun place and we were all completely broke.

1958 Clydesdale party - Natalie left middle with necklace

Ma Williams was well impressed with my freshly brushed, dinner jacketed blonde young man at her front door. He took her breath away. She stomped heavily half way up the stairs in her white overall and sensible black shoes.

"Miss Swaffield! Miss Swaffield!" she puffed and then, "Room Nine," she yelled in her sharp Welsh accent. "There's a *gentleman* for you," and went to welcome him through the big front door, "Come in Sir, she won't be a moment." There was enough time to zip my dress and dab perfume behind my ears before descending the stairs with a bit of grace.

First we sped up the A4 in his clanging Maigret Citroën and sipped Martinis at the glitzy stainless steel airport, then raced into the city for dinner at the Savoy Hotel. The doorman was a giant, the swinging doors all gold and glass, and the carpets buried my high heels. The Ladies Powder Room was enough for me, with its scented soaps, Elizabeth Arden hand cream, fluffy towels and eau de cologne. Our table was next to that of Lord Louis Mountbatten, the great-grandson of Queen Victoria and the last Viceroy of India until Independence in 1947. My habit of staring was overwhelmingly out of control, whilst Michael chattered away and ordered wine. It was difficult to speak and the menu, all in French, was large and shiny, choosing food was a guessing game. There was a cabaret and pretty dancing girls plus Bob Monkhouse, the comedian. We ended up, late into the night, drinking whisky with Baron Nugent in the Secretary's office of the Naval and Military Club in Piccadilly. We both had fun and it turned my head towards a different life.

Next day, Michael left for Ghana imploring me to write. Apart from receiving one postcard there was no further word from him. Our post was put in a rack in the hall but nothing more arrived from Ghana. He was one person whose company was enjoyable, different from the Earls Court boys who hailed from all corners of the globe. My job at Jim's was interesting, we were a happy office, and lounged on the grass in Green Park eating cheese sandwiches during the summer months. Itchy feet encouraged my investigations into travelling to America, a good stepping stone to start navigating the globe. Through various contacts, and an interview at the Westbury Hotel, an au pair job was secured in New Jersey with a family called Cumberland. Jim and the boys were quite shocked when they opened my notice.

"But you can't go," said Jim, "We need you here." The realisation of any kind of importance within the office had never really entered my head. The two Johns and Steve were equally upset, "We can't manage without old Colander Lugs," one said with mock tears.

On my last day at Jim's office, and 18 months after Michael returned to Ghana, a telegram informed us that he was due for leave, arriving next day. It was disturbing news bringing back memories of a short time together. The only thing to do was leave a brief note telling of my American plans.

Straight off the 'plane he phoned, "Are you really going?"

"Yes, I've booked my passage and depart at the end of December, but I'll go home to Cardiff beforehand. I'm sailing on the Queen Elizabeth."

"Oh! I'd better work fast then," he sounded anxious.

We met outside Gloucester Road tube station. He was late, but still blonde, bronzed and full of smiles. We enjoyed another eventful evening including dinner at Hatchetts in Piccadilly.

Jooste une mineet Monsieur, the immaculate French waiter whispered. He tiptoed off to find a table, *Venez thees way Monsieur, Mademoiselle,* and discreetly ushered us to the shadowy rear of the restaurant. Michael was wearing a very hairy suit instead of the *de rigeur* dinner jacket. How we then got into a smart nightclub in Regent Street in such garb was quite amazing.

"Please do go in Sir," waved the doorman with a flourish as the appropriate membership card was flashed before his eyes. This was a bit different from Humphrey Lyttleton's Jazz Club, or an espresso at the Wayang on the Earl's Court Road. There was an exotic floorshow, all Busby Barclay, Fred Astaire and bubbling champagne. Then we went to a Soho club where, very late, a pretend Frank Sinatra sang *Baubles, Bangles and Beads*. We danced, tripping over each other's feet, and the song has remained as a special memory to us both.

It began as a bit of a lark, but we realised there was something more; we got on well and never stopped talking. Bursting with excitement, three days later we became engaged.

"We'll go to Asprey's," he said confidently.

"Asprey's?" The vision of the glittering Bond Street jewellers flashed into my head, it was a place to linger in a lunch hour clutching a paper bag containing a white bread tomato sandwich.

A bright young man with Brylceemed hair ushered us in, everything happened so fast, and there wasn't a single piece of jewellery with a price tag on it.

"What about this Madam?" asked a smooth assistant, offering a velvet pad on which was a single stone diamond ring. It was beautiful and looked bigger than my mother's engagement ring but, not having anticipated marriage, engagement rings were not on my shopping list, it was confusing and worrying to have to choose in a hurry.

Waving at a selection I said, "Those are pretty," and knocked the tray of loose diamonds onto the floor. Staff crawled round the carpet prodding precious gems onto their fingertips.

"Don't worry about the tweezers," they hissed frantically, "Just pick them up!"

We spent a few days in London and went to restaurants and I had my hair done every day. My best outfit was a black bouclé dress with three quarter sleeves, set off by turquoise shoes, turquoise gloves and turquoise plastic earrings. My eyes were lined with deep black pencil, and lots of mascara. Ponds lipstick and nylons with seams completed the outfit. In my bag was a packet of Guards cigarettes packed elegantly in a white, red and black box, and a Ronson lighter engraved with my initials.

We drove to Suffolk to visit his eccentric relations, all dog hair and pigs, and then Michael came to Cardiff to meet my family. My mother, already half hooked because of my engagement to the famous Cadbury-Brown nephew, had to have her say, "Will you be able to keep Natalie in the way to which she is accustomed?"

Michael looked at the china ducks flying up the wall and replied graciously, "I hope I can do better than that."

My father was embarrassed at my mother's invasiveness, "Dorritt," he said quietly to shut her up, he was brought up to accept family friends without question. He hovered around with sherry and Dubonnet and wished it wasn't all happening. He was not ready to lose me. But she didn't shut up and went on about *job, commitment, aspiration and plans, family background* and all that.

On 30th December 1959 it was time to board the Queen Elizabeth sailing to New York. Michael ordered a beautiful bouquet of red roses for my cabin and was soon a distant figure waving on the quay. He spent the rest of his leave skiing in Switzerland and visiting his younger brother, Patrick, in Canada. Before we parted, we talked a lot and planned to marry in Ghana the following year. Our favourite song should have been *Strangers in the Night,* as we hardly knew each other. My whole life turned over in about two weeks. A proposed marriage, a new life in Africa and sailing over the Atlantic to a new job, with the prospect of giving in notice on the first day. Somehow everything sorted itself out and I grew up and older very quickly.

Correspondence bonded us together as we shared ideas, thoughts and dreams. Eight months were spent in New Jersey and it was hard work looking after four children. Before I left I travelled for three weeks on Greyhound buses stopping overnight here and there. I went to New Orleans, Mexico, the Grand Canyon and California, returning across the breadbasket of America to St Louis. Speaking with a thick mid-western accent, and safely back in New York, it was time to board a Comet back to England

At home in Cardiff and, whilst packing a few belongings to take to Ghana, the telephone rang. It was Michael, "Hello! Hello!" he shouted through the crackles, "I only booked this call yesterday, and men have already swept the lines and cut the branches off the trees between my house and the Post Office!" It was lovely to hear his familiar chuckle again, "You'll soon be with me here in Koforidua," he yelled, "I'm getting the floors polished and some new saucepans." It was hardly romantic, but desperately sweet.

It was exciting to tootle around the countryside saying goodbye to all my girl friends, most of them thought me quite mad, and some even suspected I was marrying a black man and not telling. Michael warned that the company wished to meet me before providing an air ticket. The Number Two to the Director for Africa, Mr Jenkins of BAT at Millbank, vetted me, it was scary but my American experience made me feel more confident. A secretary ushered me into the big mahogany office where Mr Jenkins was pleasant and kindly.

"You have to be adaptable, that's the main thing," he said, "It's not easy living in the African bush." He must have approved, and the approval was imperative by BAT rules. Several weeks later, my single ticket arrived.

My American employers had kindly arranged for a wedding dress of my choice to be made and, on my return home, my mother added a veil of tulle and orange blossom. On the evening of my departure she helped me put on my bridal outfit and we all cried. It was hard for my parents to have their only daughter disappear to the wilds of West Africa for her wedding, which was impossible, logistically, for them to attend.

My father was a sad figure at the airport, "If you don't like it Poppet," he said tearfully, "Come home, I'll pay the fare." My mother carried little packages of special silver wedding gifts, and we stopped on the way to buy two pounds of Brussels sprouts, a Michael treat.

"Mind all those mosquitoes and bugs," Mummy hugged me with a watery smile, and walked away with her shoulders sagging beneath her mossy green tweed coat. Daddy just sobbed.

Chapter 1 – Ghanaian Wedding 1960

It was strange entering the imposing first class cabin of the Ghana flight, due to refuel at Barcelona and Kano. It was an anxious time, at 22, flying out to marry a man I hardly knew, and my insecurity must have been obvious, so the hostess put me next to a friendly lady who knew a lot about Accra. She chatted away about this and that, but where was she from?

Eventually I asked, "Is your husband with the Government?"

"No," she laughed quietly, "But he is with the *other* government, UAC."

"UAC?"

"United Africa Company," she said, "It's a big corporation run by Lever Brothers, they have trading posts all over the country spread far and wide. I know you'll love it in Ghana," and chattered away about parties, coffee mornings and various diplomatic social events; Michael hadn't warned me of such goings on.

Tema beach

At dawn, the BOAC plane landed in Northern Nigeria. There were glimpses of horsemen, of dusky women in indigo blue robes and endless dry desert. I drank some orange juice and tried to calm down, it was ten months since we had looked at each other's faces. Next stop was Ghana, traditionally known as the Gold Coast, but becoming accustomed to its new name since Independence in 1957. We landed at Accra, and it was very hot, Michael was smiling, waiting on the tarmac. He wore a brown linen bush jacket, shorts, white knee socks and chukka boots. His blonde hair shone in the sunlight. We were quite shy.

"Gosh, you've lost weight," he said admiringly.

"Yes," a bit coy but giggly, "Too much ice cream in America."

It was a long time since our parting on Southampton docks. The cardboard box containing my tissue-wrapped wedding gown was flung into the back of his muddy Chevrolet pick-up.

"Mind," breathlessly, "That's my wedding dress." He carefully moved it out of the way of an oily pump and sacks of fertiliser.

"Sorry," he said, "Not used to women's things." We drove past the Hotel Avenida and onto the busy streets of Accra. In the early 1960s it was a booming city with Kwame Nkrumah enthusiastically governing, and the Gold Coast overflowing with gold. Silly, but my first impression was that everyone was black. There were crowds of people mingling; they had smooth ebony skins, soft frizzy hair, and wore colourful exotic robes, headpieces, mammy cloths and sarongs.

"They look very jolly, smiley people," I shouted above the noise of the engine.

"They certainly are," he said, avoiding dilapidated lorries and beaten up taxis, "Oh and we're having lunch with Miles and Claire."

"Who are Miles and Claire?"

"The General Manager of Pioneer Tobacco Company. Nice chap, Irish, so is Claire. They said we could have our wedding reception in their garden."

Suddenly I felt nervous, patted my hair and looked for my lipstick. Spending all night on a plane undid the allure of a potential new bride, leaving me crumpled and travel worn. We drove into the lovely gardens of The Old Place, a bungalow on the outskirts of the city, surrounded by big trees.

Claire came to greet us, "You must be tired," she said kindly, "Or excited?"

"Both," I smiled, "But mostly excited." She took me to a bathroom to freshen up.

Miles was genial with a warm handshake, "Welcome to Ghana," he said, "Mike has been so anxious to see you." Michael looked embarrassed.

Soft footed Yoruba servants, wearing white skullcaps and crisp uniforms, offered cold beer or gin and tonic clinking with ice. They smiled courteously and made me feel at ease. Two men walked into the room dressed in dark tropical suits, loosening their ties. One was introduced as Mr Husbands, an American and the BAT Director for Marketing; the other was Patrick Sheehy who, years later, became Chairman of British American Tobacco Company. He was shuffling around for cigarettes and, having bought some Rothmans at Heathrow, I held out a pack.

"Would you like one of mine?" Michael drew in a sharp breath and Miles raised his eyebrows. Nothing was said, and Pat Sheehy took a cigarette.

"Thanks," he said looking at me quizzically as he lit up.

That was one of my worst *faux pas*, for Rothmans was BAT's biggest competitor. There was a lot to learn about Company policy, tobacco growing and etiquette, cooking, entertaining. It was all rather grand.

After lunch we were saying our goodbyes, "Take the girl shopping," urged Claire, "Give her a welcome present."

"Welcome present?" Michael looked a bit vague.

"Well she has flown a long way to be with you," Claire was insistent. So we went to UAC's Kingsway Stores and a string of Mikimoto pearls was purchased, as well as a set of Beethoven's Brandenburg Concertos to play on the radiogram in Koforidua. By lucky chance, we also went to the UAC main garage and picked up an *on order* brand new Opel Kapitan company car.

"I shall miss my pick-up," Michael was quite woeful, "But this one is nice for you."

Later we drove through Accra and up the Aburi escarpment, passing Achimota School, into the rainforest. The noise of cicadas, the thickness of the undergrowth, the shining dark green leaves and the height of the palms were straight out of a Stewart Granger movie. Everyone seemed to be on the bumpy, dusty, laterite road. Women in coloured cloths carried heavy head loads often with small snuffling *picans* bundled and tied to their backs. There were crowded mammy wagons lurching over the potholes. Painted messages on rusty tail gates careered round the corners, *The Lord is Coming*, *Untidy Driving Takes Lives* and *God Protect You*, all decorated with painted flowers.

By the time we reached Koforidua and the PWD bungalow of Mike's Irish friends, the Kennedys, exhaustion was overcoming me, but I perked up when Pat and Alan came hurrying on to the veranda and greeted us warmly. Alan was laughing, "Well done Mike!" he congratulated beating him on the back, eyeing the new car with a certain amount of appreciation. His VW

Beetle was parked just ahead.

Their cook, Atia, had prepared groundnut stew and fried plantains, "Wood stove smoky today," he apologised as he put the dishes on the table, "And sorry Missis, but pudding no set. No electric."

After supper it was lovely to have a bath and crawl under a mosquito net. It was my first night in Africa, pitch dark and full of creepy crawly noises but I was soon fast asleep. Early next morning a noisy turkey gobbling around the compound woke me. It was an ugly undernourished creature being chased by the small boy, Yarro. He was a gangly lad waving his arms, "Go for bush," he shouted, "You stupid bird, go for bush!"

Pat later told me the unfortunate turkey was to be our Christmas dinner, "We'll give it a large slug of gin before we wring its neck," she said matter of factly, "Makes it relax and it won't be so tough."

The Kennedys kindly hosted me for six weeks, they had a small baby called Hugh, and it was fun to look after him. Alan, who was to be our best man, was an engineer with the Public Works Department and employed in Ghana for only a short time, but he and Pat have remained firm friends. Pat was a real help with her quiet comment and advice and she eased my natural fears in this strange environment.

1959 Accra – Alan & Pat Kennedy

We were busy with our wedding plans and, not long before the big day, we visited Sogakofe for lunch. Mike was looking after this station as well as Koforidua and it was a long drive between the two tobacco areas. Whilst wandering around the compound, which was on the banks of the River Volta, I dabbled my toes on the little beach. A speedboat went roaring by, its engine throbbing through the frothy wash. Kwame, one of the dogs, went berserk with the noise and rushed round in circles trying to catch his tail. He missed time after time and finally grabbed on to my ankle and nearly tore it apart, it was spurting blood and badly bitten. The servants came quickly and wrapped me up in bits of grubby cloth. Someone muttered *rabies,* an alien word in my mental dictionary, and another whispered *bilharzia* which maybe was Twi for *bite.* Later they told me it was a nasty parasite caught through a water snail. Mike drove me 30 miles to the nearest clean hospital, and the ankle was disinfected and dressed, and I thought it was a good thing my wedding dress was floor length and not the more fashionable ballerina style.

We made more visits to Accra to firm up wedding plans and became so fraught that it was almost like planning a divorce. The weather was hot, traffic was heavy and everything was such an effort. Mike was busy and did not really have time for all these arrangements and I felt pretty useless. He was patient and did not get cross with me, more with himself. We enjoyed a good relationship and could discuss things, but there was not a lot of love floating around, it was more business is business and let's get it done. First we arranged for invitations to be printed and we checked our guest list. Names like Dick and Nini Dettingmeijer, Kwesi Mends, Sole Atchulo, Don and Pauline Paton, Kwesi Appiah, the Wrights, Cordy and Thompson, James Fraser, Emmanuel Laryea, Ray Pigg, Bugs Allison. Who were they? The envelopes were addressed and posted with a big sigh. It was stressful obtaining a licence from a disorganised Government office full of clerks slumped sweatily asleep over their desks; it all looked so ugly and alien. I was not having second thoughts but this process took all the excitement and romance away.

"Some expats get married in this office," said Michael as we left, "I must say I'm glad we are having a church wedding."

We were to be married in the Holy Trinity Cathedral and, as it was Advent, it was necessary to obtain dispensation from Bishop Roseveare. He was a pale man with thin mousy hair and looked as if he had lived in intense heat for too many years.

"Good luck to you both," he said kindly, "I'll make sure the choir has a few practices, they love weddings." We got into the car and Michael heaved a great sigh of relief, another job done.

"We need flowers," my suggestion was tentative, "A bouquet, buttonholes, a posy for the bridesmaid."

"Oh God! Flowers," said my man, "I hadn't thought of flowers." So off we rumbled down the earthy tracks to the tiny, but exotically bursting, city garden of Mrs Noah, a wrinkled lady from the Twi tribe, with round smudged spectacles held together with string. Ever since my arrival in Ghana, the delicate blossoms on the many frangipani trees had attracted me, their soft petals defying the tropical sunshine.

"I'd like yellow and white flowers, and do you have frangipani?" I asked hopefully looking around her shabby patch, longing for Constance Spry.

She licked a pencil stub and scratched her frizzy head, "You can have yellow and white frangipani Missy, you no worry. Or you can have pink and cream frangipani. I got one tree and me friend got the other." Mrs Noah also grew hibiscus, purple bougainvillea, white jasmine, African daisies, flocks of chickens and a few runny nosed grandchildren. She cheerfully filled my hands with blossom, "My flowers are *past Takoradi corned beef* Missy," she smiled toothlessly, meaning *the best* in pidgin English and referring to a particularly good shipment of Fray Bentos that, some years ago, was unloaded at the port. Mrs Noah made a good job of decorating the cathedral, carrying the theme through with yellow and white zinnias, plenty of orange and lemon aromatic marigolds, all swathed with fronds of brilliant green palm.

On the eve of our wedding I reminded Michael that we had no ring. He was dumbfounded, "I never thought of it," he said worriedly, "Come on!"

It was closing time and we rushed into a shop called Tissot and bought the only one that fitted me. It was a wide 14-carat band with bevelled edges costing £6. He dismissed the idea of having a ring of his own, I wanted to buy one but he said mannishly, "I'll get attacked in the park with a gold ring on my finger."

Miles McLean was very kind. After dinner he quietly knocked on the door and came into my bedroom, "Sorry to disturb you," he said in his soft rolling Cork accent, "I just wanted a quick word to say that Claire and I thoroughly support you and Mike, he is a good chap, but..." he paused and swallowed, and my heart lurched, "... but, if you have the slightest doubt that you may not be able to cope with the life of a leaf wife, you still have time to say no." His manner was not in the least condescending, but totally considerate of my situation.

Gulping at his kindness and smiling as reassuringly as possible, "I know what I'm doing. Really," I said, "Life here is enjoyable and interesting, I'm determined that we will make go of it."

"That's good," he said, "You'll be a fine pair." He gave me a warm hug and quietly left me to get ready for bed.

Next morning the birds woke me early. The dawn was lighting the sky, and there were muffled sounds from the quarters, soft voices and a whistling kettle. Suddenly I was terribly alone. What was I doing in this house with none of my friends and family at hand? Why was I marrying this man who was almost a stranger? Always headstrong, had I gone too far this time? Pulling myself together and gathering my thoughts and my heart, I gave myself a good talking to and something made me convinced I was doing the right thing. Nevertheless my hands knotted and my brain worked hard to keep the tears at bay; it was for me an incredibly lonely day. It was school holidays and both Miles and Claire had gone to the airport to meet their seven-year old daughter, Sherry. She would arrive exhausted, but really wanted to be our bridesmaid. We had agreed readily, and sent money to Sherry's aunt in London to purchase a yellow and white dress to match our theme, Michael made out a cheque to Harrods to pay for it.

The veranda was cool in the early morning, striped shades were erected, underneath which tables were draped with damask cloths with rows of glasses, and champagne was cooling in big buckets. One of the Pioneer Tobacco guests stalked up the steps and gave me a nod. Embarrassed in my flowery housecoat, I was not expecting anyone to turn up.

"Morning," he said gruffly. I knew he was Jack Somebody but we had not been introduced. "Ah! Brandy," he grabbed the bottle and poured a slug into a glass, "Cheers," he said and wandered off across the lawns. It was nine in the morning.

I was absolutely speechless and furious. My father had generously cashed in an insurance policy to pay for our wedding and it was *his* brandy. The well of tears nearly burst open and I bit my lips and went back into the house.

Pat promised to help me get ready and asked a friend to look after Hugh. She came elegantly dressed in slim navy blue with a big hat. A year previously she flew from Dublin to marry Alan and knew how lonely it was. She could see my unhappiness, particularly when told about the brandy. I was arranging my veil and not really able to speak.

"Dreadful man," she said protectively, "No manners, forget about him, you look beautiful," smoothing my white cotton dress. The New Jersey dressmaker had made it carefully and added a little appliqué on the bodice decorated with tiny pearls. It was simple and cool with an oval neckline and short sleeves, softened by the veil my mother bought for me, as well as the special Mikimoto necklace. The frangipani bouquet was delivered by a little girl, it was strangely shaped on a handle and already very slightly brown at the edges. It was a funny, lumpy thing and not the spray with maidenhair fern I had imagined.

"Thanks Pat," I gave her a hug. Gosh how I needed her support.

The night before, Alan, Mike and various bachelors had a stag party at the *Kalamazoo Go Shake Your Head*, a bar in town. Alan was a particular man but, despite his efforts, the bridegroom did not quite make the 11am wedding. Was this a forewarning of things to come? However, as planned, he roared past the McLean's house about 10 minutes late, the signal for Miles and me to follow in his big white Buick.

17 December 1960 - Holy Trinity Cathedral, Accra
Back row Denzil Parry, Pat (hidden), Claire McLean and James Fraser
Front row Mike, Natalie, Sherry McLean and Father Ashietey

It was a hot Saturday morning in December. The General Manager's driver, smart in his white suit and peaked cap, dominated the scene with his swanky car. The clergy were patiently waiting to greet us under the shade at the gate, but the driver swished past them as if they did not exist. They were warm hearted, kindly Ghanaian men of the church and did not deserve this pompous treatment. They scurried to the church door, purple and white robes flying, as the Buick stopped with a little cloud of red sand around its shiny wheels.

"I'm so sorry," easing myself out, "Mr Mclean saw you waiting for us."

"That's OK Missis," they comforted with big, black smiles, "Mr Wheatley is waiting," and ushered Miles and me from the hot sunshine into the relative duskiness of the church. Sherry, my little attendant, was nowhere to be seen, but was later spotted clinging to her mother's skirts in the front pew. She was dressed in astonishing bright blue and white which, in my fragile state, upset me.

Miles and Alan were much in command. Michael Wheatley was, as he always is on special occasions, in a world of his own. He did nudge up and give me a smile and he said and did the right things, and looked at me honestly and kindly. The whole day was a bit hazy, mainly because I was so far from home amongst strangers. The church pews were full of anonymous bodies with their backs turned against me, mainly Ghanaian, the ladies wearing beautiful hats.

The juvenile choir sang *To Be a Pilgrim* raucously, the sweating organist thumped out *Greensleeves:* the jolly African Precentor, Father Ashietey, beamed. It was a cheery, almost hand-clapping affair. Archdeacon Quartey, an amiable man whom Mike befriended in Koforidua, married us. When it came to "All my worldly goods to thee I endow" my nearly husband whispered, "One speedboat and one radiogram." And that was about it. Lavish furloughs left his bank account rather empty, good times had been enjoyed and now, at 27, he was settling down. The service over, we walked down the aisle to a rendition of *When the Saints Come Marching In* through a sea of unfamiliar smiling faces. People I didn't know gathered round us, confetti and streamers were thrown, photographs taken. There was lots of laughter and loud voices. We got into the big white car, settled back into the seats and suddenly we were alone.

"I never knew this car was left hand drive," said Mike. My magical dreams of bridal joy plummeted at this matter of fact remark, and off we drove. He squeezed my hand, smiled but seemed to have little sense of the occasion, whereas I was all fluttery and joyous, we were not sharing the same feelings. If my husband was in a bit of a dream, everyone else was out for a good time. Ghanaians must be the original party people.

The McLean's advised a *no beer* wedding and, indeed, it was very stylish. Claire decorated the garden with flowers, bowers and silver bells. Her well trained Muslim servants, in their best uniforms and hand-embroidered caps, poured champagne and passed the caviare and smoked salmon. My mother would have been Queen Bee on such an occasion, embarrassing my father who, quietly, would have loved every minute. I was sad they were not enjoying this rare day of glory in their lives, but relieved not to have to worry about them. The photographer disappeared before finishing his roll, and I was caught on ciné film chopping up wedding cake and mopping my brow. The frangipani bouquet did not bless the next hopeful bride. It was stiff and sweet scented but easily crushable and soon became bruised and brown and was left forlornly behind a chair. It was a confusing day and I tried to speak to as many people as possible. They were all friendly and kind, just new.

After our reception we drove to Lomé in Togoland for our honeymoon. It was dusk and we queued at the Volta car ferry and there was that African smell of dark and dust. It was heaving with shouting people, baskets of tomatoes, dried fish, screaming babies and rusty lorries, so we waited patiently discussing our special day, and finally boarded and crossed within ten minutes. It was a far cry from the champagne reception and the silver bells in the trees. We were exhausted and Mike was feeling sad, probably because he received little support or correspondence from his family.

From then on it was a dusty journey along inky black bumpy laterite roads, the headlights picking out village *picans* running alongside our new Opel Kapitan and furious mongrels chasing the wheels. We were dead tired when we arrived, and grateful to Claire who had thoughtfully packed ham and chicken sandwiches and a bottle of champagne, which made us giggle.

Our room was clean but spartan and already well inhabited by mosquitoes. There was no door to the attached bathroom and the adjoining wall did not go up to the ceiling. This was the first adjustment, an unexpected lack of privacy.

"No door," I quivered.

"I'll cover my ears," Michael said helpfully, "Don't worry," and yawned heavily.

Like most newly weds we were exhausted from making all the arrangements far from home. The electricity abruptly went off and my future life in Africa wrapped its arms around me.

After Accra, Lomé was very French. We liked the different atmosphere and breakfasted on bowls of coffee, baguettes, unsalted butter and cherry jam on the pavement, with the stink of the drains wafting past our noses. The hotel was modern but already infested with bedbugs, and we spent a great deal of time scratching big red bumps. The Gulf of Guinea surf was majestic and frightening. We lay under a palm tree watching the massive waves crashing and swirling, but it was far too dangerous for bathing or swimming. But we talked and laughed and began to relax. After a couple of days we headed back to Koforidua, enduring a long and filthy journey. A chunk of laterite from an oncoming mammy wagon hit our windscreen and shattered it, and our new Opel was soon full of dust and grit. When we reached our flat, dead tired, it was already dark.

"Home at last," said Mike happily and struggled to carry me over the kitchen threshold. It was a funny moment, and I was glad I dieted otherwise he may have suffered a premature hernia.

John, his Nigerian steward, was standing by the sink with a note, *Massah, Mr Momoh brot dis paper, sometin wrong wid da HooHunya pump.*

"I'll have to go," said Michael, the dust, highlighted by the electric lamp, sticking to his hair.

"I'll come with you," not wishing to be left alone in this new environment after six weeks with the Kennedys and baby Hugh burbling in the next room.

The seedbed pump at Huhunya was broken so we went together ten miles along the laterite road to the fields. Mike spent half an hour struggling, with one of his workers holding a torch, spanners and grease guns, and got the Lister going. We stumbled back over the uneven ground to the car in the dark followed by the steady chug chug chug of the repaired machine.

As we drove home my thoughts were of my father thousands of miles away, wondering if he could imagine me now, bumping through the African jungle on a starry night. He would have worried but I knew I was perfectly safe. I put my hand on Mike's knee and he patted it comfortingly.

Chapter 2 – Koforidua 1961

Koforidua was a shanty town with one main road, a few rows of shops with corrugated iron roofs, two banks and a Post Office. We lived in a pleasant rented flat over Barclays bank, it was an old wooden building with a balcony and next door to the Ghana Legion, a local bar. We put up with an almost 24-hour rendition of Pat Boone crooning *Love Letters in the Sand.* There was a beautiful frangipani tree in our small weedy garden. Sometimes we picked a flowering branch and put it in a big vase of water where it flourished with soft scented blossom, far better than my bruised bouquet.

There was a double car port and quarters for the servants. The flat was airy with shiny wooden floors and louvred windows. There was a large living room, a nice dining room looking onto the balcony, and a big kitchen plus two bedrooms with adjoining bathrooms. Michael purchased quality furniture, and the carpets and curtains were red and black or black and red; it was comfortable and well equipped.

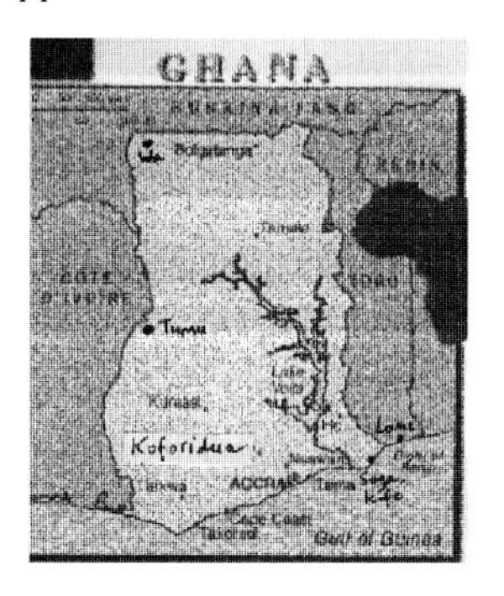

It was lonely as he was out all day in the bush, whilst my time was spent darning big holes in his long white knee socks, listening to gramophone records when there was power, and reading a lot of mannish books. There were few expatriate couples living in town, mostly traders, the rest were government or bank employees who lived on the residential area about a mile away. Mike left early to register farmers, check seedbeds, repair water pumps and find new planting areas; he was busy, young, with plenty of energy, not yet used to having a wife. He returned to Koforidua before dark and, as usual, went straight to the Club, whilst I leaned out of the window watching his car race by.

He had told me that his world was one of crashing cars, turning Land Rovers upside down and catching ferries. First he was in Nigeria, and then Ghana for six years living under the most primitive conditions, including *the hot box* at Ejura. He was a real bushwhacker and the flat in Koforidua was his first real home, but he did not seem to know how to live in it. Previously he and his Nigerian steward, John, went *for bush* for days on end. They loaded the pick-up with camping gear, tins of food, beer, kerosene stove, canvas bath and chair, camp bed, tent and all the paraphernalia to survive in difficult conditions. When they broke camp he spent weekends with the nearest Pioneer Tobacco leaf or marketing men, living in outlying places like Damongo, Tamale or Bolgatanga, or enjoyed the relative comforts of Kumasi. My arrival did not change things and it took days before I realised he had forgotten me. Each morning before he left he ordered the evening *chop* (food), making me wonder why John started cooking dinner so late and how he was so expert at keeping it hot and edible. Smells of food wafted into the sitting room making me feel very hungry, lunch was a non-event and breakfast was a hurried meal before Mike left for the day. John had his own wife and baby in the quarters and, in the evenings, he sat on the wooden steps at the top of our veranda, quietly smoking and sharing pleasantries with people walking barefoot up and down the road in the dark; he was used to his Master coming late and full of beer.

John made me feel nervous and we had not really made friends. He was an ex-boxer with big muscles and thick squat legs, and his face was wide with his nose splayed across it. New wives are always a problem for bachelor servants, it was difficult for him to have me in *his* house. The days crawled by, it was boring and miserable with nothing to look forward to except Mike cheerfully appearing late in the evening, his face bright and smiling. This always gave me hope and allowed me to forgive, but not forget. One evening at about 7-30, feeling so fed up, I telephoned the Club.

The bar boy picked up the phone. "Can I speak to Mr Wheatley please," I was feeling very anxious and nervous.

Massah playing snooker, Missis, he was reluctant to interrupt their game and the phone amplified the noise of men laughing, glasses clinking, the snooker cues rapping on the coloured balls.

"OK," weakly I put the phone down. Having to almost beg to have my own husband's company was not anticipated, so he was tearfully confronted when he came home and was sweetly guilty, "I'll pick you up tomorrow," he assured, but he didn't.

Natalie with baby Hugh Kennedy

The intrepid traveller Richard Burton (1821-1890) wrote in his *Wanderings in West Africa* that *There is no place where a wife is so much wanted as in the Tropics; but then comes the rub - how to keep the wife alive?* What was my purpose of being in Ghana at all?

Pat, busy with her baby, was aware of my predicament and Alan spoke to Mike, but it blew over his head. It was difficult to work out the reasoning behind his behaviour, possibly he was not taught to think about other people, particularly women. His mother died when he was a little boy, his grandmother died ten years later and a bully of an aunt brought him up; my immaturity found the behaviour difficult to comprehend.

Finally, there was no point in being a martyr, it was time to pull myself together and not feel so abused. In the end, I walked up the busy road every evening and into the Club. Mike was always pleased to see me, and didn't seem to realise that he should have come home first. This was the way he lived and my arrival made no difference to his routine so, giving way and quietly sipping crème de menthe and crushed ice, I yawned my way through hundreds of games of snooker.

Pat Kennedy was a lovely copper haired Irish fashion designer. With her help, we purchased a portable Singer sewing machine at the Swiss based United Trading Company in Accra, and she taught me how to make clothes. The little machine was a saviour over many years and diligently went backwards and forwards, helping me stitch all Mike's shirts, dresses and tailored suits for myself and, eventually, the children's clothes. In Koforidua there were tailors, somewhat rough and ready, who saved me the trouble of making outfits and Johan Sebastian Yeboah often made a dress by copying an old one. It was important to shrink all new material in a bucket of water before stitching and to get rid of the excess colour. Once, when wearing a newly made dress at a smart but steamy cocktail party in Accra, my warm body melted the dyes, which dribbled depressing purple and green down my arms and legs.

Vegetable Mammy Comfort and daughter

Settling into married life made me braver and it was pleasant to walk to the Post Office and to a few of the trading stores. Glimpses into the market never encouraged me in. It was always very hot, smelly and full of jostling noisy mammies, piles of aubergines, buckets of sloshing palm oil, squawking chickens and regimented lines of pineapples. There were goats hooves and horns scattered all over the slimy brick floor, bicycles arrived loaded with cow heads and hearts dripping out of bloody sacks, and fresh offal was shrouded in a blanket of bluebottles laying maggots. If we wanted meat the cook went early, and chickens were purchased alive. Other meat we bought at the cold store in Accra or, occasionally, locally at UTC. Fish came up from the sea by lorry on lumps of ice. We always kept a good supply of tins, and imported potatoes from the Canary Islands. Yam and banana chips were often on our menu, as was groundnut stew and Spam fritters.

The manager of Barclays, with the unfortunate name of John Thomas, befriended a market mammy who grew vegetables in an outlying village. She visited the bank twice a week with her daughter, and a large basket on her head. John came out of his office, spruce in his crisp white shirt and starched shorts, his legs in white tasselled stockings with highly polished brown shoes. He helped himself first and then it was my turn to choose from the small tomatoes and peppers, half grown lettuce, tiny cauliflowers, cabbages and, sometimes, a few runner beans. *I go come again Saturday Missis*, smiled the vegetable mammy whose name was Comfort. She became my first real friend. We could also buy excellent paw-paw, pineapples, oranges and bananas. Fresh milk was unavailable and we used Peak evaporated or powdered. The local diet was dried fish, fu-fu made from pounded cassava, and palm oil which was rich and red, and Michael loved this stew with lumps of beef swimming in thick oil.

Mike still ran the house, doled out housekeeping to John, pocket money to me, and ordered the *chop* (food). This system lasted a long time, responsibilities and management of the household would have been fulfilling, but it was always half a job and it took years before the freedom to drive the car was given willingly.

Nigerian John gave up trying to live with me and departed with his wife and *pican* to Lagos. We employed a new cook called Tetteh who also terrified me; he was always in the kitchen and never offered me lunch, so it was a question of creeping out in the afternoons to make a sandwich or pinch a banana. He was artistic and once worked as a steward on the Elder Dempster line. One dinner, he prepared pieces of steak and all the trimmings and served them in two dessert glasses. Another day he plucked all the flowers from our small garden and took them into our bedroom. The bed was covered with a wide pink spread and this he rolled to look like waves and stuffed little posies in all the ripples. His motive was unknown but from a torn off notebook he pencilled and placed on Mike's side, *All the World's a Stage*, and on mine *And YOU must play your part*. He was too clever for me and, when the time was right, he wandered away and we employed Boateng, a garden boy who wanted to work in a house. He was perfect; learned quickly, spoke and wrote English and made delicious bread. His forté was to wrap dusters round his feet and skate across the Mansion polished floor whilst reading *The Old Man and the Sea* by Hemingway. His arrival allowed me to take control of our kitchen and we prepared meals together.

We took in a gauche *small boy* called Samuel and, one morning, he was refilling the kerosene tank in our small freezer. He was wearing a raggy pair of shorts held up by a bit of string and, peeping above the string, was a pair of my pink Marks and Spencer panties. Nothing was said, there was no desire to reclaim them. Another time Boateng was ironing one of my cotton bras and chattering away, *knickers for up* he called them. Tetteh was the best, he ironed with his mouth full of water spraying it through the gap in his teeth to dampen the clothes. Someone else told me of a cook, who filled *his* mouth with olive oil, as it was the best way to dribble it onto egg yolks to make mayonnaise.

West Africa (WAWA - West Africa Wins Again) was always a frustrating place to live in, but there was a richness of culture and colour and very pleasant, amusing people. Pidgin English was easy to pick up and a good substitute for the tribal languages. Much later, our friend Martyn Bougourd sent us this very typical example of rich pidgin. The cook asked his Master:

Sah! You bring chop for de dog?
Yes I go bring am

Whatin you go bring?
I done bring chop for de dog, corned beef.
Ah ha! You don bring de riz
I don forgetam
Whatin then we don give de dog
You give em papati (potatoes imported from Canaries at great expense)
How de dog like the papati?
You go ask am.

The dog scampered around wagging his tail in anticipation of his dinner. The cook came in with a large enamel bowl full to the brim with sizzling chipped potatoes topped by three huge lumps of corned beef.
Whyfor you do chips for de dog you bloody man?
Sah! You no go scold me
Whyfor I no go scold ya? You no sense for de head
Sah! I go ask you how de dog he say he like chips, you say you go askam, I go askam and de dog he say he like chips.

Our first Christmas happened soon after our wedding. Mike was at a loss, he was not used to buying presents but, after much anguish, presented me with a game of Monopoly rekindling childhood memories of an overbearing and argumentative brother, who always threw me into jail without passing GO and acquired rows of red hotels. We arranged to go away with Pat, Alan and baby Hugh, plus Bill Mann, a black American who worked on a US Aid project. We travelled 80 miles to the Pioneer Tobacco Company house at Sogakofe on the banks of the Volta, and took all our supplies with us. We also took Master Whiskers, the crazy wire haired dog belonging to an African doctor friend, Frank Grant, studying in England. The ferry was particularly busy on Christmas Eve, jostling with crowds, hooting vehicles and perspiring, pushing people. Whiskers became very disturbed with all the palaver, leapt out of the car window and raced onto the ferry already pulling out into the water, his wire haired tail firmly between his legs. We were horrified; it was like losing a child in a football mob. It was dark, dirty and hot, we were all exhausted and hungry; baby Hugh wanted his feed, and it would be hours before we boarded. Mike kept his speedboat at the company bungalow on the other side, so he jumped on the next ferry and walked through the village to the banks of the river in the pitch dark, fired the engine and came over the water to rescue us. It took several trips to get all our stuff and us to the other side. The deep, black, swirly river was very scary and bound to be full of lurking crocodiles and spooky fish. The cook, Abu, was at the house and soon the generator was thumping and some food on the stove.
I get two chickens, and go mashum some yams, me brudder he grow 'em in his gardin, he said cheerfully, *Oh! and I get two tin peas*, and off he went to the kitchen.

Alan anxiously went into the village to find Whiskers, an alien posh dog amongst mangy mongrels and squealing miserable pups.
"You go see my dog?" Alan urged curious boys.
Yes Massah dat white dog with the tail under, dog he go down dis way, you see 'um? shouted a young lad in tatty shorts. Anxious for *dash* (tip) he led Alan up and down the gloomy lanes between the haphazard mud huts lit only by guttering candles and gummed up oil lamps.

"Whisker-r-r-s! Whisker-r-r-s!" shouted Alan in his Tipperary accent; some intonation must have hit the dog's ears, for he appeared, cowed but with a little wag in his tail. The boy got his dash and, to our relief, Alan found his way back with the dog who was greeted like the pooch from heaven. When excited, Master Whiskers ran in circles, and his tail wagged in circles too.

The Volta River ferry terminal

A tropical Christmas was always an odd affair with huge efforts made to feel festive, but intense heat, a lack of Christmas music, tree, decorations, (never mind traditional food,) gifts to buy, stockings to fill and a Santa down the chimney, made us all realise how we were missing home. Bill's wife, Willa, and three children were in the States and the rest of us had families far away. There was no phone or radio to hear BBC World Service. We just got on and made the best of it. We enjoyed beer, the gin-relaxed turkey, and some ham out of a tin, cherished potatoes, fruit salad and custard. After our meal the men took turns to drive the speedboat, which was fitted with a 35mph Johnson engine, and the others water-skied, showing off bouncing over the boat's wash. It was amazing how much fun we shared with so little to entertain us.

When we got back I familiarised myself with Koforidua which was a quiet place with a small European population. Many of the men trekked all week and the women were left in their crumbling government houses on the residential area. Their husbands were employed by the Public Works Department, Ministry of Agriculture or with Water or Geology. Only four of us women lived in the town, it was convenient because we could walk everywhere and, eventually, we made friends. Wendy Greenall's husband was with the Bank of West Africa and they had a little boy, Jean and Arthur Pearson were with the trading company Busi and Stephenson, Elli Potirakis and her husband, Theo, were with A G Leventis selling corrugated iron, cement and tins of tomato purée. The women filled me in with horror stories of insects, snakes and tarantula spiders. Worse was the dreaded mango fly otherwise known as the *tumbo* worm.

Elli, who was so clinically clean even her eyes looked polished, was most agitated about this creature, "You have to make sure all the laundry is ironed on *both sides*," she urged.

"Why?" what was this *tumbo* doing in the laundry basket anyway.

"A tiny fly lays eggs on wet clothing hanging on the line," Elli's black eyes flashed with excitement, her Greek coming to the forefront of her mouth, "You have to kill the eggs by ironing every article of clothing even socks."

"Socks!" in the first flush of marriage it never occurred to me to iron socks.

She continued, leaving her coffee cold on the peg table, "The fly lays eggs and, if left on your clothes, they hatch and burrow into your skin and a tiny worm will grow and eat your flesh. I was beginning to feel sick and scratchy. "When they are ready they come out as grub maggots," she paused for breath, "But not until they are really ready."

"What do you mean?" I asked weakly.

"I had three in my groin," she sighed dramatically, eyes rolling to the heavens, "They tickled as they burrowed and chopped on my flesh. Ugh! At last a sort of big crater developed in the top of the lump and I squeezed them out, they were alive and revolting."

It all sounded disgusting and, when I got home home, the boys were questioned if they knew about the *tumbo* worm.

Ah yes Missis, they assured me, *Dat's why we go iron your panties proper, we no go makeum mistake.*

Later Mike told me that the worms were long and it was sensible to have a matchstick handy to roll them around, "If they break," he said, "They regenerate."

Life revolved around the Koforidua Club up the road, and the tennis court. We were busy arranging entertainment and curry lunches. West African curries are famous for their beef and groundnut stew, palm oil chop and a huge variety of accompanying dishes of fried and fresh onions, peppers, tomatoes, yams, pineapple, bananas, paw-paw, groundnuts, coconut and everything else you can throw on a curry to make it more delicious. Sometimes we drove thirty miles to WACRI (West African Cocoa Research Institute) where there was a larger expatriate population, and we swam in their pool. Mike impressed me with his athletic swallow dives, one after the other, off the small diving board. We trekked up-country quite extensively and spent several nights a week in Sogakofe as Mike managed both stations. Sometimes he went by himself and it was awful being left alone, with servants there was very little to do. There was no diversion in a library or bookshop, reading matter was begged and borrowed. My interest in people and communication meant letters went to all my friends and acquaintances, but the replies were far fewer than the output.

Whilst in Sogakofe, we met an elderly American couple called Larry and Roxy Kaufmann who lived on a poorly maintained isolated government agricultural station. They had invited me to stay before we were married, and they lived in very uncomfortable and spartan conditions. Their's was a sub-standard government bungalow with cement floors and metal windows. Their locally made furniture was crude, there were no curtains and the bedrooms were dark and comfortless. In the windowless outside kitchen was a wood stove and an enamel bowl, It made me thankful we were not with the government. Larry was a kind man, with a gruff, macho exterior and a leathery skin. Roxy was long suffering, rather plump and soft-hearted. One evening we asked them to supper and they drove a long way over rough roads. My culinary skills were basic, so I cooked up chicken fricassée and trifle.

Mike, annoyingly, asked, "What's this?"

Larry immediately replied, "Well it's a kind of mess up."

"Hush Larry," said Roxy quietly with her southern drawl.

"Well it is," he was determined.

Perhaps socially inept, Larry made up for it with his humour, good conversation and a thorough knowledge of West African agriculture. Roxy was sweet and desperate for company, and sat at the table drinking wine enjoying the conversation. After supper Larry yawned widely and disappeared to sleep in his vehicle parked under the house, but later woke and shouted up the stairs, "Roxy you just get up off your big fat *aahse*, I want to go home." And with a flutter and a smile, she trotted off back to their mean little house in the bush.

Several civil engineers from Sir William Halcrow and Partners were working on the massive Akosombo Dam in the Volta Valley. During our travels we met them on the road and soon got together with some of the boys in remote villages where we cooked curry and drank Club beer. We also spent quite a few weekends in Accra staying with various company friends. We enjoyed going to the Ambassador Hotel for lobster thermidor, or to the open-air Paramount nightclub run by E T Mensah, well known for his use of western instruments to play African music. In 1956 he jammed with Louis Armstrong and the All Star Band on their great African tour; E T was a legend in Ghana and we were lucky to join a mass of townspeople and dance the traditional High Life, more of a shuffle than a dance, but huge fun in a big crowd.

'Please Mister don't you squish me tomato
All you do is touch up touch up
Turn your back and giv'en
Turn your back an giv'en
Baya Baya'

Ghanaians were hospitable and very accepting with big smiles, sizeable bottoms, wearing very colourful clothes and beautiful headgear. I made friends with some of the women, and Mike had pals from his bachelor days who visited us. They were always ready for a good laugh and some fun. In Accra we saw films, went to dinner parties and spent days on the beach. It was a good life and broke the monotony of the comparative dullness of Koforidua.

High Life

Chapter 3 – Middle East and Ghana

Mike with Master Whiskers

A year after our wedding we went on furlough and enjoyed a belated honeymoon. We flew to Lagos, and, by Comet, across the Sahara to Cairo. We stayed in the famous Shepheards Hotel originally built in 1841. In 1961 it was luxurious, and we had all the gear to go with it; a dinner suit, patent leather shoes, silk dresses, jewellery and attitude and we had a lovely time together. We enjoyed Egyptian food and wine and danced into the small hours and Mike was relaxed and cheerful. During the days we explored the Cairo bazaars and the tomb of Tutan Khamun. One night a guide took us into the desert for an exotic Arabic evening. We ended up in a flapping NAAFI tent, eating greasy goat with a group of woolly hatted British cyclists, and a couple of shivering belly dancers. Our smart clothes were ridiculous and we froze. Another day we drove out to Giza to see the grand pyramids and to lunch at Mena House, a former king's hunting lodge converted into a palatial hotel in 1869. Determined to ride a camel, we were soon surrounded by camel drivers who heaved me onto a smelly beast whilst I clutched my skirt and pulled my short winter coat around my knees, trying hard to keep my high heels dangling on my toes. Afterwards we climbed high into one of the pyramids, and for the first time ever I felt acutely claustrophobic. The tunnel was narrow and there were people ahead and behind; looking down the steep ladder and up the steep ladder produced waves of fear, but the wonderful fresh air of the burial chamber was a relief. We admired the remarkable tonguing and grooving of the massive stone slabs, manoeuvred into place so many thousands of years before. Mike, always fascinated with the way buildings were constructed, stroked the slabs up and down for a long time, putting himself back into the sweat and tears of the manpower that made these pyramids possible.

We had a photograph in my childhood home of my father astride a camel in front of the Sphinx in 1918. He was handsome and relaxed, aged 20 and posted to Egypt with the Royal

Flying Corps, filling my mind with dreams of deserts, Arabs in flowing robes and the mystique of biblical times. Forty three years on, we stood in the same spot, my silly heels sinking in the sand, whilst I felt so happy that our marriage introduced me to such an exciting world of travel and adventure.

After Cairo we flew to Jerusalem governed by courteous Hashemite Jordanians. It was very cold and we purchased thick, rough sheepskins with ungainly sleeves. We wandered the narrow streets seeing the Stations of the Cross, the Holy Sepulchre and Wailing Wall and looked over to the Garden of Gethsemane. We went to the Dead Sea, Bethlehem and Jericho but did not have time to visit Petra which, in those days, was well off the beaten track. Next stop was Nicosia and Christmas in Cyprus. We met up with sociable BAT people, one of whom, Alan Rands, came in from Paphos where he was growing tobacco. We went out to dinner and on to a night club where we heard Nana Mouskouri singing her Greek hit *White Roses from Athens* and Russ Conway playing *Side Saddle* on the piano. The weather was freezing and we were glad of our coarse sheepskins despite their unpleasant smell and heavy moult. We toured the countryside and coast as well as the Troodos Mountains. It was at the time of the anti-British guerrilla EOKA uprising, and the whispered dark tales of their collaboration with Archbishop Makarios. It was a restless place, but quiet whilst we were there. Beirut was palm fringed and glamorous, as was its cost of living, so we moved on to Istanbul within 48 hours. We ate tasty kebabs, visited the Blue Mosque, sailed across the Bosphorous and stayed in a dark tenement bed and breakfast, owned by an elderly lady. She made us so welcome, with fresh cotton sheets and big blankets and we bathed in the most antiquated hissing gas-fired bathroom. Athens was home to the Acropolis and Parthenon, hot chestnuts and warm weather, a wandering happy place enhanced by the charms of Plaka. Rome buzzed with Lambrettas and Vespas, volatile Italians, the Colosseum, the fountains of Trevi, Vatican City and lots of spaghetti. England was a reunion with family and friends and soon we were airborne again and back to Koforidua.

Expatriates were drifting away from the town and, when the Kennedy's returned to Dublin, they left Master Whiskers with us for several months until, without notice, Dr Frank Grant his Ghanaian owner, turned up to collect him. Frank was embarrassed and I was devastated, Whiskers was such a zany companion, but he went off with a zappy wag and without a backward glance. Our flat felt suddenly empty and I wept. Not only did we miss the Kennedys but we really missed Whiskers. The few expats remaining were a motley lot with nothing in common so we formed a poker school and spent hilarious Saturday evenings playing for small stakes.

At Easter we travelled extensively by pick-up truck first stopping at Kumasi, home of the colourful Ashanti people, who wore glorious silk kente cloths. These were strips woven on four inch looms under the baobab trees. We drove to Sunyani, Ejura, Wenchi, Kintampo and Damongo and then headed north to the bustling little town of Tamale. We stopped and watched ragged boys dangling live frogs, tied with string on their fleshy little feet, taunting swift alligators wallowing in shallow muddy waters. On to Bolgatanga, Wa, Zuarungu and Navrongo as well as Ouagadougou on the Upper Volta border, now called Burkino Faso.

On the hot, dry western borders we mingled with the duck billed Lobi people. This animist tribe, so artistically talented in carving masks and making pottery, was also known as the most primitive. The men were particularly protective of their women, forced to adopt the custom of inserting wooden plugs into their upper and lower lips and into their ears, making them exceedingly ugly. We arrived at the village of Tumu and found many disfigured women and girls in the market place, some so shy they ran away. The plugs were inserted when the girls were babies, first small splinters, a match, a piece of twig until the lip developed away from the surrounding skin and the ear lobes became hanging and floppy. We saw some women with clay lip pieces as big as dinner plates, and ear lobes stretched to the size of saucers. They did not seem to mind them, and removed them leaving loose lips and lobes dangling. They also practised female circumcision, as did many of the Ghanaian tribes.

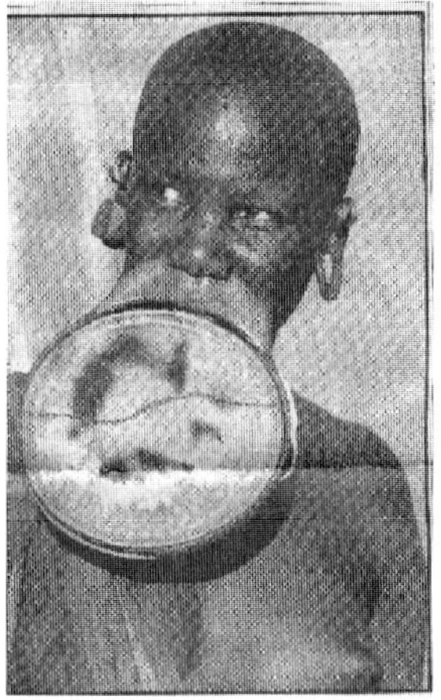

Lobi girl

We loved the more isolated areas of northern Ghana. It was less humid and crowded than the south and more typically African, the villages consisted of round mud huts with grass roofs and the women wore little else than a bunch of leaves and a few beads. They looked after the children, worked in the fields and carried pots of heavy water on their heads, sometimes for several miles, babies squawking on their backs often being doused as their barefooted mothers trod the uneven ground, dragging a toddler or two by the fingers. The men lounged in hammocks under banyan trees sipping palm wine from calabashes, or wandered around wearing striped cotton smocks and big, heavy tribal hats, smoking and chatting, whilst children played on the hard baked mud with crude wooden and wire toys.

Mike did all the driving, and loved the freedom of being away from work. With crates of tinned food and beer in the back of the truck, we purchased fruit and bread along the way. We stayed in simple rest houses with mud floors, constructed of palm trunks and thatch, and we listened to the night sounds of native drums; they whispered to me about black magic and ju-ju. Water came in buckets and long drops coped with morning duties. It was rough and ready, but always clean and swept and we carried our own bedrolls.

Back in Koforidua I was asked to take over the club nursery school, a privilege for any willing expatriate wife, especially as only three of us remained. Sixteen of the children were Ghanaian, the sons and daughters of Government officials. The others were three little Dutch girls and one little English boy. It was interesting to discover I had a natural ability to teach, and it was not long before the mornings were organised in helping children with different abilities. There were three tribal languages, Twi, Fante and Ga but we stuck to English. The children picked it up quickly with songs and repetitive rhymes and learned the national anthem of Ghana, and started the day with a jolly screeching rendition *God bless our homeland Ghana, And make our nation great and strong, Bold to defend forever.* The first of three verses was more than my little lot could manage, but the attempt went down well with passers-by on the road, who joined in enthusiastically.

My class learned ABC and numbers, English and drawing with melting wax crayons. One little three-year-old, Violet Bahwah, was very insecure and spent most of her time sitting on my lap, regularly wetting me with warm, unexpected pennies. She was petite with thick fuzzy hair pushed up into a puff on the top of her head. She was happy and chattered about her baby brother, Kwabena, and her Mummy who taught in the Presbyterian School. Another, Akosua Buta, whose Dad was Police Chief, was very bold and bossed everyone around, she was bright and did well. A stocky young man called Atsu helped with the class and heaved the see saw up and down with all twenty children on it. By then my baby bump was becoming apparent and it was good to have the mornings occupied to justify a rest in the afternoon. The salary was a huge help and increased our chance of buying a property in the UK sooner rather than later.

Koforidua Club School

Hospital facilities in Koforidua were poor and malaria hit me badly with high fever, terrible aches and pains, bathed in pools of sweat. Anti-malaria pills can cause miscarriage so were refused, but the fever was frighteningly fierce. In desperation Mike went for the Spanish Mission doctor who spoke no English but was concerned. He prescribed a suitable medicine and I recovered quickly, but it made me realise how far away from civilisation we were in case of emergency. The company doctor in Accra gave me a couple of cursory check-ups but he was not helpful about a suitable place for delivery, and in the end we took the advice of friends.

In September 1962 Mike drove me to the Basel Mission Hospital for the birth; it was about 100 miles north and way off the beaten track in the jungles of Agogo. It was awful saying goodbye and crying, feeling like a great big ugly lump. He was kind but didn't know what to do, and faced the long drive back in the dark.

"You'll be all right sweetie," he tried to be reassuring. I don't think he had a clue about the performance of giving birth, it was what women did and men kept away.

We were advised to go three weeks ahead and the baby was three weeks late. The hours of waiting were endless, hot, boring and dreary. The Swiss German staff were neither friendly, nor humorous and I was, as usual, on my own again waddling around trying to keep myself busy with none of my gadgets around me. The lamplight was dim, and the thick mosquito netting on the windows made reading at any time almost impossible. Our baby was jumping around inside me, my legs were swollen and there was no enjoyment in this lonely and uncomfortable *safe* haven.

Primarily the hospital was for the Ghanaian rural community, but there was a small guest wing for expatriates. My only company was a teacher, a British nun on retreat, and we talked seriously at breakfast. She was a nice woman and quite realistic, "I love what I do now," she assured me with a wink, "I'm perfectly happy, but don't think I haven't had fun, I have!" and there was a big twinkle in her eye. Mike came every weekend which was a huge comfort but eventually, almost screaming with boredom, he took me to Kumasi to stay with friends, the Mloszewskis, and Mark drove me to the hospital when my pains began. As soon as we reached Agogo they stopped. The midwife, Sister Dorothea, was big boned, carrot haired, unkind and refrained from speaking English. It was a dreadful 27 hour labour and the only words of Swiss German she translated via her assistant, turned out to be, *Why did you give me blunt scissors?* as she was performing an episiotomy. I was exhausted and struggling and she was getting very angry; suddenly she leap frogged onto my stomach and the baby came out with a shocking whoosh. I still shudder and was traumatised for several days afterwards, it was a brutal delivery. Susina Jane made up for all the agony, and was a perfect, pink, blonde, gorgeous eight pound baby. It was 5th October 1962 and she was born about five in the evening. I heard the housekeeper make a phone call to Koforidua to tell Mike the good news, "She's been through a very difficult time," she said in her thick alpine accent.

1962 – Company Christmas party at Huhunya

When Mike arrived next day there was a quiet pink bundle in her cot, he seemed unaware of what happened, but was so thrilled with his gorgeous daughter that he could hardly stop cuddling her. After five days he returned and drove us home, me feeling as if I was sitting on a barbed wire fence. There was no after care in Koforidua and, with only a natural instinct about babies, particularly little ones, Susina and I sorted ourselves out and she was a model child, and a great joy to us both. She was reared by a Good Housekeeping baby book and me.

We were warned of a move, Mike had been in Nigeria and then Ghana for 11 years, and I was there for nearly three. We were advised that it might be to the violent pre-Biafran Nigeria or the commodity deprived, but culturally richer, sub-continent of India. In Nkrumah's post-Gold Coast, Krobo Edusi acquired a pure gold bed and we spent our last tour driving about in a Chevrolet Impala, we ate off Wedgwood and sat on Parker Knoll. Kingsway Stores, run by the United Africa Company, had fridges stacked with Scottish grouse the day following the Glorious Twelfth. But grouse was not to be on our menu, a letter arrived from Head Office stating that South India was to be our new home. A new area was to be opened up in Mysore State to grow quality tobacco to replace the shortfall caused by sanctions in Ian Smith's UDI Rhodesia. Had we known it was to be for fourteen years we may well have had second thoughts.

On the road to Kumasi

We packed our belongings into wooden crates in Koforidua in September 1963. Susina was eleven months old and an easy traveller. Her favourite past-time was to blow raspberries at anyone who looked at her. Her little body shook with joy as the awful noises were emitted from her little pink mouth. After a holiday in Dubrovnik, we introduced our daughter to her English family. My mother was overwhelmed to have a grandchild and had looked forward to their first meeting with great impatience. Susina spent her first birthday on great-aunt Valerie's pig farm in Suffolk. As well as pigs and piglets, our baby sat astride Jersey cows and was enthusiastically licked by seven *smelly breath* yellow Labrador dogs, which were fed on fishmonger leftovers stewed for days in the bottom oven of the Aga. They farted furiously everywhere.

"Gog, Gog," Susina squealed excitedly, rolling around the filthy floor in her spruce Viyella smocked and puff sleeved dress.

For me the farmhouse was a den of germs, dog hair and dirt, but for her it was a delightful mucky paradise to explore on hands and knees. Michael and I shared a single brass bed, one leg of which was supported with a shoe. Worse was Izal toilet paper, crisp, crackly and only suitable for tracing pencil outlines, or for wrapping round a comb and humming to make a weird musical sound with a tingling of the lips. That, and being ordered to bath in blue Omo washing detergent, was a bit too much.

"Keeps the bath clean," said Valerie sharply.

Untypical of the farming fraternity, Valerie and John did not rise until well after ten in the morning and we were on the pain of death to stay quiet or "You'll wake the bloody pigs!" Once the animals heard human movement, there was uproar from the barn disturbing the snoozing dogs reminding them they needed to wee. Susina, like most little ones, was chirping at six, and it was impossible to hush her enthusiastic squeaks, creep through the house and not let the dogs out. This accelerated our house hunting so we could make our own noises at our own convenience. Mike was keen on ancient rectories with circular driveways, whilst I was more of a townie and preferred lamp posts and milk bottles outside the back door. Meanwhile we were grateful for the accommodation, despite its difficulties.

Chapter 4 – Tanganyikan Mutiny

Before Christmas we flew out to Tanganyika where East African Tobacco Company operated a Master Growers' scheme, knowledge of which would be useful in the development of tobacco in Mysore, India. Mike's twin brother, Gerald, with his wife Anthea and baby daughter Alison, were already settled at Tumbi and we stayed in Tabora, the nearest town.

NP Kumar, Muljabhai Patel, John McLean and Mike

It was central to the tobacco growing area and also home to the training HQ of the 2nd Battalion of the Tanganyika Rifles. We moved into the German owned Railway Hotel and our accommodation was too small for twin beds and a cot, so a well-wrapped Susina slept outside on the burglar proofed veranda. The room had dark blue walls, a dark green cement floor and we had to sit on the bed to open a drawer. It was constricting and we had few toys or playthings. Mike was out all day and there was nothing to do so, with her push chair, we wandered around town investigating the few Indian *dukas* (shops) and found the best shade and child playing place under the mango trees at the Gujerati Club. Card playing was the prominent sport and most members were named Patel. We employed a pleasant ayah called Julia and sometimes Mike took us to Tumbi for the day. Susina and Alison were almost the same age and played together whilst Anthea and I nattered.

The local newspaper was full of rumour, and it was becoming obvious that the army ranks were restless complaining about pay and conditions. President Nyerere, alerted to the situation, sent an urgent request for military assistance, and soon, there was a British RN aircraft carrier lying off the East African coast. The tense bubble burst in late January 1964 when the 1st Battalion Tanganyikan Rifles mutinied in the capital, Dar-es-Salaam. Not long after the jungle drums beat incessantly, whilst the 2nd Battalion askari were raging the streets of Tabora. Mike came into our hotel bedroom to pick up papers and heard what he thought was a shot. His body stiffened, "Guns!" he shouted and raced off to find Susina who was with Julia under her favourite tree. He scooped her up and brought them both to our room.

"It seems like mutiny," he muttered fearfully while Susina gurgled happily in her Daddy's strong arms, and we tried to get our minds into gear. as we were marooned in the middle of this vast and barren country. There were shots and shouting all around us, then periods of silence. It was eerie, and someone in the hotel had heard that the mutineers had locked up their British officers and families at the airport and broken into the well stocked armoury; it made us feel cold and very frightened. There was a lot of shooting by the station and near the bank, it was hard to believe it was all happening, but the shots rang out. Susina played on the floor, Julia was terrified and wanted to go home but it was not safe.

There was a lull and we went to the front of the hotel. Looking anxious were a magistrate and our manager, Trevor Tice, both visiting from Dar es Salaam.

"Doesn't look good," muttered the magistrate.

"Evacuation?" queried Trevor.

They tried to assess what was going on, and we were all feeling very vulnerable. The mayhem and shooting started again and suddenly an army lorry screeched up and out jumped several askari, guns at the ready. We ran in every direction, and pictures of another Congo flitted through our heads. Four expatriate men were caught in the gents toilet and marched at bayonet point into the back of the lorry. In an hour or so, most of the stray foreigners congregated in our small bedroom, including Anthea and Alison, who had raced along the dusty road from Tumbi in their VW Beetle. Gerald arrived last from the tobacco station and, as he was running up the hotel steps, narrowly missed being shot by a passing askari. He appeared at our door, shaking and deathly green. Anthea, terrified and unwell, immediately plonked Alison in his arms, "She wants you," she said abruptly.

Alison, Anthea, Natalie and Susina

The cramped sweaty atmosphere became very tense and we were all whispering with varying ideas of what to do. There were nine of us including the little girls; an elderly tobacco buyer called Conrad, and a young Malaysian on a leaf training course. Everyone was scared stiff and we hid under the beds and tried to keep the toddlers amused. Several tins of precious Heinz baby food were opened in a vain attempt to calm them. We pooled our money and stuffed it up the bath taps, and tried to work out a plan of action. Without us women, the men could get away along the back roads, they probably had enough petrol to get to the tobacco research station at Urambo 50 miles away.

The police visited us several times and tried to reassure us that we were safe. An East African Airways plane was due to pick up the British army officers and families and, under police escort, several in our room managed to get away.

Mike and Gerald knew the only escape for their families was by air taxi. The hotel servants had run off but we discovered one telephone was working. The men took it in turns to creep out, crawl up the covered walkway and try to contact Nairobi. Outside the angry soldiers crept and rustled around the caged verandas. Troop-filled Bedford trucks roared through the streets, the mutineers shouting and brandishing guns. There was neither order nor control, we were sitting targets.

"Missis, please let me go," Julia wailed and the little girls started scrapping in the highly charged airless atmosphere.

We were visited by Gabriel Mandara, Gerald's colleague in the company, and he reported that the soldiers burst into the schools and the hospital, making everyone run in circles whilst firing shots at their feet. Most foreigners working in the town experienced the sharp end of a bayonet or had their vehicles stolen. Late into the night, we got a phone call that a small Cessna aircraft would come next day to evacuate Anthea, the children and me, and the fourth seat would be taken by an epileptic pregnant woman. I had seen her have a terrible fit in the club just a few days previously.

That night was very scary, peppered by random shooting, yelling, revving and scampering, making us all anxious for the early dawn. By that time we knew that the First Secretary from the British High Commission had arrived from Dar and was trying, together with the police, to negotiate a settlement with the mutineers, and a surrender of arms. The mutineers threatened to go through the town again, and this time they would *not* fire into the air. We decided to take the risk and make for the airport.

Chivvied along by our husbands with cries of, "Come on! Hurry up!" "Leave that bag you don't need it!" we bundled baby milk and bottles and clothes, papers were snatched from our hands, teddy bears and dollies rescued, children plonked into seats. Rush! Rush! Rush! Amazingly our car was parked outside, still with a little petrol. The journey to the airstrip was constantly interrupted by excited askari, some very drunk. They had built road blocks and were aggravating everybody but we cajoled our way through with a lot of false hearty laughter. Our daughters were fractious and hungry, we all needed hot drinks and breakfast but that was an impossible dream. Tilly, the bossy manageress of the hotel, had locked the larder before finding her own safety and we had eaten everything in the fridge. We would have to wait. The tiny airport was alive with police and military and the single engined four seater Cessna had just landed.

The pilot, a young Canadian, was anxious to take off again. "Don't care for this place," he said, looking at the milling askari, the earth airstrip and up into the rain clouds, "We'd better go before the weather closes in and the strip becomes a sea of mud." The epileptic lady was carrying a dressing case in one hand and clutching her husband's arm with the other. She had golden auburn hair and soft green frightened eyes. Her yellow cotton dress revealed a more noticeable bump than mine; I guessed she was about five months gone. Her husband was calm and reassuring, "Just hold her hands and talk to her if she has a fit," he said, "It won't last long." My sister-in-law was recovering from post-natal depression and I was suffering from morning, afternoon and evening sickness. It was all horribly confusing.

Mike fumbled in his shirt pocket and handed me a hastily written note *This is My Last Will and Testament.* He didn't know what to say, nor did I. It was pathetically short, leaving everything to Susina, *our unborn child,* and me. The magistrate had witnessed it before he got away on the civil airline. It was a dreadful moment. Mike was 30 and life for us had just begun. There was a scuffle of soldiers behind us.

"Come on," shouted the pilot, revving the engines. There was time only for a brief hug, Susina gave her Daddy a butterfly kiss and popped her thumb comfortingly into her mouth. She was stuffed on top of me in the co-pilot's seat. Mike and Gerald waited like twin toy soldiers as our plane took off. Tears blurred our vision but we waved until we could no longer see them.

"We're headed north-east at seven thousand feet," the pilot shouted, "We'll pass just west of Mount Kilimanjaro, it's about four hundred miles as the crow flies." Susina, already rather independent, obviously thought she *was* the co-pilot, as she grabbed the dual control with her strong little arms. The plane rose at a sharp and erratic angle.

"For Christ's sake!" shouted the pilot furiously, "Keep her off the dual." He struggled to steady the wings as the small plane made a steep climb; Susina cried and sucked her thumb. Thank God for her thumb. I was shaking with a certain amount of fear and desperately needed the loo.

"Sorry," I shouted inadequately. The noise of the engine was overwhelming, the two in the back were screaming and anxious; little Alison was exhausted and had fallen asleep.

We flew across the Serengeti Plain. The pilot had a map strapped to his knee and was anxiously scouring the bush below for familiar trees, tracks or a lake.

"There's a wide river over there," I waved my hands to the right looking at the water snaking its way across the parched land.

"That's no river lady," he shouted above the din of the engine, "It's a migration of zebra." There were thousands of the striped animals zig-zagging round the anthills, avoiding clumps of thorn trees, treading round rock outgrowths and determinedly tacking their way to lusher grazing grounds. We skirted the deep Ngorongoro Crater in our flimsy aeroplane looking into the rocky vegetated interior. Despite the desperate situation it was absolutely thrilling. We crossed the border and flew over Kenya's romanticised Rift Valley before landing in Nairobi. Anthea was terror stricken because she couldn't see the airport as we came into land. The pilot did everything to calm her, "It's OK lady, it's there, terra firma, you'll be OK."

Susina and I stayed several weeks with a couple called Parsons-Smith who soon brought us back to reality with a gluey meal of oxtail stew and carrots, making me realise that oxtail was actually a *tail* with a bone in the middle. It reminded me, as a child, of a cow's tongue leering through a butcher's window, and I never ate a tongue sandwich again. Our hosts were anxious to attend a cocktail party, whilst I struggled to eat and Susina had a banana. They waved goodbye repeating the news that the Ugandans had called in British troops, as their own battalions were also restless. This made the situation for our husbands in Tabora more vulnerable than ever.

Three days later Mike managed to get through on the telephone but was barely audible, "The Tanganyikan Rifles are all mustered, fully armed, in the barracks and we expats are five minutes away from evacuation," he shouted over a dreadful crackly line, "We have nothing but shotguns and elephant guns!" His voice petered away and the phone went dead. I felt complete despair.

Later we heard that the Tanganyikan commander had managed to keep control of the troops and, that afternoon, jet fighters from the aircraft carrier appeared in the sunny clear skies above Tabora and made threatening passes over the barracks. At the same time 42nd Royal Marine Commandos made a co-ordinated landing at the airport in Beverley transporters. Highly trained, like bullets popping out of a gun, many landed, disarmed the mutineers and took over the town. Over the next few days helicopters with nets flew over the bush catching stray mutineers. The small town of Tabora was suddenly invaded by several hundred hunky Marines.

Susina with Julia

It was unfortunate that this unrest and subsequent mutiny should take place after Tanganyika's Independence in 1961 and Zanzibar's in 1963, but in April 1964 they became the United Republic of Tanzania. Most African countries had a sincere respect for their army and its practices. Mike's experience with the Kings African Rifles in Nyasaland (now Malawi) had taught him that regimental bands, with their precise marching and smart uniforms, cast a great cloak of confidence on the population, both in towns and remote villages. Army personnel were looked up to and people felt safe when they were around, but the armies became politicised and a pattern evolved where their officers were selected from the ranks of the ruling party.

Several days later, Mike telephoned that it was safe to return so I went to a Nairobi dentist, had a pre-natal check-up and bought Susina two pairs of red buttoned Startrite shoes. We took baskets of strawberries back for our men and had another exciting journey across wild East

African landscape with the same skilled pilot. The rains had been heavy, and Tabora airstrip was a deep and rutty quagmire after the landing of the enormous Beverleys.

"My God," he breathed while we circled, "This Cessna is about the height of that Beverley wheel." The landing was bumpy but we stayed upright and he manoeuvred the fly-sized plane between slippery ditches, bouncing along the sticky churned up mud, which completely obliterated our windscreen. Finally we slithered to a stop. The pilot took no time to unload our babies, our things and us.

"Rather you than me," he waved cheerily as they pulled the chocks away and he took off erratically, but as safely as he had landed.

The Marines stayed several months. The Top Club was littered with heavy belts, revolvers and machine guns, which were lodged behind the bar before drinks were served. The men consumed copious quantities of Tusker beer and taught us to Hippie Hippie Shake. Maybe it was that which brought on a near miscarriage. A wise Indian doctor put me to sleep for four days until I recovered.

Mike's orientation with the Master Growers' Scheme was complete and we were anxious to leave the confines of the Railway Hotel. Susina, pretty with silky blonde hair, was quite at home as she danced up and down the sunny verandas chattering in baby Swahili. She knew each of the hotel staff by name, and had even charmed the bristly German manageress, Tilly, into a smile. The six-month stay had not improved her appetite; hotel meal times were becoming a battleground.

When we finally departed, we flew from Dar-es-Salaam to Aden in an un-pressurised Dakota which was agonising on both little and big ears, and Susina screamed. Amazingly in Dar I bumped into Caroline Hancock, we could hardly believe it as we had last been together sharing a flat in London and, in Aden, I met Sue Thomas to whom I had handed over my job at Jim Cadbury-Brown's before I flew to America. They were both married, had babies and husbands in the Army.

After two humid days in Aden we boarded the P&O liner, SS Orsova. Our crates had been loaded at Takoradi and shipped to Tilbury to catch the Orsova and ensure we would all land in Bombay together. Hooray! Eager to settle into a home, it was good to know that all our household and baby necessities were in the hold.

As we sailed towards the Gateway of India a Maharathi passenger, leaning alongside us on the ship's rail, muttered: "They are today celebrating Buddha Jayanti, it is Buddha's birthday. Happy Birthday Buddha! Public Holiday, everything closed, no?" He went away sniffing, pulling his dhoti round his hairy legs and flapping his leather chappals on the deck.

"I can't bear it!" I shouted, "I can't bear it! When are we going to see our boxes?" Susina was concerned at my anger and frustration, and tucked her hand into mine. We disembarked into all the noises and smells that we had feared, the customs hall was like a hen house, steaming with people. We queued patiently, Mike holding Susina on his hip; I was fraught and exhausted, hot and depressed. The days on the ship had not brought the expected rest or peace, Susina hated being penned in and we had not had a decent night's sleep. She was a fractious demanding toddler, already uncomfortable with too much moving. I sat on a pallet and pregnantly wept, it was all too much.

The company had sent their shipping clerk, Mr Mahindra, *Sorry sah,* he said croakily, his Adam's apple pulsing nervously, *Today holiday, no chance to clear your saman,* (baggage) *just you'll have to wait sah. Thank you sah.* Last seen roped under canvas on a Ghanaian lorry, we did not unpack our belongings for another year.

We stayed overnight in Bombay, and boarded an Indian Airlines plane. It felt as if it had flown too many miles through too many monsoons, and a piece of the overhead trim was loose and dangled above our heads. The stewardess tapped it back, but it fell out again. We were given a cardboard box with a white bread sandwich of curried meat, and a pasty filled with coconut and jam plus a bottle of nauseatingly sweet mango nectar.

At Bangalore airport we were met by a driver in an army styled Willy's jeep. He handed us a terse note from our new British manager, Ken Barlow, *No suitable accommodation Mysore City, Room 17 at Metropole Hotel reserved in your name.* Another hotel! This was too much. It was May 1964, I was 25, Susina was 17 months and the next child was due in August. I clung on to my daughter, and wondered about the new baby inside me, strangely quiet after all our travelling.

We stayed overnight with Tony and Maureen Sparrow, who were welcoming and comforting. Mo was brought up in Ceylon and Tony had been with Imperial Tobacco Company, working in various factories, for many years. He was presently recovering from chronic hepatitis and off sick for months. Mo, noticing my bump, immediately said I could come and stay with them and have our baby in Bangalore. This was a sweet and thoughtful offer.

Chapter 5 - Arrival in India 1964

We enjoyed a leisurely breakfast with the Sparrows and were treated with great respect by their old-fashioned bearer Bullen, in his white tunic and *puggaree* (turban). They all waved us goodbye, including the *mali* (garden boy) who was busy sweeping up leaves. We were off to our new life in Mysore, and it was a comfort to know we already had some real friends; Mike and Tony were BAT pupils together in Southampton in the 1950s.

Tipu Sultan

Our uncomfortable 100 mile jeep journey across the Deccan Plain was hot and dusty. Arthur Wellesley, later Duke of Wellington, marched over it from Madras and used all his brilliant tactics to kill the evil Tipu Sultan at Srirangapatnam but I was not in the mood to be impressed. Water buffalo wandered lazily over bright green paddy fields, the water shimmering between the shoots, and we drove through acres of sugar cane, straw huts and random cattle crowding the roads. Indian poverty was horribly apparent with ramshackle villages, rutty lanes, creaking bullock carts and very undernourished people. I didn't like it and just wanted to go home, our baby wriggled uncomfortably inside me and wanted to go home too.

The over-crowded road was steaming with carts pulled by blue-horned bullocks, belching buses with bent chassis, extravagantly painted lorries and laden trucks driving fast and close. We passed several wrecked vehicles; the accidents caused by swerving, speed, dropping off to sleep or carelessness. We arrived exhausted at the hotel, ate a warmed-up meal, unpacked and tumbled into bed, and were woken early by noisy crows and starlings on the veranda. Susina was stuck in her big wooden cot in the corner.

"Out! Out!" she demanded shaking the sides. I lifted her out and she was soon running around exploring.

"Daddy *seeping*, Daddy *seeping*," she peered at him as he tried to cling on to his slumbers, but her little fingers were poking his ears and he sat up with a grunt. She was such a sweet child and always so amiable.

It was a big room with windows at each end, a dirty coloured carpet, two beds with bedside tables and a sofa by the wall. Behind a dividing curtain was a wardrobe and dressing table and, because it was dark, clouds of mosquitoes. Attached was a large white tiled bathroom with a bathtub, loo and basin, and a back door leading to the laundry lines and dhobi ghat. Compared to our room at the Railway Hotel, this was generous but we would have preferred a proper house. At the front was a wide tiled veranda on which was a round table and four wicker chairs. We did not know it, but Room 17 was to be our home for the next year and the first home of our second child. We settled in and the friendly staff soon learned our names, and Susina became their little star.

The Metropole Hotel, Mysore

The Metropole, formerly a Maharajah's guest house, was twinned with another hotel at the Krishnaraja Sagar Dam. This was a magnificent piece of engineering and the damming of the Cauvery produced water and electricity, and also resulted in the most beautiful stylised Brindavan Gardens with fountains and waterways, all illuminated at night. Our hotel was on Mysore's Jhansi Laxmibai Road and was an imposing double storied city building, with arched colonnaded verandas. We stayed there through all the seasonal changes, and the *tatties* (shades) were rolled up and down to protect us from the harsh sunlight in the winter and summer seasons, and from the thunderous monsoon rains in the spring and autumn. When up, the place was light and airy, when down it was cool and dismal, making our room very dark but at least dry. The brown patterned mosaic tiles were carpeted with coir strips and our room, together with Number 18, shared a large portion of the end of the veranda. The building had a semi-circular driveway and a garden full of hibiscus shrubs and umbrella shaped red flamboyant trees. On Saturdays the obsequious snake charmers came with their cobras and squeaky coconut violins.

Paisa, paisa Memsahib, they whined producing ear splitting twangs, their snakes pirouetting lethargically out of messy baskets. Every Wednesday a huge painted Palace elephant with pink spotted ears ambled up the drive, its big brass bell donging round its neck, its trunk searching aimlessly for banana skins, weaving beneath the wheels of parked black and white

Ambassador taxis.

"Gog Gog! Gog Gog!" Susina ran up and down the veranda on her little legs, excited at seeing such a big dog. She was soon chattering in baby Kanarese to the garden girls, the bearers and the kitchen staff. It was only to Joyce, the Anglo-Indian housekeeper who lived in a small cottage next to the dhobi, to whom she spoke English. The dhobi bashed and banged sheets and towels all day. He was a wiry white haired man who never stopped working, he beat the laundry on his granite stone with a rhythmic slap, slap, slap. Fond of an over use of Reckitts Blue for its whitening agencies, all the sheets and towels soon lost their original colour and became grey. To dry them, the dhobi fixed their corners between two pieces of twisted rope across the back yard of the hotel, and they flapped in the bright sunshine. The rest of his day was spent endlessly pressing with a clanking charcoal iron.

The hotel was run by the Ritz group and managed by an Italian, Enzo Vizioli. There was plenty of bolognese on the menu, and a distinct lack of mulligatawny. Europeans must be Europeans and it was a long time before we discovered the delights of real curry.

Each morning the room bearer, Pakisamy, arrived with a smile, patting his white turban.

Salaam Memsahib, and how are you today, and how is Baba? He was a kindly man and padded through to open the back door to let the khaki-clad sweeper in to slosh out the bathroom. The sweeper was a shy boy. He held a stick broom, a galvanised bucket and a few scraps of cloth. His ration of Vim was solidified into the bottom of a rusty Kissan jam tin, tamped down with a bundle of coconut fibre. He swept and clattered, scoured and swabbed and left the floor awash. Meanwhile one of the girls came in and scratched the floor and carpet with a bunch of twigs, whilst the bearer smoothed the beds. A few flaps of Pakisamy's grimy cloth completed the dusting.

Word got around that we were in residence and curious Indian ladies came to call. They heard there were Europeans at the hotel and appeared in Ambassador cars with their drivers. They'd completed their cooking for the day, had their *head baths* and washed their bodies, oiled their hair, and prayed to their own particular deity in the puja room, lighting oil lamps and arranging blossom in strategic places. Their hair and make-up was immaculate, eyes ringed with kohl, a colourful *bindi* in place on the forehead and, always, a dusting of talcum powder settling into the creases of their necks. Their crisp cotton saris were brilliantly coloured and their toes had rings and painted pearly nails, whilst diamonds winked in their ears. The scent of sandalwood emanated from the moisture of dusky pores. They sat uneasily, feet parted on the coir matting, knees decorously covered by the folds of their saris.

Conversation was stilted, black eyes widened and heads waggled from side to side in the Indian fashion, as they tried to understand my accent, my bulbous shape, my short dress and my little, very blonde, daughter who chattered non-stop. After powdery chicory coffee with the skin of the boiled milk floating on top and tasteless Marie biscuits, they went away often never to be seen again. But I did manage to ask them about ayahs.

"Difficult," they replied with expressionless faces, "Very difficult for *Yewro-peeans* not knowing *lang-wage*."

The hot weather made pregnancy uncomfortable and we needed someone to play with Susina and wash our clothes. After making a few enquiries with the hotel staff, within a day Pushpa came brightly to our door. She was young, with a pretty face, white and even teeth and a cheerful smile and a rich orange marigold stuck into her black oiled plait.

“Hello sweetie,” she said cheerfully in perfect English to Susina, crouching down to toddler level.

Susina smiled and said, “Come play,” making for her scantily filled toy basket.

Morose mutterings overheard here and there during the next few days substantiated that Pushpa was definitely suspect. She wore a glittery nose ornament and big earrings, glass bangles tinkled on her wrists and her feet were patterned with henna. My new found lady friends tweaked their saris disapprovingly, “Too pretty,” they tutted, “Not a good girl. Loose living."

Stereotyped European trained servants annoyed me, they were too set in their ways and usually too bossy. In Africa we were happier with the boys from the bush and, as soon as we were able to share their tribal language, we made friends and they felt confident in our home. Pushpa's lifestyle and health caused a little concern so we sent her to the Mission Hospital for a medical check-up.

‘Please test for syphilis,’ was boldly requested in the note. She came back *All is Clear* so we shut our ears to the rumours, we liked her cheerful, willing ways, and her sing-song voice. We paid her a generous £4 a month. Her salary quickly went on a new sari, another dozen glass bangles or a pair of glitzy gold coloured earrings.

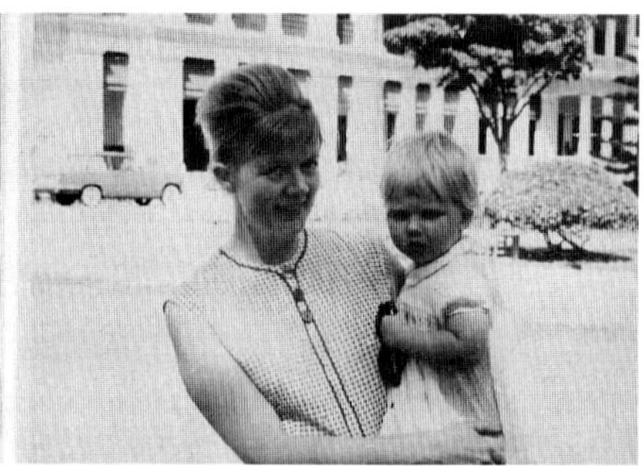

My pregnancy was very public, and my shift style dresses did not hide my bump. Mike started lengthy travelling and Susina and I were constantly alone, getting used to living in a big hotel which accommodated a constant mixture of guests both Indian and foreign from aid organisations. Permanent residents, including us, were two British and two American families occupying the largest rooms. Two were above us and one was next door. Our neighbours in Number 18 were Betty-Jo and Benton Bristol. Unable to find a house with a western bathroom in town, they opted to stay in the hotel. They crammed the room with their own dining, sitting and sleeping furniture, as well as plants, books, lamps and a record player. Benton worked at the University and Betty-Jo spent much of her time sewing. Their lives were mundane and they knew little of life in India and, seemingly, had no interest. She was a quiet sweet woman, and both liked children and sometimes played with Susina. Occasionally we pushed our chairs together to chat on our shared veranda. They never took tea or coffee, but I always requested a mid-morning drink and my round table was spread with a steel tray with a matching coffee pot, milk jug and sugar basin. These shiny things were a lure for beady eyed crows constantly swooping on the tray, four or five at a time, teetering on the edges whilst they flapped their big, black wings and stuck their nasty beaks into the sugar and milk. Sometimes Susina flapped her little arms to chase them away; making me nervous that one might land on her with its sharp, strong claws. They were a menace.

At lunch the British and Americans sat on opposite sides of the high ceilinged majestic dining room. It was the height of two storeys with a balcony at the top, and the wooden floors echoed. The bearers wore stiff white turbans, stained uniforms and soup-soaked gloves. Over-sized portraits of the big eyed Maharajah, his father and his grandfather stared solemnly down as we ate our western styled meals. Susina was very difficult about hotel food, and it was easier to give her a selection of tastes in our room. Mike was away most of the time so did not share many dining room experiences. The Americans picked at their meals, worried about their stomachs, and drank endless pots of tea.

The other British family were Mike's boss, Ken Barlow, and his wife Rosemarie and their little daughter, Nicole, who was a year older than Susina. Ken was an agricultural research graduate and employed by the Indian Leaf Tobacco Company (ILTD) to start up the Mysore project. Rosemarie was much younger and a good-natured Austrian. Life for her was lonely and she was very occupied with Nicole. Each day, when we met for lunch, she told us graphically of Nicole's most recent bowel movement. Nicole's *shtools* took precedence whilst the food before us cooled and became glutinous, the *shtools,* on the other hand, were soft, sticky, green, slimy or *vairy vairy shtink*.

Rosemarie made friends with another friendly Austrian, Mitzi, who was married to an Indian Air Force officer, Squadron Leader Purushotam. They helped us get to know people as there were few expatriates in the city, and the sociable Mysoreans seemed to be set into two separate groups. There was the steady, stoical Irani camp, and the more lively swinging 60s Bedi camp. Farrokh Irani was a prosperous Parsee who owned and managed the Jawa motor cycle factory in conjunction with its Czech mother company, which assisted with technical skills and finances. The two-stroke bikes buzzed all over India and were ideal in traffic and on muddy rural footpaths. Sheila Irani was from the English speaking, minority Anglo-Indian community which originates in India. She was a kindly, powerful woman with a commanding voice. Sheila and her gang of eager friends were involved in good works, as well as cards, gossip and over indulgent tea parties.

The Bedis were a Punjabi Sikh family who owned the Mandya Paper Mill near Srirangapatnam, which used sugar cane waste, *bagasse*, as its base product. An orthodox family, the older men were turbaned and bearded. They lived on the outskirts of town close to the imperious Lalitha Mahal Palace and near the racecourse in one of a colony of bungalows rented from the Maharajah. Their bungalow was called Kismut, set well back from the road in a large compound with a semi-circular drive, and a deep trellised veranda. We never entered the parents' part of the house and the mother and aunts were a mere splash of rich silk, moving quietly in the front quarters. There were two sons, the large one was nicknamed Gigi married to Deep and the shorter one called Gogi (or Mohinder) married to Meera, a fellow student who came from Sind. They had met in America and their's was a love match, frowned upon by most elders as being unsuitable. Gogi gained a degree at Berkeley in California and returned crew-cutted and shaven, liberated and straining against the privations of sensible life in Mysore. It was a very proper city, unused to the western wafts of the emerging Beatles, the sounds of *Roll Over Beethoven* and the decadence of flower power. Meera felt swamped by communal living and escaped most mornings, wearing slacks and a sweater, her long plait swinging to her hips, to ride the Maharajah's horses stabled in the ornate block across the road. She enjoyed the precision of dressage.

The young Bedis swept us up with glee. They wanted our liveliness, our booze and our conversation. Gogi and Meera lived in an apartment at the rear of the house, trendily decorated with purple curtains, steel shelving and a music system from San Francisco. They also had two sweet little girls, Amrita and Nandini, with big brown eyes and long, long lashes. Their music got better and better, crowds drove in from Bangalore and the parties grew wilder and wilder, with people leaping into the murky swimming pool and dancing all night. We drifted away before it all got too much. Meera was such a gentle person and she and I always remained good friends, although she was ostracised by so many in the town. Educated and humorous, she was good company and fun to be with. The family became so dysfunctional that the business went to the wall, the marriages floundered, the children scattered and Kismut became just a shabby shell. Many years later I met Meera by chance in the Tollygunge Club in Calcutta. It was a brief huggy reunion, she had married a Bengali and was happy.

Near Kismut was the club and we were advised it was important to join, not necessarily for its social amenities, but for the reciprocal advantages of being able to use other clubs. At that time there were few western hotels, so a comfortable club with shabby but clean facilities, servants whose eyes rolled with memories of the *good old days,* and English breakfasts with papaya and fresh lime slice, scrambled eggs, toast and marmalade were not to be missed. So we joined the Mysore Sports Club which affiliated with many of the south Indian clubs although, sadly not the Ooty Snooty from which we were always barred.

The club was used strictly for cards by permit holding men who drank Black Knight whisky. The state government imposed tough prohibition rules, and it was difficult for anyone to get alcohol anywhere else. Often during my lonely evenings on the hotel veranda, two or three Mysorean men turned up to visit. It was difficult as Mike was not around, and they sloped along the passage and hovered, not knowing what to say.

Madam, have you got your permit yet, have you got it? one Professor finally asked, having bombarded me with the headlines from the Deccan Herald, the Hindu and The Times of India to keep me up to date.

"Permit?" I queried.

For liquor, please, he prompted expectantly, hairy eyebrows twitching, *Have you got your units, most important?*

"Oh, you mean alcohol?" Someone told us to go to some government office to get a permit. "No, not yet," was my reply.

Well, when you get, please remember me Madam, I am Vital Rao, Professor of Yinglish Vital Rao, and having wonly one unit per month, wonly one. Now you, you foreigners, normally will get twenty units monthly, no? Too much for you, not needing, isn't it? he giggled embarrassed, *But you can share and boost our short supply. No? I am asking, can you share?*

"I'll have to wait until my husband gets back," wishing he'd go away, "Ask him when he comes to the club."

Wokay, Wokay, said Vital Rao sadly, *But please remember Madam, I am Vital Rao and need a few units please. I am only asking, listen please,* and off he went, scratching his bottom through his dhoti, to join his friends in the Metropole Permit Room, a badly lit bar at the end of the hotel frequented by traders and businessmen alike. Social drinking was only enjoyed in private homes behind closed doors.

The following week, egged on by the new found thirsty whisky drinkers, we were soon directed to the appropriate government minister. Bulky in unflattering maternity clothes, at a time when the mere whiff of gin made me feel quite sick, I was reluctant to admit a dependency on alcohol. The stone stairways were littered with dust, straw and scraps, the walls soiled with that worn-on grime look, the corners well splattered with generous gobs of red betel juice. There were people everywhere scurrying around with sheaves of beige folders covered in sealing wax. We walked through filthy rooms littered with heavy wooden desks until we reached the dingy office crowded with curious clerks and typists. Dust laden cardboard files tied with string seemed to hold the building together. The rooms were crammed with wooden desks piled with rough grey curling papers slumped over by sleepy clerks.

The Commissioner was stern but compromising, "You want units? I'll give you, but how much do you need, how much do you drink Mr and Mrs Vitley? Are you dependent?"

We smiled nervously and admitted we needed to drink every day, and to entertain liberally. He agreed knowingly and with a flourish of a signature we came away with, as expected, twenty units each, an allowance of forty bottles of spirit per month. No wonder we gathered so many followers.

Chapter 6 – Mysore City

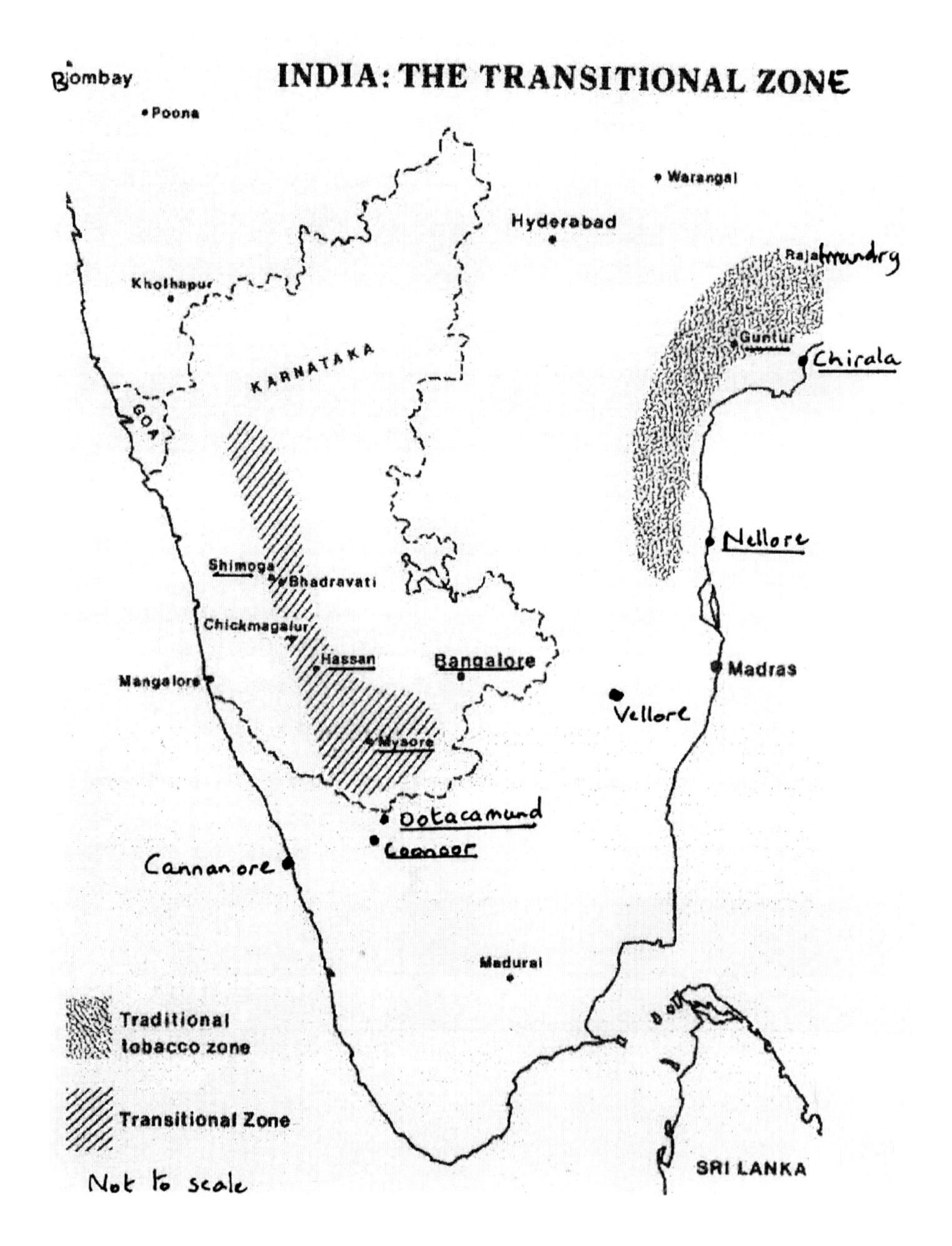

Shortly after our arrival, on 27 May 1964, Jawaharlal Nehru died and the country was in shock. Born in 1889, he married at the age of 26 and fathered his only child, Indira, who later followed in his political footsteps. Like his father, Motilal, Jawarharlal came under the spell of Mahatma Gandhi and was part of the *Quit India* movement spending 18 years in prison. He became India's Prime Minister at Independence in 1947.

Jawaharlal Nehru in 1947

In 1954, with Chou-en-lai of China, he drew up an agreement of peaceful co-existence, but his trust was completely betrayed by the Chinese invasion in 1962, the spirit went out of him and, later, he suffered a stroke. After his death he was succeeded by Lal Bahadur Shastri and, in 1966 by his daughter, Indira, married to Feroze Gandhi. She held office twice, until she was assassinated in 1984. The death of Nehru caused severe disruption at a time when we were trying to settle down, and were not yet used to India's constant dramas.

Nehru is remembered for reorganising the states on a linguistic basis, Kanarese in the case of Mysore, and for industrialisation, the burgeoning city of Bangalore being a good example, as well as the vast irrigation schemes co-ordinated under his premiership.

Mysore is a languid city and a major centre for incense manufacture. It has a central avenue called One Hundred Foot Road with the proportions of a Parisian boulevard. Most of the avenues leading into the centre are lined with red flamboyant and purple Pride of India trees and the public buildings are imposing, mainly built of red stone. Until Independence in 1947 the city was the seat of the Mysore Maharajahs. The ruling family of Mysore State, the Wodeyars, were well respected and did as much as possible for the people and Mysore was known for benevolent rule. The University of Mysore was set up in the late twenties and the state was the first where electric power was available.

Central to the city, the walled palace crowned with domes and turrets, arches and colonnades, is a veritable treasure trove of exquisite carvings and works of art from all over the world. It was built in 1912 and continued to provide a family residence for the royalty of Mysore. The imposing Durbar Hall was designed with a particularly ornate ceiling and built with sculpted pillars and marble floors, all enclosed by silver doors and, at the famous Dussehra festival, the magnificent golden throne was on view, all 280 kilos of pure gold. One section of the palace was open to the elements, tiered with seats which provided a theatrical backdrop for performances and processions on the parade ground. During festivals the whole palace is outlined and veiled in a myriad of tiny light bulbs, a truly beautiful sight.

Before the festival of Dussehra took place, the city was spring cleaned and coloured lights and floral arches were erected over the wide streets. Statues were scrubbed and buildings whitewashed. There was an impressive procession of flower decked images of deities, cavalry, liveried retainers and richly decorated elephants accompanied by brass bands. The Maharajah, affectionately referred to as His Heaviness, was very rotund and sat in a golden howdah aboard a painted elephant covered in gold cloth and clanging bells. Little boys ran behind picking up the hot dung with their hands and filling baskets. Sheila Irani, the Chairman of Mysore Arts and Crafts, invited us to watch it all from one of the windows of her Emporium. This was a grand sandalwood and incense perfumed building stuffed with rosewood tables and elephants intricately inlaid with ivory and other woods. In the evening we attended a Durbar at the palace, in the presence of the Maharajah, whose plump neck was covered with onion sized pearls, and whose podgy feet were encased in slippers made from real gold. After the Durbar there was a long procession lit by flares which climbed Chamundi Hill, past Nandi Bull carved out of solid rock, and up to the Maharajah's summer palace to the very high Sri Chamundeswari temple at the top where final obeisances were made. We were impressed with the pageantry and opulence, soon to fade into a memory as political conditions made it impossible for Maharajahs to continue to prosper.

At Independence, 287 princes were granted privy purses under the Constitution, and received tax free and generous allowances from the government dependent on the size of their principalities. This privilege was severed abruptly in 1971 when Indira Gandhi requested the president, V V Giri, to vote against them by presidential proclamation. The shock for the royal families was devastating but added *crores* (one crore = 10 million) of rupees to the Exchequer. It was a real betrayal of promise.

Close to the Arts and Crafts was the library. We had no books and I was desperate for something to read, so registered in the gloomy, musty building. There is nothing like the smell of old, well used Indian books, it insidiously permeates a building, a place, a house, and an atmosphere. Books and paper were so precious that volumes of any value were repaired, restored and never discarded even if falling to bits. The paper had the odour of death; the pages were soft and discoloured, the printing faded and illegible. I went to the desk and coped with the usual Indian bureaucratic questions, natural shyness providing an unhelpful expression on the librarian's face.

"What is your native place? What is your monthly upkeep? Husband's name? Caste?" The woman could not meet my eye, she was embarrassed and touched her plait, decorated with browning limp jasmine. The questions were brusque and I responded with as much politeness as I could manage. Three tickets were issued and, whilst wandering amongst the tall wooden shelves in the cavernous room half lit by mildewed windows, imagine my despair to discover all the books were re-bound centuries before and identified only by numbers. I questioned the librarian, "Where can I find the titles of the books please?"

Because she was unused to foreigners and to my English accent, her demeanour was stern and unfriendly.

"In the files," she replied fiercely, eyes down, "Those wood cases near the walls please."

Opening one or two drawers made it obvious that the card index was in a worse state than the books, very old, thumbed, and a difficult system to follow. I gave up and went to the shelves and picked out one or two books, but they held no interest and I was not ready for the challenge of the Mysore library again. Gradually I got to know various women involved in paperback exchange, mostly Mills and Boon or Barbara Cartland. These were locally and shoddily printed on poor quality paper, with broken type and oily ink. The sentences sloped across the pages, there were uneven margins and rusting metal staples. More irritating was that avid English scholars underlined significant words, expressions even whole paragraphs, absolutely ruining any concentration on the story. Desperate I read them and pined for a decent bookshop.

It took several years before we could purchase what we would describe as modern consumables. It was a difficult time to adjust and bring up a young family after the refinement of our life in Ghana, where just about everything was available. Indian coins from the colonial era still carried the head of George VI. When we arrived the money was traditionally in *annas* and *rupees* although the flimsy, light metal *naya paisa* coins had just been introduced. However I got stuck into the anna habit, sixteen to a rupee and, because of their love of nick names the rupee was, more often than not, known as a *chip.*

Quite near to the palace was New Statue Circle, lined with small shops selling cloth, metal ware, medicines and saris. One was Sreenivasa Stores where our company, Indian Leaf Tobacco Development Ltd, arranged for us to cash cheques. Mike opened a bank account at National Grindlays in Calcutta but was unable to obtain one in my name. For the next 14 years I was dependent on handouts finding it incredibly tiresome as he was away so often, and failed to remember many times, despite *chits* (notes) in his shirt pocket, telephoning him at his desk (phones rarely worked) or leaving messages in his jeep. In the end I developed my *envelope* system in a locked cupboard, saving notes and dividing them into *servants, food* etc. Mike scoffed, but it worked, there was always some cash stashed away somewhere, and this could be borrowed until he came home again.

The ILTD rented a small outbuilding in the hotel grounds. There they established an office employing a frog-faced stenographer called Narayana Rao. He was neatly dressed in sandals, tight green trousers and a clean *tericot* shirt in yellow and brown checks. His forehead was smeared with limey stripes and he stuck a little red shiny *buttu* above the bridge of his nose. His hair was thick and wavy, well oiled and never out of place. He was a helpful man if a little diffident. He tapped methodically on a vintage Remington, trying to keep the carbon paper the right way round. When he got the chance he would nip outside to smoke a *beedie*. This was a thin hand-made cigarette, the cheap tobacco held together by a tendu leaf (*Diospyros melanoxylon)* and tied by a tiny length of thread. He lit it and cupped his hand and inhaled the smoke through the hole between thumb and forefinger. It was a very normal way to smoke, and afterwards it was very normal to clear the throat and produce a massive great gob of phlegm, which would land, sizzling and steaming, wherever it was aimed.

Mysore State (now Karnataka) was in the south west of India with Goa and Maharashtra to the north, the Bay of Bengal and the Coromandel Coast to the east and the Arabian sea and Malabar Coast to the west. It was a particularly agricultural area with at least 75% of its population involved in subsistence farming. Andhra Pradesh was the traditional tobacco growing area but, in the early 1960s, was threatened by the proposed construction of the massive Nagarjunasagar Dam which, when completed, would swamp several hundred thousand hectares of the black cotton soil area into an irrigated zone. Irrigation produces high chlorine in tobacco making it *off type*, unsuitable for processing. As well, another situation had reared its ugly head and that was of the potential shortfall from Rhodesia, soon to be threatened by Ian Smith's Unilateral Declaration of Independence and crippling United Nations sanctions. Mike's job was to locate suitable tobacco growing areas large enough to replace these huge shortfalls, so maps were purchased and studied, plans made, areas chalked out and he soon started on his survey work. Indian bureaucracy was probably at its worst at this time, the country was in the transition of the aftermath of the British Raj and the Chinese invasion, somewhat in limbo, clinging on to the British system whilst trying to evolve its own. It was not until 1970 that expatriates started moving in to take up advisory and consultative roles and joint ventures, usually on a contract basis. Meanwhile it was a muddle between Indo and Anglo.

A Gowda farm

Unbendable government clerks nationwide stuck grimly to the old rules, and information gathering at *taluk* level (a sub-section of a District) was frustrating. Rainfall was always recorded in colonial times, but obtaining the figures from the *Tahsildars* (officials) was an exercise requiring great patience. It was at a time of severe rationing and everything needed authorising by *No Objection Certificates* required by all government departments, whether it was wireless and driving licences, liquor permits, dog licence, a sack of rice or a bag of cement. The No Objection Permits were produced and signed by all sorts of officials such as the Block Development Officer, the Tahsildar or the local Police Inspector. India was awash with purple indelible ink and weighed down by rubber stamps.

We soon discovered that there was a great courtesy given to British people by the Indian majority. They treated us like best friends and had the highest regard for our reliability and trustworthiness and, at times, it was difficult to match their expected standards. Once Mike got busy he was impressed with the governance of the state, although some of it was shambolic and a few of the newer government officers were unhelpful, mainly because they did not know any better. But there was a basic structure of departments of horticulture, agriculture, education, health and so on. It made research a little easier than in other areas, like Andhra Pradesh, where the system had fallen apart.

Mike and his driver Dorai Raj, a spruce ex-Army corporal, with a clipped moustache and bright smile, went off in the Willy's jeep, designed with high wheels and canvas door flaps to keep out the inclement weather. They travelled thousands of miles on rough roads and tracks in this Army exercise vehicle, which jarred and jolted every bone in the body. Together they explored *taluks* during the days and shared nights in filthy government rest houses and *dak* travellers bungalows; bare shells of places providing the meanest of facilities. Dorai Raj proved a competent guide and camp cook. He disjointed skinny chickens and simmered the bony birds with peppers and onions, accompanied by boiled rice, and tomato and potato stews served with slices of sugary baker's bread. Bananas and oranges were plentiful and in some places they could occasionally purchase biscuits, eggs and salt bread. Cooking was done over three stones with damp wood and often there was no water or light. They slept either on infested rope charpois slung from iron ceiling hooks or rock hard steel bunks. A bath was a bucket of cold water, the toilet a hole in the ground. Both carried bedrolls and wore thick jackets. Mysore State, at over three thousand feet and during a heavy monsoon, could be dank and chilling.

The weeks were tediously long for Susina and me. He left very early each Monday morning and returned exhausted and late on a Friday night. The telephone system in the main towns was erratic, in the countryside it was non-existent so there was no contact. There were two months before the baby was due and still we were homeless. Mike had found two poky flats in the suburb of Yadavagiri with western style bathrooms and manageable kitchens, and it was agreed to take these on lease for the Barlows and us. Construction was stopped due to lack of cement, the owner promised completion in six weeks, all we could do was wait but the six weeks never came.

"Better find out where you can have the baby," Mike smiled encouragingly as he left on one of his trips. Susina and I waved dejectedly and felt very alone.

We heard that Dr Angie Stephenson was the best consultant for a safe delivery. "You will like her Nataleee," urged my lady friends, "We all go to her, and even our cousins come from Bangalore to have their babies here."

Angie was a small, matter of fact Malayalee gynaecologist. She was well into her sixties and delivered Royal babies, planters' babies, foreign babies, jockeys' babies and lots of Mysorean and Kerala babies. Her fame flew far and wide, and pregnant women booked into the Planters' Wards at the Holdsworth Memorial Hospital in their droves. She was cheerful, full of energy and common sense. I liked her immediately; she was a far cry from the carrot-haired, cruel Swiss midwife who extracted Susina from my body at the Basel Mission Hospital in Agogo.

I waddled into her consulting room which was old fashioned and dingy. There was a brown leather couch covered with a rumpled sheet, a deep porcelain sink and terracotta tiled floor. The windows were high, the building old and light rationed. A young nurse in a stiff white sari and starched cap fluttered until given instructions. Angie sported a well used stethoscope and wore a long white coat over her blue cotton sari. Her eyes smiled behind her steel rimmed spectacles and her grey hair was pinned up in a bun. Her voice was gentle but with an air of authority.

"Big baby," she breathed as she prodded my swollen tummy and listened intently with a brass trumpet, "Heart is OK," she smiled, "And your blood pressure is normal. Off you go and come back in six weeks." It was a relief to have found someone who gave me confidence, more so when we discovered that she qualified in London as a Doctor of the Royal College of Gynaecologists. We looked at the Planters' Wards, two private rooms with antiquated bathrooms, birds nesting in the lights and concrete floors. They were rather grubby with super clean starched nurses on hand. Well, if everyone else went there it must be all right.

"Better than Agogo?" asked Mike wanting my approval.

"Definitely no birds nests at Agogo," I answered. Holdsworth was tolerable but it was not the London Clinic.

Simon arrived at 8am on 24 August two days before his due date, which was a relief as I was almost bursting. Indian babies are small and delicate, so my monster at 10lbs 1oz was especially cheer making. The evening before, we went out to dinner and it was an astute Deep Bedi who whispered, "Natalie are you in labour?" I nodded and hushed her, the pains were light and would go on for some time. We got back to the hotel before midnight and asked Pushpa to stay and sleep, well wrapped up, on the veranda. At 3am Mike telephoned Angie as it was silly to wait any longer. "Come straight away," she urged, "I'll be in the labour room."

Mike, half-asleep, dropped me off, patted me on the shoulder with a "Good luck sweetie," and returned to the hotel, leaving me alone again.

The labour area was a primitive badly lit room with murky metal windows and a rusty fan. The nurses, always looking as if they could not bend they were so starched, fussed around me like butterflies. Their tiny fingers were well meant but useless, I longed for Mike's strong hands to rub my back. Finally we got going with pushing and puffing and our son was born after twenty hours of labour with his cord around his neck. Quickly Angie released him and marvelled at his size, "A Maharajah!" she said with glee.

There was no rest and I was soon busy looking after our baby. The nursing skills were airy fairy and every bottle of milk prepared was boiling hot and I was up and down changing nappies, bathing Simon and feeding him. The room was simple, not clean, and full of twittering sparrows, as well as long legged spiders and cockroaches. Bits of straw and grass and non-hygienic débris fluttered down. The sparrows woke at 6am, and continued cheeping well into the evening, and plenty of curious visitors came and went and presented us with pretty handmade shirts and shorts. Producing a boy gave me a new status, but they were all rather alarmed at Simon's size. As far as Mike and I were concerned he was a cracker, but I wondered why Mike referred to him as *she* for several months after his birth; in his heart did he really want another girl?

Mike brought Susina to see us. She liked her *bubby* very much, but did not even give me a glance, she was angry and unsure, maybe because it was a strange place. Next day she came with Pushpa and was more amenable. No matter how hard you tell a child about a soon-to-be-born new baby, it is still a shock when it arrives, and she was only 21 months old. We returned to the hotel after about three days, Simon with the inevitable tummy bug and on anti-biotics. He slept in a canvas baby bed behind the wardrobe whilst Susina had restless nights in her cot. No matter how quiet we were, or how low the lights, she was disturbed by our mere presence and, when the baby cried, she cried.

Simon had very few belongings, there was really nothing in the shops except Johnson's baby powder and satin outfits covered in stiff gold ribbon. One problem was baby milk powder. My *Good Housekeeping* book insisted that once baby was on a formula it must not be changed, and the invisible author in leafy England wagged her finger at me as I mixed up yet another brand. In Mysore it was impossible to follow that maxim as stocks of milk were scarce and we grabbed what was available. Mike was wonderful, journeying, around the state visiting outlying medical shops to buy up tins of Ostermilk, Nespray or Amul. The latter was local, made of fatty buffalo milk. Simon took to it all and thrived so there was no point in worrying. Feeding Susina was another matter, she was a strong willed toddler who had travelled too much without routine. Hotels did not cater for babies and toddlers, the food at Tabora was highly flavoured and textured, and in Mysore even stronger. No good for little tummies and she survived on mashed bananas and bread, supplemented by powdered baby milk, I did not trust fresh milk from the hotel kitchen nor the half washed metal milk jugs. Clean filtered drinking water was another problem and the bearer did not convince me that, "Yes Madam, the cook just boiled this water Madam, truly please."

In the end we started importing infant food at great expense from Singapore. For ourselves we brought in shampoo as all the Indian bottles were laced with coconut oil and made our hair very greasy, rather than clean and shiny. We managed to buy a second-hand electric ring on which to boil water, heat baby bottles, and warm up baby foods. We kept it in the bathroom, where we finally moved Susina's cot so she could get some peace. No doubt we were frowned upon as in India the bathroom is almost as sacred as the puja room, and only used for bathing and the toilet, but living in one room was proving a dreadful experience.

Several months previously our kit was sent from Bombay to Bangalore cigarette factory for storage. We decided to extract the pram, baby changing table and the bigger cot for Simon, our radiogram and some toys. Mike went up in the jeep and discovered all our boxes had been rumbled by customs at Bombay. He opened every container to find the things he wanted. However it was worth the effort and made our lives a little more comfortable and cheerful. We were able to listen to our long playing records of Ella Fitzgerald, Frank Sinatra, and Louis Armstrong and, for me, the Brandenburg Concertos.

Like Susina, Simon was a sweet and easy baby, his start in life was good and he was soon thriving and giggling, and became a hotel favourite. He had a stuffed giraffe and loved it so much he almost sucked the animal's ears off. His own little ears protruded so I resorted to sticking them to his head with Elastoplast. Residents and hotel staff did not approve of this method, the plasters were stiff and left black rubbery marks all round his baby ears, but we persisted for a year and put up with all the criticism. It was primitive and effective and Simon has flat ears.

Pushpa played endlessly with Susina and also proved to be an excellent baby ayah. Susina soon cuddled up to me again, stroking Simon's head as he fed. In the morning she ran to his cot and smiled, "See *bubby*, see *bubby*," she said happily. She was talking more, calling herself *Seena* and saying "Naughty, naughty," when she threw all her food on the floor. She hated Mike going away each Monday morning, she watched the old jeep pull out of the drive, waved the last wave and sadly say, "Daddy gone, Daddy gone."

Susina and Simon in 1964

Chapter 7 – Tobacco

For the best part of a year Mike, and his driver Dorai Raj, travelled the entire state checking rainfall, testing soil, farmers' skills and transportation. Life without him was very humdrum but Susina was usually lively and full of beans, enjoying stories and games and we shared a lot of home-made fun. Simon was amiable and slowly learned how to turn over and watch the world from a different angle. They did not escape fevers and illness. The weather was changeable, sometimes very wet, or hot, or windy and they caught colds and suffered high temperatures. Simon became really ill with a fever and was pitifully miserable and weeping. The doctor prescribed the usual anti-biotics, and these controlled the temperature, but it was against my nature to use such strong drugs.

In November the festival of light, Diwali, occurred. It is the happiest of all Hindu festivals, when thousands of oil lamps are lit to show Rama the way home from exile. For five days firecrackers burst everywhere, and the ground before doorways are decorated with swirly chalky designs, new clothes purchased, oil baths taken and sweets exchanged. Mike took a rare day off and, as the Barlows were on leave, we used Ken's comfortable 1957 Plymouth car (assembled in India), and went with the children and Pushpa for an outing. We took a hotel picnic and it was all a wonderful treat. We drove to a star-shaped temple at Somnathpur, built around 1260 AD during the heyday of the Hoysala kings. It was small and superb, covered with intricately carved stone sculptures depicting tales from the Ramanaya and other stories. No two scenes were the same and it is still a little gem in a perfect paddy green rural setting. The countryside was quite flat, but heavily cultivated with pulses, grains and mulberry bushes for the silk trade. The villages were squalid, highlighting the poverty and lack of facilities, and the over population of India was apparent. We drove to the Brindavan terraced water gardens at Krishnaraja Sagar, laid out on the side of a great dam near the confluence of three rivers - Cauvery, Hemavathi and Lakshmanathirtha. Susina loved scampering along the footpaths amongst the geometric flowerbeds red with cannas. At night the gardens were illuminated and the cascades and fountains danced to the rhythm of music.

Our boring life at the hotel suddenly became exciting when an MGM film unit arrived to make the film *Maya,* in partnership with an Indian company. The film was about a little boy and an elephant and made in the foothills of the Nilgiri mountains. The production team used the Metropole for a base, accommodation and offices and their packed lunches. Clint Walker was the big star, Jay North the little boy and two Indian stars, Jairaj and I S Johar, provided local interest. Mary Chipperfield from the circus family flew out with a tiger, a leopard and a cheetah, and the animals lodged in the zoo. It was an exciting time and there were plenty of spectators peering over the boundary walls, and I was offered secretarial work which kept me occupied earning some cash to fill my envelopes. Money was tight and we got few perks.

An eccentric, friendly lady, Kitty Buhler, who handled Public Relations, told me she was 41 and a Hollywood screenwriter. She was scrawny with cropped hair, big teeth and a huge personality, and she fell madly in love with baby Simon. I typed letters to her stockbroker and tried not to giggle whilst she dictated: *Dear Beautiful Man, My soul is yearning for you and it will not be too soon for me to come back and take care of you. Darling boy, I hope you realise that my shares have lost 5% in the last few weeks, please buy 3000 Cosmat and put them up to 62. You delicious thing you...*

Kitty became ill with a bad stomach and, Dr Bell, the old-fashioned English missionary physician from the hospital, was summoned. He courteously knocked on Kitty's door and was instantly invited in.

"Men queue to come and see me," she purred whilst he, highly embarrassed, questioned her bowel and vomit movements. Strong anti-biotics soon put her right and she minced up and down the veranda in one of her new saris. Kitty had been a United Press correspondent, a lecturer and had written some of the most popular television shows such as *Dragnet* and *My Three Sons.* Shortly after she left Mysore, Kitty was married for the third time to the five-star General Omar Bradley, who served under General Dwight D Eisenhower in World War II. He was a 73-year old widower and they met in Okinawa in 1950 when she was a freelance writer. Kitty was a devoted wife and edited many of Bradley's writings. He died aged 88 in 1981, and Kitty died on St Valentine's Day 2004 and is buried beside him at Arlington National Cemetery.

Metropole Dinner – Mike, Kitty, Mr Ahmed, Enzo Vizioli, Jairaj, Natalie

On return to the US she did not forget Simon and wrote: *I have his adorable face propped up on my desk and look at him constantly both with love, and a deep disturbance, with the knowledge that he is living on watered down buffalo milk, goat and rotten carrots. I am sorry that you, Mike and Susina have to put up with all that, but you are inflicting a direct cruelty upon me exposing Simon to this. I will send you everything here in America. Send me Simon.*'

Construction work on the Yadavagiri flats dragged on, it was almost a year since they were located and it was obvious that we would not occupy one. Our future was becoming more certain, Mike finally finished the survey, wrote a lengthy report and new areas for tobacco growing were selected. These were in Hunsur, Hassan, and Shimoga. It was decided we should move to Hassan, but to take advantage of our local leave in the hills first. Anything was better than hotel living with two small children, so the move to a permanent home became a bright spot on our horizon and, for Mike, the large area meant a challenging leaf growing job. Apart from a sprinkling of coffee planters in Coorg, around Saklaspur and in Chikmagalur, few Europeans remained in those districts. There were small clusters of industry, but the land was mainly used for subsistence agriculture farmed by *Gowdas* living in hamlets, clearing their fields with hand hoes and tilling the heavy soil with pairs of yoked bullocks and wooden plough hooks. Their produce was carried to *shandy (*weekly market) by creaking carts.

I have always been impressed with the responsible way in which BAT, and the subsidiary companies all over the world, have grown tobacco. When we were married none of us had any idea of the detrimental effect of tobacco on health. As a management pupil in Nigeria, Mike was trained to work alongside small farmers operating in scattered rural communities. The farmers, who were registered and their records documented, were taught new skills and provided with seed, fertiliser and other supplies to improve soil, water conservation and to encourage growth yields. Wood was used for curing and re-afforestation methods were quickly introduced. The agricultural practices usually ensured a food crop grown on the residual fertiliser after tobacco harvesting. Whole families were involved with the work but young children were not encouraged on the sites.

Hassan – Ken Gill and Mike

The peasant farmers of Mysore were not familiar with tobacco as a crop and needed training. The ground had to be well prepared and *stumped*, or cleared of tree roots. The seeds, smaller than grains of sand, were sown through the roses of watering cans and nurtured on raised beds, then the plants were set on ridges and constantly inspected for suckers and useless leaves. Harvesting from the bottom of the plant was fastidious, and the work unpleasant as the leaves are very sticky. For the flue-cured variety, barns were built; flue pipes installed and furnaces constructed. Curing is a technical process which goes on 24 hours a day and needs constant monitoring. At the beginning farmers were recruited from Andhra Pradesh to help the Gowdas with the first cure. The ILTD had been heavily involved with tobacco growing in Andhra since the 1920s.

Cigarette making started in a big way in America, and the American Tobacco Company was established by *Buck Duke* (James Buchanan Duke). By 1885 it was well established but the American government did not like either monopolistic companies or smoking. Undeterred *Buck Duke* bought into the British market, his first catch being Ogdens of Liverpool, then Players of Nottingham and Wills of Bristol. The British, in true British fashion, closed ranks against *The Duke from New York* and in December 1901 the Imperial Tobacco Company (of Great Britain and Ireland) Ltd was formed. Battle began between *Duke* and Imperial (GB&I), involving price slashing, bonus schemes and new advertising. In 1902, both American Tobacco Company and Imperial (GB&I) declared an agreement and marketed each other's brands but did not invade each other's territories. A new organisation, British American Tobacco Company Limited (BAT), was set up and registered in the UK to handle overseas trade, with two thirds of its stock owned by American Tobacco Company and *Buck Duke* its first Chairman. The American government persisted that monopolies such as American Tobacco and Standard Oil were against free trade and they were ordered, under the Sherman Anti-Trust Act of 1891, to be broken up. American Tobacco sold off its majority shareholding in BAT, and plans were made to develop operations abroad. Those in India - Peninsular, Indian Leaf Tobacco and Imperial Tobacco Company - were eventually amalgamated into the Imperial Tobacco Company of India Ltd, becoming India Tobacco Company Limited and finally ITC Ltd.

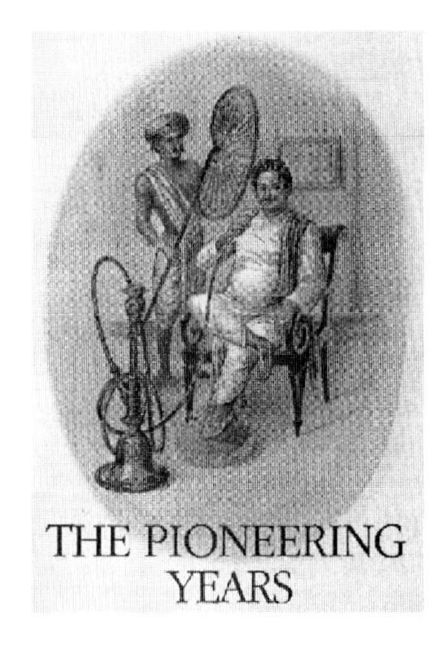

Tobacco was not new to India; it was smoked in beedie (*biri*) form, as well as hookah *hubbly bubbly* and sniffed, chewed and spat out for centuries. There was not much indigenous tobacco grown but the company imported tins of Wills cigarettes and was anxious to encourage the more profitable habit of smoking cigarettes. A small cigarette making factory operated from 1907 in Monghyr, Bihar, but could not produce enough to cope with potential demand. The idea was to *teach* the Indian people the pleasure of cigarette smoking, an idea today that would set the world shuddering with horror. Once the desire to smoke cigarettes was achieved, the desire for good quality tobacco was implemented and a local organisation, Indian Leaf Tobacco Development Company (ILTD), was formed in 1927, its registered office in the Isle of Man, becoming a division of ITC in Calcutta in 1975. Trials to produce quantity and quality in Bihar were not successful, so south India was chosen and the South India Leaf Area (SILA) in Andhra Pradesh became the main source until Mysore was developed. The establishment of increased leaf growing in the area acknowledged the company as a prime contributor to the welfare of the farming area. And so it also became in Mysore.

Mike has always been good at locating houses and started negotiating with the Church of South India to rent the old colonial 1860s Hassan Mission House on Racecourse Road, the races long forgotten as, almost, was the church. Reverend Ken Gill, his wife Edna and three young children were being transferred and needed a reliable tenant. Ken, later Bishop of Bangalore, was moving from pastoral duties to start up a broiler chicken farm at Tumkur, not too far from Bangalore. He was a character, pure Yorkshire, the son of a lorry driver who called a spade a spade. After living in Tumkur for some months he came to stay.

"How are your flock," I asked.

"Flock?" he queried, "I don't have sheep I only have chickens."

"The human flock, Ken!"

"Oh them," he said rather wearily, "The chickens keep me busy all day and all night, no time left for much else."

The Mission House, Hassan

Before we went on local leave, Mike took me to Hassan to see the 100-year old whitewashed house which was long and rambling with blue painted windows. Ken and Edna were waiting at the entrance. They told us that the roof was constructed from Mangalore tiles lined with smaller tiles patterned with flowers. Ken mentioned that the roof *leaked a bit* during the June and October monsoons. He was right, the rain dribbled through various areas of the dried out tiles and developed into steady trickles needing buckets to catch the water.

The charming building had polished terracotta tile floors, thick lime-washed walls and dark and high wooden rafters over the six rooms. The doors were all double with heavy brass knobs and hinges. Ken was keen for us to take on the lease, and some of the really lovely antique furniture. The dining room had a dumb waiter and a solid rosewood round table and, in the sitting room, was a hand crafted corner cupboard with drawers beneath. In the cool spacy bedrooms were narrow brass handled teak campaign chests, the drawers with flat brass handles fitted into the wood. These were transported by ship from England as cabin trunks, holding the camisoles and petticoats of Edwardian ladies. The beds were iron, shaky and squeaky, with upper frames for cotton mosquito nets to be tied and tucked under the mattresses. Architecturally the house suited our formulating taste for the traditional and antique.

Practically it was not so suitable as there were no identifiable bathrooms or any running water. The kitchen area at the back had no resemblance to a kitchen, it was merely a murky hole within a lean-to space with a rough bricked floor, large enough to store buckets and boxes, cleaning materials and sacks of rice. In the corner stood a fridge, and next was a large galvanised tank with an immersion rod in the base, this was the *running hot water.* The window spaces were fitted with a cob-webby open metal grill to stop intruders. There was a double door leading to the small back garden, a bulky granite dhobi stone and water tank. Across the compound was a row of dilapidated servants' quarters. The large L-shaped bungalow was divided and the rather fierce Superintendent, Estheramma, of the CSI girls orphanage occupied the L. Fifty poor little girls lived in Dickensian outhouses, spartan and ancient buildings with absolutely no comfort whatsoever.

During our visit Edna said she was going to leave her many pots of multi-coloured geraniums. She also said the soil was good for vegetable growing and advised, "I should get bullocks in to do the ploughing".

We asked Ken about employing servants, "Don't 'ave Christians," he said heartily, "Unreliable lot." They told us that up the road was the Redfern Memorial Hospital run by Methodists with an expatriate doctor and two nurses. This was comforting news. We drove back to the hotel and the children, and felt a sense of relief that we could finally settle down.

St Margaret's, Ooty

Before we moved we were due a month's local leave in Ootacamund in the Nilgiri Hills about 100 miles south of Mysore. We drove across the flat plains along the tree-lined road and climbed through the bamboo and teak jungles of Bandipur, and between coffee plantations always on the alert for any wildlife. We often saw spotted deer, birds, monkeys and the occasional elephant, albeit with a chain round its neck. It soon became chilly as the mountain air hit us, the highest of the range, Doddabetta, reached 8000 feet. Ooty was chosen as the summer headquarters of the Madras government in the early 19th century. It was a bolt hole for the sahibs and memsahibs to escape the fierce heat of the plains. Before that it was the home of the polygamous and buffalo worshipping Toda tribe, whose population dwindled considerably on the arrival of the British. Originally, many stone cottages with pretty wooden fences surrounding flower gardens were constructed on the green hillsides. There were winding lanes and eucalyptus trees, and the lemony citradora variety created a small industry for local people who sold the oil in their little shops. The British built stone churches, private schools and the terraced Botanical Gardens whilst the Maharajahs built palaces. It was the principal hill station of south India with beautiful scenery, cool air and far reaching views.

The panorama of the intense terracing was magnificent, every inch of the land cultivated with acre upon acre of mossy green tea bushes stretching as far as the eye could see, their planting neatly divided into gardens and run by different companies. Nilgiri tea was a fabled luxury and hard to obtain except at Harrods in London. As well as tea, potatoes, some coffee and vegetables were abundant, whilst fat milky cows roamed munching on fresh green grass. In Ooty there were treats like fresh butter and cheese, home-made chocolates, strawberries, globe artichokes and Brussels sprouts. The children developed rosy cheeks and enjoyed all the new tastes and it was a joy to watch them.

Our company bungalow, St Margaret's on Monte Rosa Road, was a commodious colonial building separated into four self-contained flats. The ceilings were high, there were wooden floors, fireplaces and old fashioned bathrooms with geysers. It was always very cold inside and the small rusty electric fires relied on a low fluctuating voltage which, often, could not even power the light bulbs. The house, surrounded by cliffs, was built on a flat plateau which was a lovely flower garden. The caretaker, the wily Raju, was a keen gardener and won many prizes at the annual flower show. Susina at two and a half was keen on picking *pretties* which made relations between Raju and us somewhat strained.

Ooty is famous for the very snobby Ooty Club or the Ooty Snooty where, it is said, snooker was invented. The building is grand and pillared, festooned inside with trophies, portraits of British royalty and photographs of the hunt, situated exclusively on a little hill. We visited this last bastion of the British Raj, but they refused to let us enter although Mike has been, since aged 18, a member of the Naval and Military Club in London.

"Sorry Sah," said the uniformed bearer, quietly shutting the door in our faces.

On the downs was a golf club and sometimes we watched the pink coated hunt galloping by. Further down the mountain towards Coonoor was the Army Staff College at Wellington, which had a friendly club and provided a social life when we were holidaying.

We made friends with some Indian tea planters working for Brooke Bond, Ranee and Kutti Kuttaiah. Ranee was a larger than life person in bright saris with huge eyes, big jewellery and a booming friendly voice. Both came from Coorg, a small principality nestling in the Western Ghats. Coorg has produced some military elite over the years, having sided with the British during the battles to seek out and slay Tipu Sultan. Latterly they were honoured by Queen Victoria and given dispensation to carry arms without licences. The Kuttaiah's invited us for tea on their estate, Thaishola. It took nearly two hours to reach, but the area and house were magnificent with a large flower garden and glorious views. They were a most hospitable couple and not only served us tea, but dinner as well. On the return journey we passed a jackal, a porcupine, a hare and a wild pig.

Leave over, the children having enjoyed pony rides, walks in the woods and paddling in boats on the large lake, we returned to the heat of the plains and to get on with our life in Hassan.

Life in the Hotel Metropole for a whole year had shielded me from India proper and cushioned us in a clean environment, surrounded by servants who were not ours, and basically no responsibilities except to care for our children. So moving to an alien town, a large uneasy house and grounds, plus a whole lot of new Kannada speaking people, a kitchen to run and marketing to achieve, was going to be quite a changeover.

Chapter 8 – Servants and Shopping

Our Willy's jeep crawled over the dusty pot holed road, behind lines of lazy bullocks pulling creaking wooden carts with big steel bound wheels. It was May 1965.

"How much more Mummy?" Susina bounced up and down on the rear bench seat, held firmly by the driver as we made our uncomfortable journey. Jeeps have no doors and no passenger protection. Simon was nuzzled on my lap and held tight.

"Not far," was my reply, "Not far," having no idea how far it really was. She popped her thumb firmly into her mouth and heaved a big sigh of boredom, "I want there Mummy, tell me when..."

"We'll soon be there Susie," Mike shouted comfortingly over the rowdy noise of the engine.

We honked our way through carts and cows and hundreds of people into the small town of Hassan. There was a roundabout with a centrepiece of a concrete bullock, complete with removable metal testicles dangling on a hook, garlanded in dehydrated orange marigolds. Around the edge of the circle, vendors flapped flies behind pyramids of sapotas, sweet limes and green bananas. A rickshaw with a battery powered loudspeaker cycled lazily by, Kanarese music screeched from the brass horn and the billboards, displaying busty women, advertised the current film at the Hollywood Talkies. It was nearly midday and hot.

We drove past the Traveller's Bungalow shaded by brilliant red blossomed flamboyant trees, their orchid flowers fluttering into the flotsam and jetsam of the tangled gutters, on to the dusty shoe repairers, the men flattening rusty tins and a dozy woman with a wooden tray of cigarettes and *beedies*. We drove a little way up Racecourse Road, our new home was on the left behind a high brick and concrete wall. There were balls on the gateposts, and the gates were of slatted wood sloshed with blue peeling paint. Mango trees, tall and darkly foliaged, made a spooky orchard, it looked a good place to play until we found the snakes and the hornets' nest, and the crumbly termite mound. Later it was Out of Bounds when one of the children nearly fell down a disused well, covered in undergrowth and grimly deep.

The single storey elderly house fitted its site very comfortably and, at night, looked like a ship at sea. Brilliant cyclamen and mauve bougainvillea cascaded over the entrance and the long verandas had pillars, round and firm, supporting the lean-to roof, and there was a low wide retaining wall. In the evenings we sat there with a beer, or a gin lime soda, and listened to the *muezzin* (call to prayer) from the onion turrets of the mosque, muffled by the density of the mango trees. The constant demands for prayer, the caw-caw-caw of crows and the yap-yap-yap of dogs were permanent sounds, always there. So much so that their repetition became buried in the psyche and silenced in the brain.

The garden was big and rambling and great for children. It was enhanced by three Flame of the Forest trees capped with exotic brilliantly red flowers, each bloom fashioned like a delicate orchid. The others were Pride of India, bell shaped and covered in mauve trumpet type flowers. Whilst exploring the orchard several days after we moved in, I stumbled over a small gravestone and stood back shocked. There was a very faint inscription:

Michael John Chaloner
Born 6 November 1928
Died 8 November 1928

Our own children were on the veranda, chattering and giggling, and the discovery of this grave made me feel terribly sad. Little Michael must have been the son of a missionary or of a government officer. Later it was moved to a more suitable resting ground.

The kitchen was a dark hell hole in the back quarters. It was tiny with two galvanised topped tables, three wooden shelves and a dreadful sink hewn out of a bit of scummy rock with a plug hole, but no taps. Light came through a narrow greasy slit, water was in a refillable tank, and it was incredibly difficult to consider any form of hygiene. On one table was a two-burner gas stove, under the table was a canister of gas.

Opposite the kitchen was a large locked store cupboard with lots of shelves, which was a good dumping ground for everything that wouldn't fit in anywhere else. Outside the store was a normal fridge but no freezer. It was all so much better than the hotel, but it was a horror story of adjustment. Each morning and evening the municipal water supply ran into an open tank outside the kitchen door for a scant two hours, sometimes less. We shared this with our servants and various hangers on. The laundry was washed on the granite stone using buckets, the garden was watered in the dry season and the jeep kept clean.

The Mission House was freshly whitewashed and the tiled floors polished with red Cardinal, as were the unbelievably primitive bathrooms. The bathtubs were shallow cement holes dug into the ground with little retaining walls, the basin was a blue enamel bowl on a cement shelf, the running water came out of a small galvanised tank with a little tap on it. Hot water for bathing was cooked up by electricity in a drum near the kitchen, carried in buckets and tossed into the *tub* on the floor.

The first evening I gingerly stepped into the hole and sat down, but could not understand why the surface water was covered in globules of red grease. The Cardinal polish had melted and was floating around sticking to my skin. My towel was covered in red oxide and I was an orang-utan with a red bottom and elbows; it took weeks to get the polish off the tubs, our sheets and us.

Our untrained houseboy was taught to fill the buckets of water from the drum and carry them into the bathroom. He was shown how to put in the plug, which was on a chain, and how to fill the tub with water. Much head waggling. Next evening I put in the plug just in case, and he tottered through the sitting room with precious hot water. He removed the plug and poured in three buckets, which gurgled down the drain, and then he replaced the plug. His complete lack of English and dumb expression made me realise what hard graft village servants were.

Once settled we welcomed innumerable Indian overnight visitors who used our guest bathroom, equipped with a large zinc tub in which to sit. The boy was used to filling this and then overturning and emptying it after use. Only later we discovered that Indians do not like sitting in their own dirty water, they feel defiled. Not one of them complained or explained that they found this method of bathing unacceptable. We asked Sikh friends about correct bathing habits, and they laughed at our dilemma.

"Simple," they said, "Take the tub away, give them two buckets of warm water, one dipper, a bar of Hamam and a bottle of shampoo, they'll be happy." If they were they never said, just adapted to sloshing and washing from the buckets. It made me wonder if our educated friends wanted us to think that we knew better than they did? Was this a throwback from the severe governance of the British Raj? The truth, of course, was that they knew everything better than we did, but were never going to let on.

The purdah pans were back to front western loos with seats. After use they were flushed with water from a metal jug. The septic tanks worked well but the loos stank and, on enquiry, we discovered that the internal waste pipes were made of porous instead of baked clay, and the pipes grimly retained odours. It was particularly unpleasant when Susina locked us both in the bathroom (who put the bolt on the outside?) and the whiffs flew up through the pan almost suffocating us. No one heard our cries to escape until she got fed up and started yelling too.

The livestock which shared our house were bats hanging from the rafters, mice scampering all over the place and kumli poochies. These were dark furry caterpillars with long fine hairs; they dropped indiscriminately upon us, onto our beds, into the toy box, and amongst the cushions on the sofa. On the slightest contact with human skin their caterpillar hairs produced angry weals and an itchy rash. We also suffered an infestation of big, shiny, dark cockroaches, which were easy to stamp on as they rustled by, they cracked and oozed repulsive innards and were loathsome with their black round droppings, prolific breeding, big shiny wings and their whispery, waving antennae. Less invasive but equally startling were the see through pink geckos that clucked in the rafters. A soft *plop* indicated one had tumbled from a great height, either on to the floor, or a bed or chair, a baby cot, or a head. They always recovered from these massive falls and, beady eyes flashing, scampered away on their little five-fingered padded feet. If a gecko fell on an Indian, and they frequently fell on everyone, he or she was horror struck with fear and immediately looked for a place to strip off clothes and sluice the badness away with water. If a dog or cat snacked on a gecko it soon became very sick, but most of the little lizards were welcomed as they gobbled up many insects. Every house we occupied in India had its own little family of birds, usually sparrows, which zoomed in and out twittering noisily. Field rats were constantly scrabbling to get in, and often did if they were not already firmly resident. Another hazard was sleepy snakes slithering silently and hiding, inconspicuously, under beds.

Sadly, because of family commitments, Pushpa was unable to come with us, as was her sister, Chandra, so we beat the jungle drums, sent out the runners and, eventually, starched ayahs arrived from Bangalore and Mysore, and khaki clad cooks came from the coffee estates seeking work. There was little choice, no references and, one by one, we employed them on trial. They all spent hours in the quarters preparing their rice meals over damp wood fires, or they disappeared mysteriously to the bazaar or *bathroom Ma*. Working round them was worse than not having them, the ayahs cuddled the children, but would not wash their clothes, the cooks made sponge cakes in mud ovens, but refused to scour the pots.

Madam this is too much, they wailed, *Yev-ry Madam must have chokra* (pantry boy), *sweeping woman and bearer, I yam not able to manage Madam, too tired please.* So then followed a constant procession of unsuitable sweepers and *chokras*.

Rebecca, bent and grey haired started as a sweeper. She cleaned the purdah pans and did all the other mucky jobs the others refused to do. Because she spoke English she was probably desperate, and not of the sweeper caste at all. She was the only rice earner in her family of one sick husband and four out of eight surviving children. She was a loud belcher, all garlic and unbrushed teeth. One afternoon she was caught in the kitchen helping herself to groundnuts from a jar.

"Rebecca, you are stealing," I accused.

"No Madam," she looked at me unwaveringly with soft brown eyes, "Only taking."

She stayed until ill-health took her away; she was gentle and kind and worked hard. It was so difficult not to take people like her under a huge wing and care for them forever; dealing with poverty keeps the conscience on the alert and the compassion at danger level. It took me years to understand that their ignorance was due to malnutrition, they were the product of undernourished mothers, riddled with worms, who produced very little milk. Lack of health and hygiene education meant that little babies struggled to survive polluted water, infectious diseases such as cholera and typhoid, not to mention unsuitable food, worms and constant diarrhoea. Unfairly I became very irritated by their stupidity, but it was me who was stupid, having not considered *why* they were so listless and forgetful. Rural India was very difficult for new expatriates, and there was no one near for us to discuss these problems. Unqualified, we were living at the sharp end of illiteracy and ill health, the learning curve was slow and difficult but, in the end, we developed a new tolerance and a better understanding of a struggling humanity.

Raju the mali with Simon aged one year

Hassan was not the ideal place for *city* servants to move to, as it was a small dull town. The quarters we offered were appalling and no better than cow byres. The roofs were repaired, the mud and dung floors freshly swished and the rooms whitewashed, but they were medieval with one evil toilet serving about seven little properties all in a miserable row.

In six weeks, cooks called Joseph, Swamy, Krishna Rao, Mohan, Matthew, Thomas and various others passed through our portals until we took on an ill-shaven man with deep lensed spectacles called Samuel. At first he was pleasant but soon became very demanding and bolshy. Instructions were ignored, mistakes were made and it was a question of anticipating what *he* was going to do, because *he* did what *he* wanted to do not what was required of him. Thought reading became a part of my life and it was agonising trying to be one step ahead. Samuel demanded coffee, bread, a bed, blankets and an umbrella, a warm coat, electricity and cooking fuel.

“Would you like cream cakes as well?”

He looked quizzical but, not to miss out, "Yes Madam, I want those too."

Servants did not come alone; a job for one provided a roof for many and there were always camp followers described as sisters, cousins or brothers-in-law, and each one came with emotional baggage, health and education problems. In south India there were several languages to cope with, including Tamil, Telugu, Kanarese and Malayalam. They all held on to their roots, their religions, their food, their customs and their families, and were pretty unbudgeable. So a series of unsatisfactory people meandered around our house flicking dusters, wielding stick brooms and stirring soup, never mind bashing nappies on the stone and ironing Master's work shirts in the dining room where there was only one suitable plug. Noise was another problem; servants are not quiet; they are verbose and full of rattle and information. They smoke, sniff, spit and cough and all have very strong opinions. Good ones are jewels to be treasured.

The hunt for an ayah continued until we ended up with a large, older woman called Rukmini who wore stiff white cotton saris. She was a typical *English* ayah and a far cry from the lively Pushpa. Rukmini was confident in her childcare and definitely more knowledgeable than the Memsahib. She was very determined about her rights, intelligent and kindly, but not really my sort of person, however she was trustworthy and sensible.

The Gills left Raju, their garden boy, who was from the local Gowda farming community, he was a good looking strong fellow who helped in the house and kept the garden tidy. He had a rusty old bike and managed to do the vegetable shopping. His lack of English was a drawback and it was not long before I started to pick up Kanarese. William joined our household as a *chowkidar* or watchman, he was young and pleasant, with a friendly dog called Tommy and turned out to be an excellent child minder and good companion. Later he became our driver, as Dorai Raj wanted to return to his home comforts in Mysore. We liked William, married to a sweet wife who produced a baby girl but, like his father, he was hooked on the bottle. He was very attached to us, and stayed for years, but in the end he lost his job, his home and his family and slid down the slippery slope.

Hassan Market

The situation with Samuel became worse and there were several unpleasant rows, not helped by Susina standing in the middle saying, "Stop it Mummy, nice Samuel. Stop it Mummy, nice Samuel." But he left and, soon after, Rukmini walked out and caught a bus home, angry because she was not given butter for her bread, something we were unable to buy for ourselves.

Soon after we arrived at the Mission House, Dorai Raj took me shopping in the bazaar, crammed with agricultural hardware, ropes, iron goods and a vegetable and fruit section piled with purple aubergines, hairy coconuts, sweet onions, fiery red chillis, green mangos and lumpy, pungent marmalade oranges. The shops were poor, there was no cold store and hardly any tinned goods, everything was bought loose including oil.

Apart from the three medical missionaries, who became good friends, there were no expatriates, and our Indian neighbours made no move to be friendly, they were not used to foreigners. In the five years we were there, the only person who called was a Coorg lady from the Coffee Curing Works on the Mangalore Road, but she was shy and nervous with English so conversation was very difficult.

It was necessary to learn Kanarese and get my nose further into the ground, so helped by a book, *Kannada made Easy* which contained archaic phrases such as: 'Do not beat the horse'; 'Brush my hat' and 'I intend to go to Persia', and examples such as: I am - *Nanu iddene.* The language was a nasty cross between Latin and German declension, and lots of wiggly writing to go with it.

We employed Pundit Devaiah who came each morning at seven o'clock. He carried a little plastic bag which remained firmly zipped, and we sat at a table on the veranda. He was a jovial Brahmin, unshaven with white snowy hairs on his chin like an upside down halo. He wore a dhoti and a wool shawl, with a length of holy string tied across his body. His head was shaved with a little pigtail sticking out at the back. His sandalwood and red caste mark was finely painted down the centre of his forehead, and he had three thicker marks above his eyebrows indicating *the feet of the Lord.* mixed from refined mud, sold in little cakes in the bazaar. He got muddled with his *b's* and his *v's*, but was very sincere and determined, and spoke very clear *Yinglish.*

1965 Mike in Hassan

"*Mr Vitley,*" he enunciated, "You must *exameene the grammaire, the lang-wage* needs you to open your bowels and speak *werry, werry* clearly please." Mr Vitley struggled to keep a straight face and tried to open his A E I O Us. Mimicry comes easily to me so I was able to hear the accent but not understand the grammar, which always remained a mystery, as did the script. However within a few weeks I was jabbering away in kitchen Kannada and Mike learned how to say tobacco - *hoggesoppu,* and spinach - *tota kora,* and want - *beku* and don't want - *beda. Namaskara* covered many greetings during the day plus *tumba sari* meaning well done, thank you and anything else you wanted to say. Sadly neither of us reached the dizzy heights of Mr H R Rao's book which taught us to express in Kannada: 'I have had four motion'; 'We took possession in the city on the very first charge'; 'Are you at leisure? 'Is there a steamboat running from here to Paris?' and 'Do you like my new hat?'

My new found language gave me the confidence to brave the bazaar and mutton market alone, and I paid a little boy to carry the round basket on his head. We pushed our way through the brass pots, garlands of flowers and heaps of charcoal, jostled by people and bullocks. I became more confident with my smatterings of Kanarese, the smiles came and the vendors helped me complete my shopping. Gupta Stores cashed Mike's cheques, the dusty little store overladen by the sickly smell of *asfoetida* (an aromatic root resin used in Indian cooking), dried garlic and knobbly ginger. They packed up rice, wheat, salt and lentils into newspaper cones twirled with thread.

Susina was much smarter than me and soon picked up the language from our new ayah, Sarpinamma, and spoke it all day. Only when she was with us did she revert to English. Sarpinamma, who appeared one day like a miracle, was well educated and her Kannada was superior to the Gowda slang. Mike's staff congratulated Susina on her grasp of the complicated Indian language, but we couldn't understand a word she said.

Sarpinamma was a Christian, who had worked for the Gills, then retired but was now on hard times. She may have had polio as her body was twisted, and she had a club foot, but she was tiny, strong and wiry with grey wispy hair and deep wise eyes. She was a real mother with pleasant teenage children, Joyce and David, and a husband who was a mechanic. They moved into the largest of the quarters and were a decent, quiet family. Joyce and David loved our children and played with them endlessly, and the husband was a retired cook and helped us out in his spare time. He was a quiet dignified man whose main claim to fame was icing a birthday cake with salt, which made him overcome with embarrassment. Local meat was so tough that trying to mince it burnt out our Kenwood mixer, but we could get decent potatoes and carrots, cabbages and lots of fruit. We ate endless meals of thick soup jazzed up with crisp croutons. Susina loved that, Simon ate anything and never stopped smiling. Sarpinamma adored him and he her, she fed him. I was not very hungry, beginning to feel unwell but put it down to stress, moving and worrying.

Susina aged three

Chapter 9 – Settling In

Considering our boxes travelled from Ghana to India not much was broken and, after two years, it was a joy to unpack. We had little company furniture, and it was sometime before we visited Bangalore to order carpets, curtains, beds and chairs. Susina and Simon enjoyed their new home, freedom of the garden and the big front veranda, which we covered with mats and spread their toys around. Toys? There was very little available and most of that was cheap, dangerous tinware, plastic had not yet arrived in India. We really missed colourful books and good paper, the local stuff was rough and difficult to write on.

Mike had a small office at the end of the veranda and was busy planning and anxious to get his seed beds sown. There were five, 50 miles apart, and he drove round in his jeep urging the farmers to prepare the soil and construct raised beds. His days were long and exhausting and the rigours of thousands of miles of jeep riding were beginning to manifest themselves into aches and pains. Each night he came home in the dark covered in dust and laterite, unfortunately I was not very comforting as I was not feeling well.

The first batch of seedlings were poor and were replanted, then scrapped and re-sown. The local Gowdas, unused to tobacco cultivation, were nagged continually. Set in their ways this *hogge soppu* (tobacco) was not a crop they enjoyed. It was a difficult time, we were unable to compare notes with other staff, we had no phone and distances were great. The June monsoon started with torrential rain, heavy skies and cold breezes, at 3600 feet we needed wood fires and eiderdowns but had neither. Mike was away and one evening, feeling incredibly ill, I asked the watchman to call Dr Robb to the house. She was a stressed Northern Irish missionary with far too much to do, and was cross as I should have gone to her surgery. Once she examined me she was more sympathetic and suspected jaundice but later, after blood tests, she diagnosed infective hepatitis.

"That's awful," remembering how ill Tony Sparrow had been.

"The only cure is complete rest," she said kindly, "I'd like to admit you to hospital to be properly nursed."

"I can't leave the children but promise to rest," having no option as staggering to the bathroom, hanging on to bits of furniture, was all I could manage. My bile count was 41, normal is about five and my skin became a disgusting shade of yellow, with eyes like fried eggs. My illness frustrated Mike and, at low moments, he told me to *snap out of it*. The shopping trip to Bangalore was cancelled and I lay in our bare house willing myself to get better. It took three months for the bile count to reduce to 12, and then to five, and still my energy levels were very low. The cause was probably strawberry guzzling in Ooty, strawberries like watermelons and cucumbers, suck up ground water.

I lived on Bovril and lost ten pounds in less than three weeks, moved into the spare room and eventually outside onto the veranda. Visitors were few, there was no radio, hardly any books and nothing to watch except the occasional head bobbing above the front gate. Sometimes a Hindu wedding procession broke the monotony preceded with a piercing brass band, a turbaned groom on a bony pony garlanded with marigolds, and a trail of friends and relations all dolled up in their best. The postman came in his khaki uniform, sniffing loudly and blowing his nose noisily, wiping the mess on his trousers or occasionally on the door. Blowing noses into the air was common practice amongst the uneducated, it was considered disgusting to blow into a handkerchief, wrap the contents to put into a pocket. The newspaper boy was another bright spot on my horizon, on a bike, whizzing up the drive and flinging the Deccan Herald onto the doormat. The only page I read with interest was the *Matrimonial* columns. There were advertisements placed by anxious parents on behalf of their *on the shelf* sons and daughters: *Alliance invited for fair Tamil Iyengar girl, 35, 5ft, Central Govt employee, Delhi, innocent divorcee. No encumbrances* - or ambitiously - *Strikingly beautiful, soft spoken caring, deeply religious Tamil girl required for affectionate broad minded, well known reformist intellectual teaching USA, settling India in future, art lover, 36, 5ft 8", boyish, very young looking, (looks under 30) Tamil language enthusiast, classical dancers, artists, writers especially welcome. Will fully support your interests after marriage. Financial status, wealth, caste, horoscope irrelevant. Shall gladly bear all marriage expenses,. Girl's qualities only consideration. Full details first instance requested.* There were over 400 of these ads every day and it put a whole new concept in my mind about Indian arranged marriages.

Simon at one year

Dr Dorothy kindly visited me every Tuesday afternoon after she completed her town clinic near the post office and we became good friends. Susina and Simon accepted my new bed ridden role and Simon romped around his big playpen. His vocabulary at nearly one year old was limited to *I* uttered in a very deep voice. After trying to teach him *Da da da* and *Mum mum mum*, he only said *I* or was it *Eye?* and smile. Susina climbed in and out of my bed, and we read the same stories endlessly, but she just wanted to talk. One afternoon we made a cassette tape on the recorder, her baby talk was so sweet, and she sang little songs and chuckled. I wrote letters to everyone in my address book, "Mummy always *liting*," said Susina, "*Liting, liting,*" like a Chinese she had not yet mastered her r's. Her other favourite expression was *My God!* She was a dear little companion, always cheerful running in and out, chattering away whilst I stuck in photographs, edited and spliced 8mm film, embroidered a tray cloth, copied recipes into a cook book, played with the children and dozed. Someone left an Indian published booklet on household hints which included cooking and beauty. Looking at myself in the mirror was a shocking experience so reading: *For enlarged pores on the nose make a paste of equal parts of glycerine, oatmeal and lemon juice, leave on for a few minutes and then wash off* - was a pretty disgusting thought. Cooking was another dimension, *Indian corn eggs* consisted of hard boiled eggs placed in creamed corn and covered in cheese sauce. We had eggs, but no corn or cheese ditto flying pigeons for the suggested steamed variety. There were household hints too: *How to use up coal dust – make into balls with rice water* - and - *If shoes squeak, spread a thin layer of castor oil on a large plate, stand shoes in oil, leave several hours and they will never squeak again.* I threw the book away.

There was nothing to read, the missionaries brought me what they could and everything was absorbed, India embellished my reading enormously. A new friend, Frances O'Brien, wife of a coffee planter popped in occasionally on her long journey between their estate at Balur, and Bangalore. She was a bright minded woman and loaned me her set of the Alexandria Quartet - Justine, Balthazar, Mountolive and Clea by Lawrence Durrell. They looked inspiring and I was prepared for a challenge. One of the words constantly used was French, *mœurs* but we had no French dictionary and it was weeks before Frances was due again. So I wrote to my linguistic mother in England who replied, *Mœurs - customs, habits, manners, morals,* and it was only then that I buried myself in the strange atmospheric story. Frances told me they were romantic and experimental novels and once I got stuck in, the books presented four perspectives on a single set of events and characters in Alexandria, Egypt, before and during World War II. I later discovered they were an exploration of relativity and the notions of continuum and subject object relation, with modern love as the subject, a convergence of Eastern and Western metaphysics, based on Einstein's overturning of the old view of the material universe, and Freud's doing the same for the concept of stable personalities, yielding a new concept of reality. Well! Looking and feeling like the proverbial vegetable, I was not at all sure if I fully understood this concept, the reading was difficult with constant interruption from servants and children, but the books had an impact on me at a frustrating time when I was yearning for mental stimulation.

Frances O'Brien and her four daughters at Goorghully Estate

The constant stream of company visitors continued but they generally ignored me and I relied on the cook at the time to produce meals and do the shopping. The day brightened when Mike's jeep lights hovered up the drive. How familiar I became to the differences of jeep, and later Ambassador engines, instantly recognising *our* vehicle on its homeward journey. He was always dirty and tired but, after a bath and a drink, he brightened and we ate our meals together in my bedroom but the children did not see much of him.

Gradually I felt stronger and was anxious to get to Bangalore, the house was so gloomy without lamps and curtains, it was a barren echoing place, so we made the journey and took the children with us. We stayed with the Sparrows who, as always, made us very welcome and comfortable. We ordered a three-piece suite, and handloom material for the loose covers and curtains which came in lovely colours and weaves.

Bangalore in those days was known as the Garden City, situated five thousand feet above sea level and once part of the princely state of Mysore. The Mysore Royal family were as rich as the *Nizam* of Hyderabad, but not so indolent. As rulers they had a real responsibility and a great pride in their state and their people. They developed good irrigation systems, built schools and colleges and planted shady roadside trees. The city was well designed with parks and lakes, the *Lal Bagh* Botanical Gardens and an imposing *Vidana Soudha* (city hall), constructed from granite in the Neo-Dravidian style housing the legislative chambers of the State Government. Although dominated during the Raj by its military cantonment, Bangalore preserved its British past. On the edge of Cubbon Park was Queen Victoria's statue and Sir Mark Cubbon astride his horse, whilst the red stone Gothic High Court building was mighty in its architecture. In the 19th century, ladies in palanquins stopped every hundred yards for a change of bearers, but in our day mechanical horsepower and strident Klaxon horns overtook horses. The climate was also changing with increased industry; an aircraft factory, HAL, was in full swing as well as the Imperial Tobacco cigarette-making complex in Fraser Town.

Bangalore had two commercial centres, one near the city market and the other closer to the more affluent Mahatma Gandhi Road. Commercial Street was where we purchased most of our goods but there was no western fashion. It was difficult to find a reliable tailor and I ended up with Mr Mohan Rao in his little workshop at the rear of The Green Shop. He sat at his treadle machine, wearing only a dhoti and a thread of Brahmin cotton across his chest. He usually greeted me with a naughty smile, "Madam has put on." He made beautiful dresses from Mysore silk, trouser suits and pretty blouses, but they were never ready on time and I waited months for a telegram, "Dress ready, collect immediately. God be with you. Mohan Rao." He got fed up with me as it was months before my material, my dress and I were reunited and he was given his money. The tailors, always orthodox Brahmins, were very shocked with the modern sixties mini skirts, "Madam cannot have that hem up *another two* inches," they chastised. But Madam, aged only 27, insisted and the hem was shortened again. This was very immodest in an Indian culture and usually only worn at home or in European company, generally I wore trousers and *kurtas* (long shirts) and kept myself reasonably covered. Having my hair cut was another problem, often doing it myself standing back to front to the mirror hacking it the wrong way because, being directionally dyslexic (not knowing my left from my right), the result was dreadful. It was easier to let it grow and have a pony tail or pleat.

The Sparrows lived on a company compound in a very large ground floor flat, close to the Bangalore Club; we were not members but occasionally went there for lunch. The magnificent club building was in a poor state at the time but originally, when it was established in 1868, it had sweeping lawns and a curved driveway and was a grand blue washed colonial building with circular rooms. The imposing entrance with a columned portico led off to various high and airy receiving rooms with tall, arched windows and the distant whisper of fans. Large antique lamps and chandeliers, and exuberant flower arrangements masked the shabbiness of the interior. The Ladies Room offered gentility with dressing tables and hairbrushes, carpets and reclining couches. Formerly it was the Bangalore United Services Club and described as one of the oldest in India in the best traditions of English country clubs, their food however did not come up to such standards. Winston Churchill was in Bangalore in 1896, he called it *a third rate watering place* and spent his time reading intellectual books on philosophy, history, economy and biology. He became very impoverished and proof of this is a Minute Book in a display case in the Bangalore Club with a list of members *who have outstanding dues,* the name of one debtor being Lieutenant W S

Churchill with the sum owing of 13 rupees (and still owing).

As well as the club we went to a few Indian restaurants such as the Kwality Inn, but there were no bars so we were excited when a night club, The Blue Fox, opened, but were so broke that we could only afford a bottle of Kingfisher beer. This we watered down with a bottle of soda and it lasted the two of us the whole evening. We didn't mind, the music was western and Beatle orientated and the air-conditioning was freezing. Two or three days in Bangalore rejuvenated us, but were rare and we visited maybe only two or three times a year.

Shimoga was opened up; it was a hundred miles to the north, John and Helen Maclean, a Scots couple from Campbelltown, were posted there and often came to stay, or dropped in unexpectedly for lunch. John appeared once at eight in the evening when Mike was away, so the cook was called to make some food and asked John if he would like a bucket of hot water for a bath.

"Och no," he smiled, "I'll have a dry clean on the sheets."

The Byerley Stud

There were very few expatriates in our area, and those were scattered in the foothills of the Ghats on well established coffee estates. Jim and Christine Gunn worked two estates for Volkarts - Karadibetta and Arabidacool, the former nearer to Hassan. They often called in en route to and from Bangalore and were a pleasant couple but emigrated to New Zealand to farm sheep as they felt their life lacked quality in India, and they hardly saw their boys. Frances and Gerald O'Brien and their girls lived on Balur Estate, quite some way from us. Fred and Shelagh Foster lived at Goorghully and afterwards moved to Ossoor Estate on the Bangalore Mangalore Road just east of Saklaspur. Shelagh, described as *half horse* by some of her less kind friends, was the daughter of a racehorse trainer who spent most of his life in India. On retirement she and Fred set up the Byerley Stud.

They found a beautiful tract of land, built a house and stables and mowed lots of paddocks edged by poles. Fred invented a methane gas machine for cooking using horse dung, and also distilled eucalyptus oil and grew coffee. They bred many horses and were pretty successful on the Indian racetracks. Visiting Byerly was to be amongst green fields and paddocks, fat and shiny pregnant mares snickering for carrots and sweet soft foals gambolling in a splash of sunlight.

One day Shelagh gave a coffee party and invited all the planters' wives from a 25-mile radius, the ladies were in their best saris, nose rings glinting, excitedly playing rummy and gambling furiously and I opted for Scrabble with 15-year old Caroline Foster, out from UK for the school holidays. The game did not last long, my little friend Susina decided to upturn the board and we crawled around on the Kashmiri rug picking up the bits. Mike collected us and we enjoyed a lovely tea of home-made brown bread and jam, scones and sponge cake, the Fosters always had tea - cucumber sandwiches and little cakes at four o'clock, served on china plates covered by cotton netting umbrellas to keep the flies off. They persuaded me to hang pictures, choose curtain materials and sort out their bed linen, but the most important job was to reduce the line of Fred's shoes, which spread from one end of the room to the other, and hats. They owned every form of headgear from *topis* (pith helmets) to toppers and cloth caps, all dangling on brass hooks and getting in the way.

Jane and David Hughes were with Bombay Burmah on a coffee estate in Coorg. In 1964 whilst still at the Metropole; they rescued us after our jeep broke down on the Ooty-Mysore Road and, a week later, sent a letter asking us to come and stay. The road to Coorg was rough and bumpy, and we climbed up into the hills through a lot of dead bamboo coming to the coffee estates with their forests of shade trees and hedges of crimson poinsettias. Coorgs are a warrior class, cheerful and hospitable, it was always enjoyable especially when being warmly taken under the wings of two venerable elders, Uncle Bhandari and A C (Tim) Thimmaiah. One of our favourite places was the Bamboo Club in Polibetta where the planters gathered and enjoyed mad parties. The fun loving and eccentric Hughes and their two children lived at Mylatpur, Caroline was already boarding at Hebron in the Nilgiri Hills and Richard due to go there at the age of five. We spent quite a few weekends with them over the years, and they visited us in Hassan. Despite her lifestyle in the middle of nowhere, Jane insisted on wearing bright blue pearly toenail polish and, at any opportunity, picked up drumsticks and became a vibrant and enthusiastic percussionist for any band, fired by gin lime soda and sheer frivolity.

In January 1966 Nehru's daughter, Indira Gandhi widow of Feroze Gandhi, became the third Prime Minister of India. She reluctantly dithered before taking up this position but was fired by the political motivations of her father. As a child she was frail, and a particularly tubercular and ill young woman but now, launched into new womanhood was fit and most energetic. Economically India was in a dreadful position, severe droughts resulted in food shortages leading to serious famine conditions, there was rampant inflation and a serious lack of foreign exchange. Punjabi's were nagging for a Punjabi speaking state; relations with America were at an all time low since the Americans provided arms to Pakistan during the 1965 war, and grew worse with the involvement in Vietnam.

Later in the year a disastrous event happened when the rupee was devalued by a whopping 57.5 percent. Indira made a speech, *...the balance of payments has rendered industrial capacity idle and compelled retrenchment. Small industry has been particularly hard hit. Exports have come to a rest...* Within months of her election Indira made herself most unpopular, but it was amazing how she sailed through two terms as Prime Minister until she was assassinated in 1984.

For me, in my subservient wife role, it was odd living in a country ruled by such a tough, powerful woman constantly in the newspapers. She made me jealous, I wanted to get up and be out there, using my brain and my abilities, but was stuck in a time warp. Many Indian women felt restless whilst Indira was around, wishing to get out into the public landscape, and we knew several who held down responsible jobs and earned good salaries whilst others, who were university educated, abandoned all when they married. Arranged marriages were normal, some worked and some didn't, the Hindu philosophy is not to question. A north Indian lady, Manjula, told me how she was forced to marry her cousin when she was 18, but was anxious to study at college, her widowed mother was desperate for her to have *a good match*. It was not a happy marriage, and the baby produced was *not right* as the parents' shared genes were too close for comfort. Another independent graduate friend agreed to an arranged marriage but with trepidation. She was wed with all the ceremony to an older man, from a different family background who spoke fractured English. It took some adjustment for Prema to settle but she told me, "He was always kind and gentle and made me laugh." Their partnership worked so well, they ran a successful business together, and produced two clever children. Love matches were not approved of, but I could see women were finding themselves and beginning to break out of the mould of orthodoxy.

Chapter 10 – Mission Hospitals 1966

Our home leave was approaching in the winter of 1965, and I was busy making some warm clothes for the children. First we went to my parents in Hampshire to attend my brother's wedding. This was a shambles as my mother did not like her proposed daughter-in-law, no invitations were sent and my father and I ended up meeting the newly weds in a country restaurant. Mike looked after the children and coped with my furious mother. We beat a retreat to Suffolk, keen to purchase a house, difficult with two fractious kids in the back of the car. The dogs and discomforts of Pound Farm were unavoidable, John and Valerie were kind to take us in but enjoyed the experience less than we did.

Ivy Lodge, Woodbridge

We visited the small town of Woodbridge on the river Deben, and made an offer for Ivy Lodge. It was a three-storied timber framed 17th century town house with a Regency facade, a pretty hand carved wooden filigree balcony and large floor to ceiling windows. These let in bags of sunshine with a view of the lovely garden. The sale went through whilst we bought furniture at auction and received all throw outs from the family, nothing was refused and everything was useful, and we prepared it for rental to US Air Force officers by the end of March.

Discovering I was pregnant again added to the mayhem, "Don't carry heavy weights, heave wardrobes or fit beds together," were the orders. Ivy Lodge has been, and still is, our haven and anchor, and we flew out to India well pleased with our purchase.

Already dressed in maternity clothes, people wondered why I had returned. Dorothy prodded me with her brass trumpet, "Your stomach muscles are so weak," she said in her deep Belfast accent.

"Too many babies," I said philosophically.

"Too many heavy babies!" she retorted wisely. We planned that the baby would be born at the Redfern Hospital up the road, and that she would deliver it. However that was months ahead.

Sarpinamma welcomed us, the house was clean and polished and soon we were back into our routine. There was no rainfall during our absence and ten of the twelve Mysore districts were declared famine areas. Sometimes our municipal water supply stopped for two days and Bombay had only a week's worth of drinking water. Mike's entire tobacco crop was in jeopardy, it was only in July that the monsoon broke and the ground sucked up the rain as fast as it poured down.

We had employed two new people to work for us, and then had a theft of special pieces of jewellery which were not locked away. We called the police and they reacted as if we had lost the crown jewels, they were bored and arrogant.

"Everybody out," they barked waving their truncheons and bristling their moustaches, and all the servants were hauled off to the police station for questioning, which was unpleasant as the police had rough interrogation methods. In the end the culprit was discovered to a be a dodgy looking watchman who crept indoors unnoticed one evening, and rifled a drawer.

After months of devious cooks we got a message that a man called Chinnathambi was available, as his coffee planter employer was retiring and returning to England. Chinnathambi arrived with his tiny white haired wife, he was quite old, with aquiline features and sincere eyes and he was nervous. He cooked up some pretty dreadful meals, but soon got used to the black hole of a kitchen, the battered aluminium *dekshies* (saucepans), lack of space and equipment and fiddling around with two gas rings and no running water. All the frying was done in a disgusting lard like grease called Dalda which came in big tins, and several tablespoonfuls were doled out to last him through the day. He used more when it was hot because it melted and dripped off the plate. He was a whizz at baking meringues in a tin box on top of the gas burner and made lovely biscuits. *Swimming pool* was a favourite with the children, this was mashed potato surrounding a pool of gravied mince, and another dish he introduced was *Eshepherds Pie* which was not new to us but should have been renamed *Ebuffalo Pie.* Simon took a shine to Chinnathambi and called him *Tumby* in his deep voice, he also said: *Wower* - flower, *goggie* - doggie, Mummy, Daddy, *Zoo Zoo* - Susina, shoe, poo poo, king - pointing to himself, *illi* and *tege* - Kanarese for here and take, *more* - milk, *giggy* - bicky and *Ma* - Sarpinamma. We took on Singa Raj who had worked for 40 years on various coffee estates, he dusted and ironed and served at table. He was a nice man, but a boozer and deteriorated in our employ.

There was a new Indian doctor at the Redfern Hospital, a great relief for Dorothy struggling alone, sometimes the queue to her clinic stretched down the road. Dr Susie Malaki was a small, smiling, plump Mangalorean lady with a very precise voice. She accepted the job in Hassan because her husband was on a three-year scholarship in America, and she needed a place to bring up their three children. They were such spruce and tidy children, each day they came with their ayah to play and it was such fun to watch them all running around and laughing, and made Susina and Simon very cheerful.

Feeling bulbous and uncomfortable I went to see Dr Susie as Dorothy was on leave. She listened with her brass trumpet to my stretched and bleeding stomach.

"Big, active baby," she said confidently, "I don't think there are two but we'll take an x-ray." There were only six weeks until my due date, I was so large they had to open the double doors to let me through. The x-ray machine was a new acquisition and the only person who *sort of* knew how to operate it was the desperately shy driver, who had attended a day's course in Mysore. He was particularly put off by my obvious state of imminent childbirth, my dress pushed up by my bump and my bare knees and legs. He looked the other way and said very quietly, "Please Madam lie on your stomach."

The steel table looked high and hard and brought back memories of Jim Cadbury-Brown requesting me to *pirouette on your navel Natalie* so many years ago in London. Now was my chance so, with a struggle, I heaved myself up and painfully on to my stomach. If someone had patted my foot I *would* have pirouetted and spun round and round, instead the driver hid behind the door and clicked the trigger. After quite some time he appeared with the photograph, a blurry image showing no baby at all, just the large bunch of keys stupidly left in the pocket of my dress. I went home feeling dejected and worried. Mike was dreading twins, he was already tapping his calculator and pounds, shillings and pence rumbled through his brain, totting up the prospect of two more lots of school fees, clothes, food and equipment.

Simon, Akil and Anil Malaki and Susina

I went to see Dr Angie's sister, Ivy Stephen, who managed a small nursing home in Hassan. She examined me expertly with hands and trumpet and said she could feel two heads, which was a disturbingly freakish moment, but she comforted me that the babies were literally lying one on top of each other and their hearts beating in unison. She advised me to be delivered by Angie at the Holdsworth Memorial Hospital in Mysore, so plans changed and suddenly we needed double everything, in a town where nothing of our sort of baby stuff was available and with hardly any time, or energy, to locate it.

Once in Mysore we stayed in the ILTD guest quarter beneath the Yadavagiri flats, Sarpinamma came to help with the children, as did Singa Raj who would cook in the small kitchen. Mysore was burningly hot and I was burstingly huge. We were cramped, the children were fractious and ill and Singa Raj surreptitiously drowned his sorrows frequently. Sarpinamma was just plain homesick, but very loyal. Buzzing city ladies marvelled at my size, saris wrapped pregnancies with dignity, whilst western dress broadcast big babies. They fed me with spicy chicken and cool yoghurt and lectured heavily on all aspects of twin bearing. My stomach heaved with unabated football matches, and it was decided it would be sensible to be induced in hospital before I exploded.

We spent much of our time alone, probably because I was such an embarrassing lump with swollen legs like an elephant. Mike called himself *Mike the Mahout* and used it as a perpetual joke, but it was not funny with blood trickling down my bump which heaved with heavy kicks. Zohra Chaube befriended me and we shared some good conversation together, and the Sharma's in the flat above were distantly kind and gave me sugary sweetmeats and a recipe for floor polish using mashed banana.

Mike stayed in Hassan busy with tobacco work, it was the first time since Susina was born that he was alone at home. At the weekend it rained and the jeep was in the workshop, so he was able to plant a vegetable patch hiring two skinny bullocks with clanging brass bells round their necks. They were linked to a wooden cross pole attached to a heavy plough hook, and were steered by ropes tied through their shiny, dribbly nostrils. Their driver, clad in an old jacket with a grubby towel round his head, dug his bare toes into the mud and pushed them along sticking his finger up their bottoms to make them go faster. Lots of seeds were sown and peace and quiet reigned.

The twins seemed settled with no urge to be born so, Angie agreed to induce me on the next Saturday when Mike was due to come for the weekend. I left for the hospital and Pushpa's sister, Chandra, came to help me. Although not alone, I was emotionally bereft. Susina and Simon stood at the gate with Sarpinamma and waved me goodbye, they looked such small and blonde little tots on that hot dusty day.

"Mummy having baby," they shouted, "Mummy having baby."

We carried in a large metal gas cylinder with a two burner stove and big aluminium *dekshies* to boil bottles and nappies, and also took plenty of cleaning materials and buckets. Chandra and I swabbed and dusted and flicked away the flies, cockroaches, beetles and birds and doused the place in Dettol.

The twins were induced one day before their due date and were certainly *full-term.* Birds fluttered in the fan above my metal bed, and a couple of surviving cockroaches scuttled beneath. Having spent the day scrubbing I was longing for peace but was not alone. There were three devoted Mysorean ladies attending me; one brought greasy samosas, one produced some potion her Mother concocted for flatulence and the third gave me sound advice on a post-natal diet, “Only vegetable curry and water melon,” she finger wagged. Angie appeared in a pale cotton sari, eyes sparkling behind small gold rimmed spectacles and her presence was worth all the spring cleaning.

"Well Nataleee," she said comfortingly, "Let us put in the drip." The labour room was a dingy brown cupboard and Dr Angie closed the door firmly, “Come back later,” she advised the trio. But they waited outside twittering with anticipation, the air was charged as the pains increased, and came to a rapid crescendo with the arrival of Number One.

Her healthy cry echoed in the corridor outside with a big *oh dear it's a girl* moan and the chorus, “Never mind Nataleee!” rippling under the door. Number Two was quiet and only eight minutes behind his sister, he was feet first; face up and all wrapped round with cord. Angie was quick and calm and very soon he cried lustily. Anxiously waiting, my supporters released a shout of unified joy, “A boy!” I could face the world.

Back in my room clustering round our new babies, they strapped my stomach tightly into a home-made rag corset and placed peeled cloves of garlic on my bedside table, “Suck them when you wake,” they urged, “They will clear your blood Nataleee.” Soon they departed, their silken saris shimmering in the evening breeze, leaving me alone. The twins snuffled and snuggled and I sighed, then heard the mosquitoes buzzing and got out of bed to check that the net was firmly tucked under the babies' mattress.

Compared to the others this was an easy delivery, but a muddle for Angie as the twins were large and came quickly. Andrea (7 lbs 13 oz) was born screaming at 4.57pm, a healthy little girl already with a mind of her own. David, at 5.05pm, was a breech delivery, weighing in at 6 lbs 8 oz (a small baby for me), and soon wriggling and crying. It was Saturday 3 September 1966.

At last Mike arrived at the hospital, the noise of the jeep was so familiar as he parked outside the wards. Zohra was just leaving.

"Congratulations Mike," she greeted him, "You have two beautiful babies." There was a pause.

"Oh so it really was twins?" he sounded rather surprised.

"Yes Mike, perfect babies," and she went off to look after her own children.

He was pleased we had got through the ordeal unscathed, and admired his little bundles with an affectionate proud smile. He was tired and did not stay long, as we were both worried about Susina and Simon at the flat. Next day he brought them to see their new siblings. Simon ignored them and just cuddled up to me, saying, "Baby, baby." Susina was thrilled and soon claimed her new sister as, "Mine baby."

I was left to cope with my two little ones who, on the whole, were not too much trouble apart from demanding me all night and sleeping on and off all day. I felt well and was up and about almost immediately. Chandra was such a help with laundry, boiling bottles and generally caring for me. The nurses wafted in and out, so stiff and starchy, thin fingered and mildly attentive.

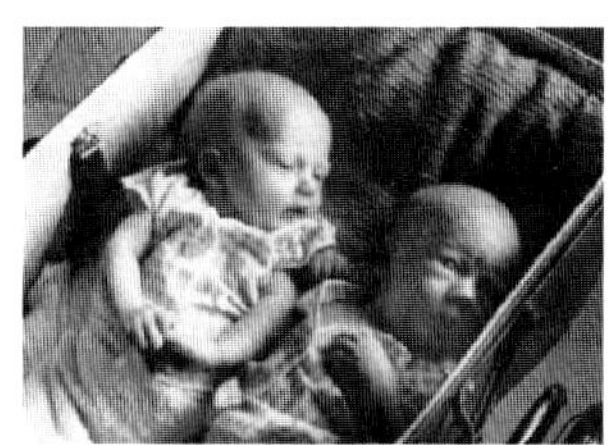

Andrea and David

After giving birth on Saturday, Wednesday was the day planned for my sterilisation, a difficult decision which, finally, was left to me. Angie had been consulted and always sensible, "I would not do it unless you had babies of both sexes," she said firmly. Well, we did, two of each, all under four so the decision was made to go ahead. Although only 28-years old we felt that more children would not be a good idea, and my health and strength, including hepatitis, had been given a severe test with three pregnancies so close together. Our marriage was stable, our lifestyle very difficult and our finances not too secure, as we were unsure how long the India job would last.

On Wednesday morning Angie came to see me, a worried expression on her face. She said, "Nataleee, I am so very sorry, but we have no anaesthetist today." I was a bit shocked. "I can do it without anaesthetic," she said, "I can give you a local, but you may feel, you may..." Now was the best time whilst my fallopian tubes were high, when would it be possible to get away from my children again and have this operation?

"I'll trust you," I smiled.

"You're a brave girl, you'll be all right."

I felt dreadfully alone, but I wasn't, there were two new, squeaking and beautiful children to care for. The nurses came in and out and prepared me for surgery. Chandra was left in charge of Andrea and David and a nurse wheeled me along the sunny verandas to the operating theatre. Suddenly there was some disturbance behind me, and the sound of running feet.

"What are you doing?" a female voice shouted, "Why are you having this operation, you wicked woman!" I recognised the voice; it was Hilda Baker, a stout nursing sister and devout Christian. She was panting behind my trolley, her ample bosoms heaving beneath her pinafore, and perspiration running off her face, wispy grey hair unravelling from her missionary bun.

"Killing God's little children, that's what you're doing. Killing them," she shouted. The nurses were useless in the face of authority. They pushed me along and tut-tutted but did not intervene. I was speechless and half-drugged.

"Go away," I said muzzily, "It's my business."

"Wicked, wicked woman!" she continued as the swing doors were pushed aside and the nurse wheeled me into theatre. Angie was absolutely furious. Furious! But could not criticise a colleague apart from apologising profusely. Her face told another story, there would be repercussions later. Angie was small of stature but loud of conviction and voice.

It was a dreadful operation. Expatriates require a lot more injection or anaesthetic than Indians do. She did not give me enough local and so I felt everything, the knife, the fingers, the cutting, the stitches. Worse I could *see* everything in the multi-angled spot lamp above me, but all juggled up into angular shapes, it made me feel quite faint and immersed in dreadful pain. "What are you doing?" I asked.

"Don't worry, its only the peritoneum," she said, her little fingers busily sorting and stitching. There were two nurses at my head stroking me gently, whilst I needed a rope through my teeth and a leather belt to pull. Instead I was offered the hands of children and the strength of nobody.

It was over, it was done and it was successful and there were no regrets apart from a sore tummy, and I never saw Hilda Baker again.

Chinnathambi

Despite my hospital spring cleaning, David was hot and feverish and on anti-biotics. I wanted to get him home so, three days after my operation, Angie said we were fit. Mike expected visitors and telephoned that he was unable to collect us, but we could travel more comfortably in the Plymouth rather than the jeep.

"You can't go alone with two little babies," Angie was horrified.

"The driver is a good man, we'll be all right, it's only 100 miles," although I wondered how to hold two babies in my arms on the rough road.

"I'll come with you," she said impulsively, "There are no confinements due and I can visit my sister, Ivy," she smiled placidly, "I don't see her often and I'd like to do that."

We drove into the Mission House by lunchtime; Susina, Simon, Sarpinamma and various others were all jumping about on the veranda. Angie held one baby and I held the other and we went into the cool of the house and settled them in. Chinnathambi came with a happy smile and two glasses of iced lime juice and Angie was soon on her way to visit Ivy, passing two vehicles on the drive, one with Mike. The operation and the journey made me forget that six company men were due for lunch. Mike jumped out and tried to greet us, but was too busy thinking of guests, food and everything else. Like most ILTD wives, I felt married to the company and not to a man at all.

I made a brief appearance and helped to pour drinks, but the arrival of our two new babies was ignored, so I withdrew like a Victorian housewife feeling weepy; the children demanded cuddles and the twins wailed for food and peace. It was long after eight in the evening before Mike stroked the little pink faces, and asked me how everything had gone since he had seen me the week before.

1934 Chevrolet - Bonnie

Life at the Mission House settled down and there was plenty of company entertaining to do. The servants worked well together and, for once, all was calm. Travelling with six of us in the jeep was impossible so Mike looked for a suitable car. Then India suffered a terrible shock when the rupee was devalued, eventually we got a 50% salary rise to cover the increased income tax but still ended up with less money. We had no savings but owned a Johnson 18hp outboard engine, which we had shipped from Ghana. This proved a perfect financial match (£250) for a 1934 Chevrolet car, christened after the film *Bonnie and Clyde.* Bonnie was in almost original condition with spare wheels on each side of the bonnet and long running boards. All the dials worked and the upholstery was good. The front seat was cramped, big enough for a chauffeur, but there was plenty of room in the rear with a metal rack on the back to carry a trunk. We were the sixth owners and there were six good tyres, six cylinders and three forward gears. Mike bought it from a Muslim planter near Shimoga, drove it home and it was soon parked under our portico. Just after Susina's fourth birthday we took it for its maiden voyage. Bonnie carried us thousands of miles over many years but, eventually, was sacrificed and sold to pay school fees.

Sarpinamma came limping in one morning looking particularly bright-eyed, "Ma," she said in her firm tones, "There's a nursery opening just close by."

"Nursery school?" I asked.

"Yes Ma, good for Susina baby, Muslim woman opening, she's a good woman Ma." Susina's Kanarese could have carried her throughout the state so there was no fear of her being unable to communicate. She needed company and missed Doctor Susie's family, transferred to Bangalore.

The Muslim lady, Fatima, was plump, pretty and welcoming. Her house was spotlessly clean but there were few teaching aids.

"My school is of English Medium please," she told me earnestly. "I am having nearly thirty pupils, all fee paying." The fees were five shillings a month.

Susina came home every day chanting *Waash yor ya-ands, brush yor ya-air, clean yor ty-eeth and be kind and be good to yor py-arents*. She was at the school for months but did not learn how to write her name, or they failed to teach her. Her fluent Kanarese helped her fend off the jibes of the other children, and to learn their games. She was not unhappy and was becoming more independent, a quality which would help when she started boarding school the following year. After months she could just recite her letters in a sing-song voice.

Chapter 11 – The Mission House

The children spent Sundays scampering around new seed beds, half built tobacco barns and corrugated iron stores. Gowda farmers, their heads wrapped in voluminous turbans, taught them Kannada games; how to play *Pick up Stones* and how to make *Cow Pat Cakes*. We were still dedicated to the tobacco leaf and Mysore State proved to be a flourishing growing area. Mike registered farmers and instructors were employed, supervisors trained and management lectured on pot watering, ridge building, barn construction and the benefits of residual fertiliser on ragi and sorghum. I became familiar with topping, suckering, air-cured and Oriental varieties, lugs, hand tying and barn poles. Life in the field was fraught; the farmers constructed their barns and tried to understand the rudiments of flue-curing. Mike was doing the work of ten men, coughing his head off and slogging all the hours that God gave, but still they were not enough. One day, with Susina, we went in the jeep on a site visit.

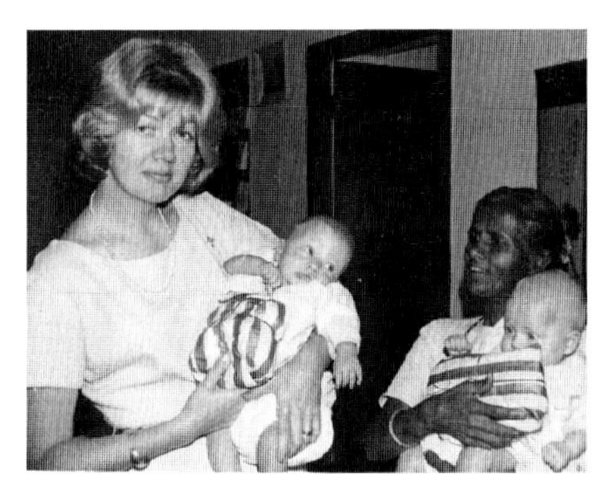

.Natalie, David, Sarpinamma and Andrea

"Oh my God," yelled Mike, "The idiots haven't hung the tobacco to air-cure." And there it was in steaming heaps, so we all set to, the indomitable little Susina stacking the best piles, with a group of eight inept head waggling labourers *not knowing* how to handle soggy leaf. Afterwards we drove in the jeep to Chikmagalur, 36 miles away, a small town in the foothills of the Western Ghats, and joined the Kadur Club where we bought beer and a few groceries. The average age of the expatriate coffee planter members was 75, and they were scattered around the area, just about hanging on. One had died leaving a coffee plantation worth £300,000 (nearly £4 million in today's money). Two British men remained in the guest quarters but had not spoken to each other for over two years. The other planters were up-and-coming Indians who were sociable and enjoyed the infrequent parties. Susina ran around with the bored bearers, and we sat drinking tea on stuffed leather chairs surrounded by tiger skins and antelope heads, reading old copies of the London Illustrated News. My expectations of dance dresses and cocktail parties withered away

We were baking, making squashes, jams, pickles and chutneys and brewing wine, hampered by sugar rationing and an allowance of only four pounds a month, the rest was bought on the black market and scarce. When sugar was melted, the syrup became densely black and full of straw. We bought Bangalore Blue grapes in the market, squashed them in plastic buckets leaving the *must* (grape skins) beneath sheet plastic which expanded if tied on with pliable knicker elastic. It was a primitive but an effective airlock system, the bloom on the grapes was natural yeast and a little sugar was added to start the fermentation. The wine fizzed away until the *must* became flat and dull. We squeezed the juice through clean muslin and stored it in three gallon earthenware Parry's sweet jars, using the same plastic and elastic method to allow continuing fermentation. Hassan had the perfect temperature for wine making and our store was roomy and cool; the entire process took about four months. The grape treading for children was messy fun; it made their feet tickle and their fervour increased the quantity of juice. When the red wine was just about ready to drink, it was tasted and applauded by a few special guests.

The *Good Life* and lack of money became more intense when a recipe for floor polish was found in a book, and we were soon grating beeswax, candles and soap, mixing it with kerosene over the gas in a large tin and stirring well with a bamboo stick; a lethal method but nothing blew up. We planted tomatoes and supported them with sticks, the sticks grew and the tomatoes died, but the vegetable patch at the back of the house produced buckets of green beans, piles of *tota kora* (spinach) and enough fresh and dried lima beans to last a couple of years. We erected a wire fence to keep out the cows and planted potatoes at the side of the house, but the monkeys leapt over the fence and tore out 235 plants. A helpful Kanarese visitor told us how to get rid of the wild monkeys, it was easy, *Just catch one,* he said excitedly, *Grab it and dip it in a bucket of whitewash. Then,* he held his breath, *just let it go and the others will run away, they hate white monkeys.* Another visitor wagged his finger knowingly, *Yew must understand that the monkey is the most sacred of our animals, yew know we have Hanuman, the monkey god? Are you understanding Hanuman? If yew drop a monkey in a bucket of whitewash you will cause a riot, isn't it?*

Returning from Bangalore we visited Ken Gill on his chicken farm in Tumkur and collected eight laying white leghorns to live in our red brick chicken house and coop. The car broke down and the chickens, with their feet tied, were resting several hours on top of a large basket of black grapes we were bringing from Bangalore's Russell Market. The resultant brew turned out to be the best of the vintage and was re-christened *Chicken Shit Wine.* The chickens thrived and I enjoyed taking out a bowl of mash and c*luck-cluck-clucking* before collecting warm eggs for breakfast.

Simon, Mike, Natalie and Mo Sparrow

Christmas 1966 was spent with the Sparrow family in Bangalore and Mo kindly took a lot of black and white photos of us as a family group when the twins were just over three months old. With four under four, it was all quite overwhelming. Then we went on local leave in Ooty, passing through Mysore and we had made an appointment to have the twins vaccinated against smallpox. The vaccine was Russian and very strong, however Doctor Angie decided to scratch it into both of their tiny insteps.

"It doesn't take too well on the feet," she said knowingly, "Not like the upper arm."

Afterwards we drove up to the Nilgiris in Bonnie; a monstrous journey double de-clutching all the way, but she sailed the hairpin bends like a bird and hummed her way to great heights through the eucalyptus forests. The smallpox vaccination was terribly strong and the reaction fierce with swollen blisters that came up in the arches of their feet, almost too bulbous to look at. Both babies became feverish and next evening we called Dr Gopal Raj, who was playing Bridge at the Indian Institute in town. He hurried down the St Margaret's drive in his bull-nosed Morris and came agitatedly into our flat, his eyes flashing, bald head shining under the dim light bulbs.

"Rotten Russians," he yelled, washing his hands, "Poor babas." He handled them gently and was concerned and kind, and returned to town and brought back medicine to treat them for *vaccinia* (cowpox). Their little feet looked as if they could not tolerate any more swelling or soreness. Susina was not well and developed a very high temperature which resulted in convulsions. We were completely terrified as her jaw clamped and she passed out. We cooled her down and within minutes she opened her eyes, drank some water and went to sleep. Next day she developed a rash. The children recovered from their illness, the sore feet healed leaving huge scars on the insteps and Susina was no worse for her frightening experience. It was stupid of me to have left behind my bible, Doctor Benjamin Spock's *Baby and Child Care,* he was an essential part of my luggage. Tough little Simon was a bystander to all these antics and firmly remained strong and healthy. He got into his bed and ordered us to "Go," which meant he was up to some mischief and, as soon as we disappeared, he got out and was coating the bedside table with zinc and castor oil cream and polishing the floor with Susina's dolly's clothes.

The nights were arctic cold and we lit wood fires and cuddled under lots of blankets. The days were fresh, sparkly and sunny so we went on picnics and for long walks, and the children rode ponies through the silent forests. We boated on the lake and shopped in the vast Ooty market, bursting with wonderful vegetables like artichokes, green peas and great big cauliflowers.

We visited the Army Staff College at Wellington quite frequently, one Saturday there was a big dance and we met up with some of the 176 officers attending a seven month course. They came from all over the world and Mike spent time with a Ghanaian Lt Colonel who was one of the prime movers in the ousting of Nkrumah. We got news of many of our African friends, some of whom were thrown into jail. We nearly killed ourselves *shaking* on the dance floor and got back to St Margaret's at 5-30am. Sarpinamma proved her angelic self, coping with the kids next morning, taking them into the sunny garden to play on the swings.

Susina was due to start at Hebron School in July 1968, so we made a visit. It was pleasant and friendly and *the Nest,* the first dorm for tiny newcomers, was cosy with bright bed covers. The missionaries, many Plymouth Brethren, were plain and frumpy with no make-up or fancy clothes, but were kind and caring. Susina was not impressed with the visit and did not want to go to *sleeping school,* ever.

In March 1967, some time after we got back to Hassan, a bear with a bell appeared at our gate, standing on two feet, snuffling its large nose and waving sharp claws. The children jumped up and down on the veranda squealing, "A bear, Mummy! A bear!" In my *don't be ridiculous* fashion, I locked the store and wandered out to join them. Not only was there a bear, but three elephants ambling up the drive chewing our nurtured gerberas and zinnias. A little boy thrust a poster in my hand, *CIRCUS* it announced, *Near Lock Up!* and he scurried after the elephants and held on to the bear with a piece of chewed rope.

"Circus! Circus!" all the servants were gathered and Susina was beside herself with excitement, so we said we'd go. The flapping Big Top, held up by huge poles and ragged lengths of rope and wire, was surrounded by crowds who had travelled from outlying villages, their heads encased in every type of towel and scarf. Babies bobbed on mother's backs and children, eyes plastered in kohl, scampered around wearing prickly nylon clothes which stuck to their hot little bodies. They darted everywhere, fists full of sticky sweets and fly spattered candy floss.

Inside was the thick smell of sawdust and excited sweat, rough benches surrounded the ring and Susina and Simon, thrilled beyond belief, sat and dangled their legs wearing embarrassingly white socks. Drums rolled, bright lights flooded the area and the ringmaster strode in cracking his whip. A spotlight focussed on a little girl in vivid orange, who climbed a wire stretching from sawdust to sky but with no harness or safety net. It was heart-stoppingly awful to watch as, slowly, one tiny foot after another, she struggled up to the apex where she twirled, swayed, wobbled dangerously and made her careful descent. Meanwhile a black bear beneath careered around on a motor bike, nearly colliding with an elephant shambling through the worn out curtains with a lion on its back. Horses and dogs, all dressed in frilly pants and pinafores, did their tricks and made way for the knife throwing act. The band reduced its blare to a soft and incessant roll of drums, a mauve spotlight fell on a blindfold girl wobbling on a tightrope hurling lethal, flaming hatchets at her sobbing sister strapped to a revolving wooden wheel. It was unbelievably dangerous but real. Lions and tigers padded about attached by thin chains to their minders, their snarls and roars showing their dissatisfaction. The animals jumped through hoops, padded across tightropes and played pat ball; they yawned and groaned, huge fangs gleaming yellow in the lights. The finale was two shiny, black hippos who ambled in and immediately marked their territory by twirling their tails emitting explosive faecal discharge, showering their mess all over the local dignitaries in the ringside seats, who shrieked in horror at this unexpected torrent. As quickly as it started it ended, the national anthem Jai Hind, blasted from the orchestra and everybody left

Halebid

We received an invitation addressed to *All Your Family and* Friends to attend a nearby Muslim wedding. The bride was swamped in a crimson sari and veiled in jasmine flowers, it was impossible to see her face, and the groom was in another room. We sat on the ground and ate a delicious feast off fresh green banana leaves which Mike always found difficult. Neighbours tried to be friendly and invited us to various functions but, apart from the hand folding *namaste* greeting, did not involve us in any conversation. It was so difficult to communicate with them, smiles were not returned and English was fractured. A local MP asked us for dinner. His house had five fancy bathrooms and a urinal and wash basin in the dining room. His wife spoke no English but had attempted a *Yewro-peean* dinner. A particular delicacy was an aborted unborn lamb cooked in rich gravy, and the other guests were seriously sucking marrow out of bones and scoffing innards and offal. Our hosts were kind and welcoming but it was a difficult evening.

The Barlow family departed from Mysore, Ken off to grow grapes on the Isle of Wight. He was a dour character, never very happy and too much of a loner and scientist rather than a man-manager involved in a massive new project. Later he and Rosemarie divorced. He was replaced by Leo Been, a Dutchman, ex-Malaya *the land of milk and honey.* India was a big shock to him and he did not stay long.

The Hassan area was not being expanded and Mike was given an advisory capacity, and spent more time away bouncing around in his jeep covering the whole state. Shimoga was opening up managed by John Maclean, who lived there with his wife Helen. One weekend with Susina we jeeped the 100 miles north to Shimoga. The Macleans were very welcoming, theirs was a lonely existence. As we arrived a farmer delivered two squawking chickens to the cook lady, as we drank our first beer she was out in the garden with a large knife cutting their throats and, as we drank our third beer, the jointed chickens were curried and plopped into a dish, "Lunch ready Madam," she called.

Caroline and Toby Sparrow with Susina

Mo, Toby, Caroline Sparrow, Susina and Natalie

Other visitors were Tony and Maureen Sparrow with Caroline and Toby and they drove 250 miles from Bangalore in their super 1926 Bentley roadster. Mo stayed for a week with the children and we visited the famous temples of Belur and Halebid. It was a lovely day out with a picnic, but did we admire the intricate carvings on the famous Hoysala temples? We were too busy chasing little ones, finding toilets and putting on shoes and socks. On later visits we took more time to appreciate the creation of these two temples; Belur out of soap stone, its exterior showing a variety of intricately carved sculptures and friezes, the most stunning being those depicting different *bhavas* (moods of love) of the Bharatanatyam dance form. The material was so soft when quarried in the 12th century, and the sculptors worked on elaborate details, before the stone hardened in the elements. Halebid, more intimate and a supreme example of Indian temple architecture, is full of glorious friezes. The lowest frieze has no less than two thousand elephants with riders and rich trappings, and the exquisite dancing girls have been so finely carved that each bead on a necklace looks separate from the others. In 1967 there were few tourists and the beauty and peacefulness was really appreciated. We were sad that the Sparrows shortly were transferred to ITC in Bihar, a shock after the delights of Bangalore, and we missed them terribly.

Tony Sparrow's 1926 Bentley

Susina was finally speaking to us in English; maybe she was translating it from Kannada and said, *I want to hair my wash* or *Simon why are you teething your brush?* In August Simon started at the Muslim school aged just three, clutching a new green school bag, a slate and chalks, juice and biscuits with Susina's protective arm around his shoulders. He came home with the same old chant *Wash yor ya-ands, brush yor ya-air, clean yor ty-eeth and be kind and be good to yor py-arents,* so nothing had changed since Susina started 18 months earlier. Simon didn't learn much except nursery rhymes, which he chanted repeatedly in his very deep voice.

Baa Baa Black ship, 'ave yew yany woool
Yes Sah! Yes Sah! Tree baags fool.

The weather was hot and the twins were smothered in itchy prickly heat; they were almost raw. The monsoon arrived preceded by the blossom showers, an essential ingredient of successful coffee growing, as they adhere the sweet and sickly blossom to the plant, if the showers were too late the berries fell off and there was no crop. The rain poured through our roof making everything damp and we had no little heaters in our wardrobes to stop the clothes going mouldy. The children's room was a flat roofed extension which did not leak, but getting the washing dry was almost impossible. One weekend there were 59 wet nappies and one dry one, so Mike went out and bought a crude washing machine, it was a cylinder shape with an impeller at the bottom, and a ten inch hand driven mangle which squashed everything flat. It was better than a woman bashing clothes on a lump of granite, but equally destructive. It was a tough machine and a rough machine, and chewed the unfinished seams of our locally tailored clothes into shreds; clothes I disliked were washed twice filling the inside of the impeller with wads of mashed material.

1966 Susina (back row) at Muslim School

Then men arrived with armfuls of pipes and plumbed us in for running water. They did a *kutcha* (poor) job, but the water ran. We were also re-wired with consequent mess, muddle, dust and garrulous shouting from several *maistrys* (workmen). Neither pipes nor wires were tastefully hidden but on show for all to see. It was common practice in Indian households to have the fridge in the dining room, to prove that you owned one. Also the Godrej, a steel cupboard used for storing expensive saris and jewellery, was a thing of beauty and acquisition. Newly manufactured liquidisers, coffee percolators and Kenwood mixers became display objects usurping pieces of silver or brass ornaments.

A telephone was installed, Hassan 380, which made us more accessible to the company, before we had relied on telegrams for instructions and these were delivered by hand. Every time the phone rang the excited servants jumped up and down.

Pone! Pone! they shouted, *Ma! Pone ringing!*

One day Sarpinamma reported sick and did not come in, on the table was her letter of resignation and I burst into tears. The children, hungry for breakfast, were concerned.

"Mummy *k-ying*? Why Mummy *k-ying*?"

Chinnathambi shuffled around feeling awkward, not helped by an infected leg which I was dressing every day, "Breakfast Madam?" he asked hopefully, pretending nothing was happening, whilst heaving the twins into their high chairs and pushing the other two up to the table.

It came as a dreadful shock, but was the normal behaviour of many true and trusted servants. Something was wrong, they wouldn't say, it would simmer and be discussed at length in the quarters and, finally, a nasty letter. My little world was disintegrating; Sarpinamma was such an essential and decent part of our family life. After simmering down I went to the quarters and reasoned with her. First she said it was the ironing but it was more and, in the end, she admitted it was the travelling, she was unwilling to accompany us any more. We most needed her when we went away but her stays in Bangalore, Mysore and Ooty had made her decide never to leave

Hassan, her husband and her children ever again.

This could not have come at a worse time as our life was beginning to change. Mike was getting vibrations from Andhra Pradesh that he was needed for seasonal work, the lot of most Leaf Buying Managers (and their families) who were moved from pillar to post to make up for a shortfall in staff in the main ILTD growing and packing area. Eventually with much persuasion Sarpinamma agreed to stay with us until we were due for leave in February 1968 but would definitely not accompany us to Andhra Pradesh. She was a good, kind woman and a real loss to us all.

David, Natalie and Andrea

Chapter 12 – Hassan and Guntur

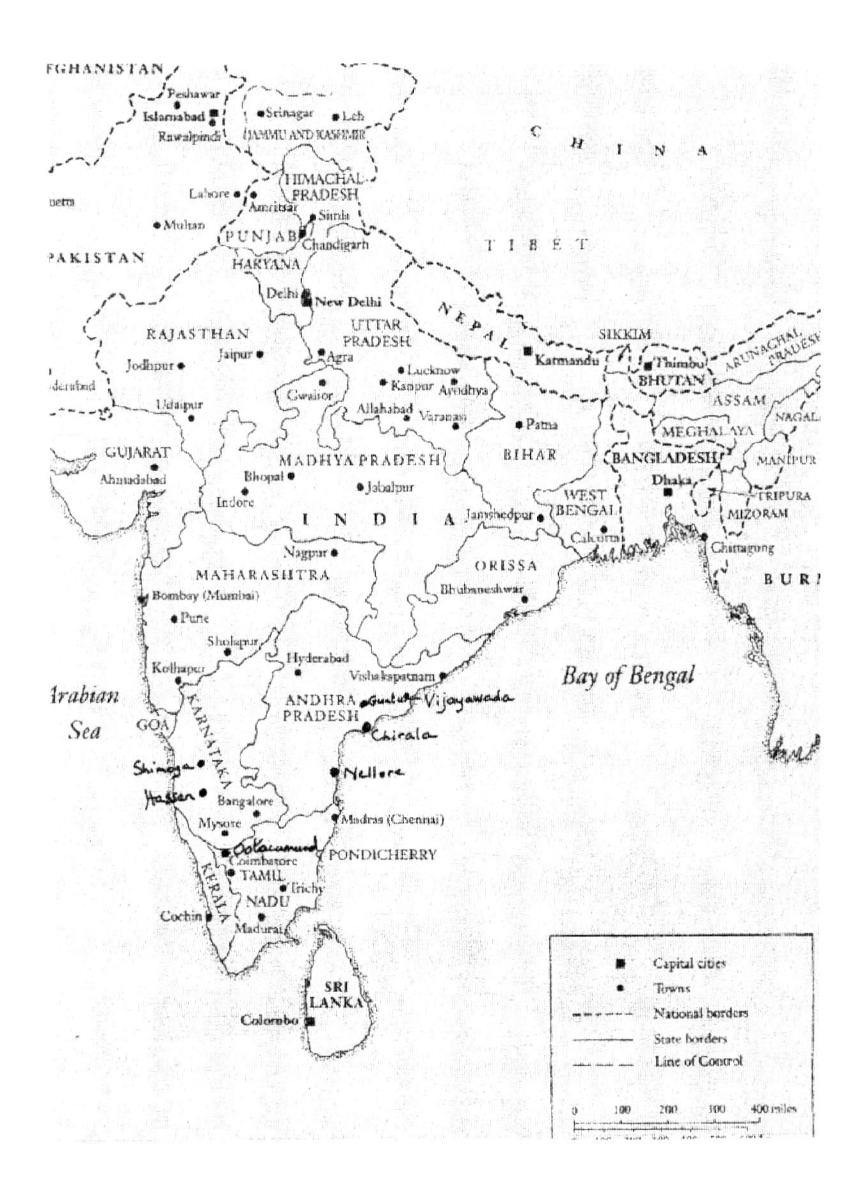

Mike spent more time in Mysore and Shimoga and we were alone. A new Leaf Assistant, Anand Murch, was posted to Hassan and came with his Mennonite wife, Sunita, and baby daughter Nandita and they were cheerful company. Anand was an orphan brought up, with eleven other children, by an English missionary called Miss Murch, always referred to as Mummy. She was a formidable but loving lady, respected by her adopted sons and daughters who spent a happy childhood in Naini Tal in the northern hills.

When Mike finally got home the children were so excited to see him, dancing around and shouting, demanding his time and attention. Although affectionate and loving, he was never good at playing, telling stories or occupying them probably because he got little affection as a child, his mother aged 32, died of TB when he was 11, and he and his three siblings were dependent on a father who distanced himself and a crabby aunt who loathed children. Their saving grace was their white-haired Nanny who looked after their mother as a baby; she cuddled them but was always aware of her position, so not a real substitute for the acceptance and love of natural parents.

There were a couple of American Peace Corps nurses in town and Mike picked them up one day while they were sloshing through a heavy monsoon storm. Alice Neuendorf, aged 28, was small and Beth Furlong, 24, was tall and dark, they came from Iowa and lived in the Basic Training Institute which *was* basic and unpleasant. They were running a hygiene and birth control programme and, in their white uniforms, travelled to various villages with an interpreter, explaining how to avoid pregnancy. Babies, particularly boys, were the future of an Indian family and birth control frowned upon. The nurses showed the men how to use condoms by stretching them over the handle of a broomstick. A couple of months later they came back to find the condom still on the broomstick, "Not working," one man was adamant, "Wife vomiting every morning." They tried to explain Dutch caps to women, meeting with total incomprehension. The condoms were blown up as balloons on sticks and the caps became flying saucers and casual drinking vessels. Birth control was becoming an issue and, later, in 1976, things became more serious under the State of Emergency when the government initiated a National Population Policy to lower the annual birth rate. Previously births were controlled by disease and natural phenomena such as flood and drought. Now it was sterilisation of both males and females, a radical and unnatural step and Sanjay, the wayward son of Indira Gandhi, was behind this vote seeking plan. Vasectomy clinics were set up and men were rewarded either with a tin of cooking oil or a transistor radio, and women were unreasonably persuaded to have tubectomies. The poor peasant farmers objected to this regime, children were a valuable resource but, in a period of five months, mostly by force or bribery, over 3.7 million Indians were sterilised.

Alice was a broad-minded Catholic and had her set her sights on marrying an Indian. She got to know people from Kerala, the majority of whom were Catholics and, quite soon, met a polite young man called Walter Machado and persistently wooed and pursued him. He succumbed and we attended their very formal white wedding at the Roman Catholic Cathedral in Bangalore and Beth soon returned home

After Leo Been left, Eric and Zohra Chaube became frequent visitors to Hassan and we stayed with them on our trips to Mysore. Zohra had Pomeranian dogs, which were frequently talcum powdered and brushed and, once the pampering was complete, we spent happy afternoons smoking our heads off and chattering about everything. Sometimes we went to a Satyajit Ray movie, he was a far sighted film maker known for his humanistic approach. He made all his thought provoking black and white, classic films in Bengali, and Zohra was able to explain the story and spiritual sense of the film to me in hushed whispers in a darkened cinema.

She was an excellent cook but had no written recipes, Indian women have a strange sense of recipe measurement using the sections of their fingers to apportion quantity. A piece of garlic is the thumb pushed up against the first section of a little finger, ginger is the three sections of the middle finger, and powders are measured in a similar fashion, the methods passed down from their mothers. Zöe and I devised a way of writing them down into cubes, teaspoonfuls and even ounces, making the quantities much easier to understand, and then Chinnathambi and I were able to serve our guests with tasty north Indian curries. Eric was the only boy from a family of six girls and came from Lucknow. He was domesticated and, when I had a lot of entertaining, particularly in Shimoga, he was a huge help to me with cooking and serving, even taking morning cups of tea to our guests. He was comfortable and hummed a lot, and we all shared hilarious evenings when he quoted from Chaucer with panache and belly laughs. Zöe was the daughter of a Muslim father, Yusufji, who converted to Christianity and they came from Jabalpur in Madhya Pradesh. She was well educated, bright and good company.

Eric, Zohra and Pravina Chaube

Susina, now able to write her name in capital letters and to sing a selection of pretty songs, celebrated her 5th birthday in October 1967. Somehow we mustered 13 children and 12 adults to enjoy her party – mostly her favourite servants and families. Cooking on two burners, turning out buns, biscuits and savoury snacks, never mind a suitable birthday cake, proved a challenge. Both Sarpinamma and Chinnathambi were stricken with flu', so it was all hit and miss. Life continued fairly sociably despite our limitations. Jane and David Hughes came from Coorg for the weekend and we invited Fred and Shelagh Foster over for a hilarious Chinese dinner, "Better than the Chungking" declared Shelagh. We all went over to their stud farm next day and lolled on oat sacks, drinking beer and eating curry, but returned early to Hassan to bath and change for a dinner in Coorg to celebrate the wedding of Uncle Bhandari's son, Anil. We expected a buffet for 50, instead it was a feast for a thousand with all the accompanying lights, shimmering saris, glittering diamonds, pandals, marquees, cooking pots and 54 cases of Scotch.

In early December the GM, Ray Pritchard, came to stay and invited us to Guntur for Christmas. "You want to get out of here," he said, half joking. "You're getting very parochial."

Parochial? What chance did we ever have of getting anywhere with so many visitors and Mike racing from point to point all over the tobacco development area of Mysore State? It was a generous invitation so we graciously accepted, but wondered what to buy people we did not know for Christmas. There were five Pritchards, seven Barbys and various other Brits celebrating the big day in Helvetia, the company house on the Grand Trunk Road. Sarpinamma was not coming but luckily Zohra offered her ayah, Kamala, who would help whilst they were on leave in the north. The Sparrows had left Bangalore but Gill and Tony Drayton, who had a little boy of 18-months and another on the way, kindly put us up while we did our essential shopping. The quality of goods was so sub-standard, toys either fell to bits or were made with lethal pieces of metal and hideous prongs. Wrapping paper was in short supply and of such poor quality that a package burst before it was stuck with glue.

The 600-mile journey to Andhra Pradesh was uncomfortable with six of us squashed into Bonnie and we spent one night in Bangalore and one night in Madras at the transit flat. The 1934 car was designed to be chauffeur driven, so was narrow in front and roomy at the back and we stacked plenty of luggage inside, covered it with blankets and the children sprawled on top. The bumpy roads were crowded with lorries gushing exhaust fumes and filling the air with their loud Klaxon horns, whilst rickety *tongas* (carriages) rattled alongside pulled by skeletal ponies. So desperate were we for expatriate company that sometimes we spotted a white person on the roadside, unusually squatting under a tree. We shouted and waved and Mike slowed the car, before we realised the person was an albino with no pigment in his seriously white skin, ash blonde hair and pale eyes squinting against the bright sunshine. It was embarrassing but the albinos, who normally did not get much attention, responded with pleasure and waved back.

There was so much livestock; it was like driving through an endless farmyard. Galloping bullocks were yoked in pairs with chunks of wood tied between their front legs, buffaloes waved sharp horns and waggled big bottoms, black snouty pigs squealed with fear and mangy dogs put their tails between their legs whilst vulnerable scraggy chickens raced willy nilly, squawking for their miserable lives. We rattled on for miles with everyone moaning, we were not used to this type of rough travel and could not locate toilet facilities or anything to eat en route, street food was unsafe and drinking vessels unhygienic. We spotted the odd *Military Hotel*, but on closer examination they looked dirtier than most restaurants, because they served meat. We managed on fruit, biscuits and water. On further travels, with more confidence, we found a few clean vegetarian restaurants where we enjoyed freshly cooked *masala dosais* (thin savoury pancakes made from fermented rice and lentils), rasam and sambar, the Wheatley children's idea of heaven.

We met up with Kamala, our borrowed ayah, in Guntur and the children soon took to her. Getting them to bed was not so easy.

"How is Father Christmas going to bring our stockings?" Susina was genuinely worried and Simon soon picked up that he might be missing out.

"I want Pa Kissmass! Pa Kissmass!" he jumped up and down on the springy bed, almost falling onto the polished terrazzo floor.

Looking quickly round the room I said, "Air conditioner,"

Con-dish-ner? they chorused, "Where's that?"

"Up in the wall, see," and pointed to the square box blowing out cool air and a soft hushy noise. "Father Christmas will come through that." Bewildered and exhausted they accepted the solution. It was Simon's third Christmas but he was not going to miss a thing, Susina was matter of fact and put her empty stocking at the end of the bed and snuggled under the covers.

Kissmass air con-dish-on, Simon wafted off to sleep.

The holiday with the Pritchard family was hectic, sociable and very different from our own family life in Hassan. We took 24 bottles of an especially good vintage of Mission House wine and people looked at us with new eyes, we possessed a skill they wanted to learn and were very complimentary, and we started a cult of wine making in the ILTD growing region. We also took two bottles of expensive Scotch purchased in Bangalore but it was spurious and turned out to be sugar water, the whisky had been siphoned out through the caps by a hypodermic.

Mike carving turkey

Although it was the coolest time of the year, the weather was hot, the smells pungent and Guntur a particularly horrible sprawling filthy town. We relaxed at the beach at Vadarevu for a few days, swimming, sunning, playing games and sand yachting. The Retreat was built in 1927 by the Brits of ILTD; no doubt excluding any Indian apart from those who could cook meals or serve gin fizzes. Located in a small forest of waving casuarina trees, it was a haven of tranquillity apart from the constant night time barking of *pi* (stray) dogs. There was a main building with bedrooms, kitchens, dining room and bar and a large veranda scattered with cane chairs. In our time there was also a separate cottage, known as the *kutcha* (basic) bungalow, with two double en-suite bedrooms, a dining room, kitchen and big veranda. There were also three shacks nearer the beach, rather heavily inhabited by little pink clucking geckos, but big enough for twin beds and a partitioned primitive bucket bath and loo.

The Retreat was reached through the busy fishing village with palmyra thatched huts, and we bounced and swerved our sandy way through the palm trees and the fishing nets laid out to dry. The sense of freedom on the 23 mile stretch of white sand was wonderful, the shimmery ocean dotted with wooden fishing canoes. Some years before the ILTD men built a sand yacht which, after a few beers and a curry lunch, provided great sport sailing up and down the smooth beach. We watched all methods of fishing, from line, to canoe, to two men with an arch of netting running into the sea and pulling the two ends together, catching a few wiggly fish each time. The village was small and simple and the men went out each day in their canoes, they wore only loincloths and plonked baskets on their heads. An earthenware pot of water was wedged into the prow but they carried no food, although they were out all day in the burning sun and sailed back in the evening with the catch. The fishwives waited on the beach with their baskets ready to head load their purchases up to Chirala railway station. Children bartered with prawns and, sometimes, huge fish, such as barracuda were caught. It was a simple life and a simple way to purchase seer, bekti and pomfret for our supper. Once beached, the fishermen separated the two parts of their waterlogged canoes which had been roped together, and lay them to dry, and spent the last of the light mending their nets. The fish were delicious but catering in a tiny kitchen with a filthy fridge was unpleasant.

Fishing canoes at Vadarevu

We drove back to Hassan for a while and then returned to England which was fresh after the heat of the sub-continent. Leave was busy in our Woodbridge home with many overnight guests, and a big family party when the twins were christened at Huntingfield. Although it was cold I dragged the children out every day and pushed them on the swings in the park.

"Harder Mummy, harder Mummy," they cried as I careered from one swing to another.

A woman with a Yorkshire terrier stopped, "Are they *all* yours?" looking me up and down like a breeding machine.

"They are," I puffed.

She smiled rather unkindly, "Goodness me, quite a tribe. Come on Poppy, teatime," and walked off, her little dog yapping at her heels.

Simon was unsettled and kept on querying, "When are we going home Mummy?"

"This is our home," but he shook his head.

"Not my home," he said wearily, wandering off with a dinky car in each hand. It was a relief to return to India and our smiling servants, including Sarpinamma who came back for a while.

Simon was hugely relieved, "Home," he said happily and went off to play with two old tins in the mud. Having managed England with a sideways crabby crawl, David celebrated returning to Hassan by walking eight steps alone, and Andrea careered off into the compound with whatever wheeled vehicle she could stuff her dolls and fluffy toys into. Susina was just pleased to be back.

It was April 1968 and we were allotted an elderly, unreliable Ambassador car, similar to a

1958 Morris Oxford. It was luxury compared to our breezy, hard wheeled jeep and more relaxing for Mike and his tedious and endless travels, though it did not ride the potholes well. The Ambassador was described as the *carthorse* of India, not for agricultural purposes, but that it was the most reliable form of road transport. It drove like a tank, had the heart of an ox and was mechanically easy to repair. Mike and his driver trundled all over the state in sedentary fashion, and the Ambassador has survived for over five decades.

One month I left the compound only once to go shopping and visit Sunita Murch up the road. Labourers swarmed in to whitewash the walls, they were unshaven wearing baggy shorts with nothing underneath, and oily cloths wrapped around their dirty heads. Their bamboo ladders were held together with ropes, their clanking buckets made of bashed up bits of tin and their brushes were bundles of straw. It was mayhem with more whitewash on the floor than the walls and every room turned upside down. They came and went at whim and spent all day chewing paan, spitting and shouting at each other.

Sarpinamma with the children 1967

Susina was becoming frustrated, there were so few toys and teaching aids and the Muslim school, when term started, was one of Kanarese chanting and hardly any fun or creativity. When asked what he did at school Simon replied seriously in his deep voice, "Fighting, just fighting." At home he was developing artistically and drew complicated pictures full of interest, shape and form. He was happy for hours with a pencil and paper, or flying around on his tricycle.

We were preparing Susina to start at Hebron Mission School up in the hills at Coonoor in August when she was nearly six. We were reluctant for her to go, she was so sweet and small, but felt it was necessary to start her education. We had decided on Hebron because we knew other children who studied there quite happily, also it was the nearest boarding school, 200 miles away up mountainous roads. It was founded in 1899 by evangelical missionaries as a girls' school, taking boys up to the age of ten. We visited and liked it, but did not realise the depth of religion that threaded through the school.

The necessities list was several pages long and we provided six of each item of clothing. The climate at that altitude (6,000 ft) was often very cold and wet so there was a pile of blankets, sheets and towels. The Headmistress wrote that we should teach our child to be independent, toilet trained, able to blow their noses and tie their laces.

"I don't want to wear those, they're horrid," Susina's face was tear-stained as she examined the recently purchased heavy black Bata lace-ups, "I want pretty shoes." She was so used to running around barefoot that any shoes were an impediment. It was a struggle to impose all these new rules and we felt bleak, she was such a little thing but with a strong spirit.

20 Jan 1969

Dear Granny
I om going to
send you a
silver present.
My poor Granny
I am sorry
you are not
well.
I will come and
show you my
colouring
when I comes
to England
I hope
Grandadaddy
hold a had a
happy Birthday
with lots of
love from Susina
xoxoxoxox

Chapter 13 – Going to Sleeping School 1968

An early monsoon was in full flood and there were lengthy and frightening thunderstorms, which cracked and flashed furiously for several hours; the children were scared.

"It's OK," I comforted, "It's only Jesus moving the furniture. Whoops that was a wardrobe!" and "There goes the dining room table," it reminded me of my mother during the war, soothing my trembling brother telling him that it was *Hitler doing his exercises*. The rain came in torrents; the roof was like a sieve and the house shrouded in wet washing.

Then came a period of unexpected drought, the tobacco seedlings were stunted and the entire crop threatened, the monsoon was on and off and the growing tobacco became infected with white mould and needed more sun. We were always aware of the leaf in the fields, in the barns and on the buying courts. Tiny flies, irritating and buzzing, danced mercilessly on the rims of our eyes causing infection and conjunctivitis, and the children re-infected themselves by constantly rubbing.

The weather did not stop the visitors and we ran a permanent hotel and restaurant. At times all the servants were down with flu', the walls were damp and the floors slippery from leaks. The children were fractious and needing attention, and the staff became militant if they did not receive expected tips. The only compensation was that we were paid an allowance for meals and overnights, and this helped the housekeeping, but it was difficult to manage on a very tight rupee budget. We did everything possible to send a small quota of money home each month for the mortgage payments on our house, leaving little to survive on, so the *dhobi* (laundry man) who cost almost nothing was dispensed with, leaving me with all the ironing. With this additional workload it became even more difficult to find time to write, something I was keen to do to earn a bit of money. In 1962 I wrote an article on Ghana and it was published as a full page in the Western Mail in Cardiff, so I decided to write about the circus and sent it off to the Monthly Review, a magazine produced in Calcutta by the United Kingdom Citizen's Association. It was later published and I received Rupees 135.00 (£7). I was excited that someone recognised my ability, and contributed regularly to this publication for the rest of our time in India and, later, to Indian newspapers and magazines and in Britain. My writings were of everyday things and my style simple. It was the early start of another career.

Susina and I went to Bangalore in the hospital jeep as the driver was collecting Nurse Margaret Lamb from leave. We shopped for Susie's boarding school clothes until we almost dropped, and she was a very patient little girl. She enjoyed my unadulterated attention and we had a special lunch with cool drinks and ice cream. The date to go to Hebron was looming and we spent a lot of time talking together and trying to reassure her. She was only 5¾, and seemed to understand but, a week or so before she was to start, she frequently cried and was very nervous. Her clothes were sorted, repaired and labelled, I made and marked new outfits for her dolls and each one was given a special bath and shampoo ready for school. Her precious teddy was name taped on the underside of one of his feet. Her first stint at school would last only six weeks; it would be an ordeal for her and an eternity for us all.

We left the twins at home but Simon, very nearly four, came with us. The journey was so long and bumpy, 100 miles to Mysore and another 100 up the ghat road to Ooty. We went to Mysore Zoo and the children laughed merrily at the antics of a spitting chimpanzee. They were in high spirits and wide awake enjoying the scenery towards the Western Ghats and the mountains stretching above us, but soon it became dark and we were blinded by lorries racing downwards. We reached St Margaret's at 8-30, fed the children and put them to bed. Next day we took the school trunk to Hebron in Coonoor which was 15 miles down the other side of the ghat, a scenic journey with the little puff puff ratchet train in the verdant valley below. Coonoor was situated amongst mossy green tea bushes, a pleasant little hill town with shops, a café and a church with many British graves. The school with its red tiled roofs was built on the side of a hill and approached by a big archway with Deo Supremo written on it, and a drive curving upwards. Many buildings were wooden with balconies. Miss Angus, the elderly, plump motherly matron was waiting with Miss Hall, the Head. It was a highly religious school and the staff came from Britain, Australia and New Zealand; it seemed a happy and friendly place and Susina started in a dormitory called The Nest. We walked around and then went back to Ooty for lots of last minute treats like pony rides, rowing on the lake and a visit to the only chocolate shop we knew in south India. Susina was fine until we went under the Deo Supremo archway and she got out of the car and screamed and screamed. It was awful, truly awful. Mike did not know what to do, and stood limply on the drive clutching her little Wellington boots with tears in his eyes. Simon stayed firmly in the car. Eventually it was me who dragged her to the dormitory, a teacher offered a sweet, but Susina knocked it out of her hands and spat on the floor, and uttered the worst words she knew, "Damn you, damn you."

Unable to calm her the best thing was to run away, so I fled and left the poor little thing weeping. Our last view was of a tear blotched face at the window. It was harrowing and Mike and I shared a soggy handkerchief on the way back to Ooty, whilst Simon chatted away as if nothing had happened. We spent a depressing evening and next day phoned the headmistress who said that Susina screamed for over an hour, but ate her supper in bed, slept all night and woke in a cheerful frame of mind. We felt dreadful but slightly more comforted.

The journey home was dreary without our little chatterbox in the back. After ten long days we received a kindly letter from Miss Hall, *Since the outburst when you left she has never looked back. She seems very much at home in the dorm and Miss Angus says she is the best of the bunch for showing a happy spirit. Miss Mason (class teacher) is pleased with the way she has adjusted to the classroom situation. Susina has been telling Miss Angus that she has three brothers and two sisters and that she is the oldest!* After another two days her first letter was delivered *Dear Mummy and Daddy. Thank you for your letter. I am being a good girl. I am playing with the toys. Susina.* Most written by a teacher and copied, but it was her own little signature with a drawing of a highly coloured girl with green hair. Putting our first child so far away into boarding school was one of the worst things we have ever done. Nor did it get easier with the others.

Hebron School in the tea gardens of Coonoor

Our lives were dependent on her little notes, and they came weekly and from then on I wrote regular letters in block print, trying to describe something she could identify. My drawing skills improved with each letter using whatever colours I could find. As an absentee mother to all my children, this was the only way to communicate with them over the many years they boarded. As a child I was given a book called *Letters from the Babalog* written by a mother in north India whose children were sent to England during the British Raj. This mother was very gracious with a house full of servants and she rode around on an elephant and went to many tiger shoots. Her life was different from mine but her anguish of separation from her children was the same, but her drawings were better.

At home Simon became more independent without his big sister and started playing with the twins, previously rather ignored. Andrea was very busy, she was a clowny little girl with a penchant to wear any odd hat she could find. David became gloomy and rather angry, his best thing was to load the dolls' pram with toys and wheel them round and round the driveway. He was, at last, busy talking and saying *Baby, Mama, Push, Shoe, Day Day* (Andrea called him Day Day). His most favourite word was *No.*

My thirtieth birthday was looming in August 1968, I felt saggy and careworn, immersed by children and overwhelmed by demanding servants and chores. Mike had planned to go away.

"But it's my birthday tomorrow," I reminded him.

"Oh," he said looking guilty, and stayed at home. Hidden in a cupboard was a nice handbag he'd bought in Madras on a rushed trip to Guntur. The sniffing postman brought nothing, worse was that my parents, to whom I wrote weekly, forgot, as did all my nearest and dearest. It was a black time.

Soon after Simon was four, an excuse to have a party. Frances O'Brien shared his birthday, so she and her girls came from Goorghully to stay. Originally Simon thought he would be *big like Daddy and shave* but, as his the day loomed, he preferred to stay three. We gave him Wellington boots and a red tie, which was exactly what he wanted. He togged up in shirt, trousers, tie and boots and looked about six and the bee's knees. We managed to bake two chocolate cakes so he was in heaven. The Draytons visited from Bangalore with their two little boys, one aged four months, their Assamese ayah and their spaniel called Soda, who stayed with us whilst they were on leave. We went to Belur and Halebid but, best for the children, was a clean sandy beach on a river three miles up the Saklaspur road. They could paddle and use buckets and spades, no one bothered us and home-made lemonade and jam sandwiches completed the treat.

At the end of term, Jane Hughes and I met up in Mysore and fetched our respective children from school. I was so desperate for company, talked too much and lost my voice on the journey. Susina laughed heartily when she saw me and they said she behaved beautifully and scored two house points. She enjoyed being back at home but soon got bored and was not too upset, after a couple of weeks, when she reached the archway and Deo Supremo, and there were no more agonising screams. There was to be a fancy dress party and she wanted to be a fairy so, during the holidays, we found an early 1960s frilly petticoat and I sewed her a pretty little dress with a band to go on her blonde wavy hair. She looked lovely and it eased her entry back into school life so far away from home. But oh! how we missed her.

Our lives shuddered when a dreadful virus attacked 50% of the tobacco crop which was in danger of extinction, another dramatic hurdle to overcome, farmers to appease and expansion suddenly halted. A new English family, Mike and Vera Windus and their three very small children, arrived at Hunsur. They were accommodated in one of the recently built houses on the company research station. It was of small basic design with concrete floors, metal windows and no veranda. The site was on red hard-baked earth, without landscaping, stark to a degree and they had no transport although miles away from any medical help or a market. We had known Mike as a young man in Ghana, now a settled family man. Vera was only 19, and Mike previously had adopted her first daughter, and then they had two more, a boy and girl who were two years and two months respectively. ILTD suffered no qualms about dropping its young expatriate staff in at the deep end.

We decided to give a long overdue party when we got delivery of a new gas stove with three top burners, no grill and an oven underneath. This was progress indeed! We made a list of 24 possible guests who could travel to Hassan. Not long before, we'd enjoyed a dinner party with ten others at the O'Brien's some 30 miles away, and ended up dancing to records departing merrily at 3am with an almost flat battery. The jeep died on the outskirts of Hassan and we pushed it the last half mile, me in my mini skirt, high heels and tights.

"Whoops, can't push any more," giggling, sliding on some buffalo mess.

"Oh come on," Mike was desperate for his bed, the pleasure of the party disappearing down a pothole.

We have always taken trouble to ensure that our friends have a good time, and the Murchs pitched in to help, getting beds and blankets organised in their flat up the road, whilst we moved with the children into a dusty empty office at the end of our building. We had found some old iron bedsteads and thin mattresses, which we put in the sun to air. Chinnathambi was busily forking up egg whites by the dozen, he made mouth watering meringues and we discussed a Chinese menu. Lots of wine was bottled and there were jugs of *nimbu pani* (fresh lime) for the abstemious. Twenty one people came, all the usual friends from our wide neighbourhood, and others from further afield. The O'Briens arrived with guests from UK, all dressed up as flower power hippies. Mo Sparrow brought records of Beatles and other music from home leave, and we pranced around in our very short skirts until after four in the morning. Next day the party set out with the children for a picnic to the Cauvery River at Ramnathpuram, the trees were full of chattering fruit bats, the river was surging with bloated *mahseer* fish and we were all a bit hungover. Muslim neighbours prepared dekshies of delicious hot *biriyani* (rice with mutton, vegetables and spices) and we ate the steaming stuff from Ghanaian calabashes washed down with rum and lime. It was a good weekend.

Mike travelled regularly to Shimoga, and it was possible that we might be permanently transferred there. The town was industrial, there were no expatriates, the company rented house had a certain charm but was small and difficult to live in, and Shimoga was miles away from Ooty, Bangalore, the coffee estates or any other form of our civilisation. Fears were allayed as it was decided not to expand the area. Ray Pritchard made one of his frequent visits and invited us again for Christmas. Was it us or was it our wine? The Mission House became a wine factory and in one year we made 86 gallons, all fizzing away in the store. I collected big beer bottles like a woman demented, and we brought back a crown corking machine from England. This was serious stuff. Ray also told us that Mike was required in Chirala for two months to work on the grading system in the factory. There was a lot to organise.

Wheatleys in 1968

Susina spent her 6th birthday at school where they made her a cake and gave a little party. Her parcel contained hand knitted dolls clothes and goodies to eat. It was dreadful not to have her with us, but amazing how she made the adjustment to her new life at such a young age. Soon afterwards we visited Ooty for four days and went to her end of term Carol Service. It was performed with great fervour, and was so sweet and ear-achingly tuneless, and she got the giggles throughout the performance. Her report was very average but she was happy and did not complain, peacefulness when your child is separated from you is worth more than any academic achievement. Whilst there, we discussed Simon's future and almost decided that he start school just before his 5th birthday in August 1969, as Hebron said he may have no chance of passing the Common Entrance exam if we left it too late.

Whilst at St Margaret's Mike supervised the installation of a bore well and we were requested to check through the inventories of the four apartments. This was an arduous bureaucratic company task. Annual checking of BF&F (Bungalow Furniture and Fittings) was every wife's dread, we all had dog-eared badly typed lists of every item of company belongings, all marked with painted numbers. A complex system was set up in the dark ages, and everyone seemed to have their own version. The BF&F clerk was usually from the lower ranks, often sweaty, spotty and nervous but determined to achieve his end and have no losses or breakages. There were things like *4 chota hazri set* (bed tea), 2 commode, *3 almirah* (wardrobe), *one dozen dekshies various* (if we ever reached the dizzy heights to be supplied with saucepans), *6 cots* (beds), 6 mosquito nets (cotton) and *8 durries* (bedside rugs) and every single item was checked, marked and counted, all complicated by Simon being very ill with mumps.

1969 Hyderabad – far left Connie Pritchard with specs and centre seated, Zohra with flower in hair, Sally, Anand Lal, Shelagh Barby and (foreground) Prabha Raghavan.

The next excitement was a promised trip to Hyderabad to attend the company Triangular Cricket Match, an annual event held between Vazir Sultan in Hyderabad, India Tobacco in Bangalore and ILTD in Andhra Pradesh and each factory took turns to host the event. Desperate to go we made arrangements for Frances O'Brien to take Susina and Simon whilst the twins stayed at home with Sarpinamma, with Margaret Lamb on call at the hospital if anything went wrong.

Some months before I took a grosgrain skirt to the Bangalore tailor with a request to make me a black shift with three-quarter sleeves. The skirt was ten years old costing seven guineas when new, so I was, as usual, asking a lot from his design skills. When complete he posted it to me and surprised me with hand stitched gold sequins around the neck and in a band down the front *By the grace of God here is your dress Madam,* he wrote in this 5th Standard, lick your pencil, writing, *I am knowing you will be happy, isn't it?. These seequeens are costing you fifteen rupees (many I have stitched costing you wonly four annas for a full dozen) but they are of purst* (first) *quality and will not melit from the yiron. I send my salaams to you and the Masters. Diwali Greetings and respekfully I am your Mohan Rao."*

Not being a sequin person I was doubtful, but Mohan Rao excelled himself and it was an elegant outfit. Whilst pregnant with the twins I had lost weight, my hair was long and blonde and swept up into a chignon, and a decent pair of black stilettos was found in the bottom of a cupboard. It was so exciting and I dared any of our children to snivel, sneeze or produce a temperature. Susina went happily to the O'Briens but Simon refused point blank, *Not going O'Byan house, I stay home,* he said determinedly, and he did.

Mike had already left for Andhra on business and I was due to meet Zöe in Bangalore. It was an exhausting 700-mile, 16-hour journey. We enjoyed a wonderful weekend and felt we were in the land of the living again. We became real people, with real conversation and dropped our hill billy Hassan ways. I stupidly visited a hairdresser and landed up with the biggest bouffe held together by 160 prickly hairpins and gallons of lacquer. Mike played golf for the first time in his life and hit me in the stomach whilst trying to score a hole in one. He did! No more pirouetting for me, I hopped around pretending it didn't hurt but the bruising proved otherwise. We went sailing on the huge lake, my maiden voyage in a boat and we set out in a flimsy Laser, almost like a surf board with a big sail. All was well until we hit the strong winds in the middle of the lake and *ready about leo* we capsized and landed in very deep, cold water with dubious underwater creatures lurking beneath. Bang went my bouffe, also my handbag, Mike's new shoes, air tickets, money and various other important items. Or so we thought, but Mike had wedged them so securely in the prow that all were recoverable but sodden.

We attended two big parties with bands and danced our feet off. It was such fun, a reminder of youth and freedom, and being normal. We flew to Bangalore together, a rare treat, and motored to Hassan. The children were all right but, next day, Simon came down with such severe tonsillitis that we took him to Mysore as his condition was worrying. Anti-biotics, as usual, dealt with the problem but did not cure the cause.

1968 Susina after her first term at school

Chapter 14 – Palm Villa West, Chirala

The next hurdle was our trip to Andhra and a two month stint in Chirala. Bonnie was eased off her blocks, greased up and the cobwebs flapped away. She started like a dream and sped ten miles up the Bangalore-Mangalore highway as if she had been out all year. Before departure, Mike checked the accounts and sorted out his office situated at one end of the veranda. Our life was much more settled but the children were excited at the prospect of a change and more beach fun, and dear old Chinnathambi promised to come with us, but Sarpinamma stayed firmly at home. This was the cut off point as we could no longer retain her in Hassan, and employ another ayah in Chirala. It was a difficult time, she had been a good, honest and faithful servant and cared for the children, particularly the twins, with great diligence. We allowed her to stay in the quarters while she searched for another house and, when we returned she, Swami Das, Joyce and David had all gone.

Just before we left, some ILTD colleagues telegrammed, "We're transferred to Malaya, would you like Nanny?" Would we? I had visions of a uniformed felt-hatted lady from Norland, my expectations were sometimes ridiculously high, but other wives knew of her and wrote that she was a tiny Burmese and completely bald. Her credentials were good and we were desperate so telegrammed back, "Yes please" and arranged that she should start with us at Chirala immediately after Christmas.

Little girl spinning at Jandrapetta

We set off on 21 December and stayed a night in Bangalore and then drove on to Madras to discover a rear leaf spring needed replacing, causing a delay. On our journey we began to understand the habits of drivers on major trunk routes. The weak two-wheelers gave way to the mighty fuel tankers and lorries, and the least aware of their dangers were the pedestrians who walked three abreast, backs to the traffic, and cyclists who wobbled along with 8 foot bundles of sugar cane, five people or three bags of rice aboard. It was a noisy and tedious 250-mile drive north, this time travelling via Chirala to attend the annual children's Christmas party at the New Club. We turned off the trunk road at Ongole, crossed the Madras-Calcutta railway line and drove over the salt flats, onto sandy roads through the villages where artisans such as silversmiths and wood carvers worked, also many sari weavers. We stopped at Jandrapetta, a hamlet famous for its seven-yard handloom saris, most saris are six yards in length. It was good to get out in the late afternoon sunlight which dappled through the palm trees and we walked all round the small village, followed by the usual trail of onlookers. The cotton was painstakingly spun on primitive wooden wheels, and the hanks were treated with vegetable dyes and dried in the sun. The long threads were stretched on primitive looms, and woven with shuttles flying through them deftly handled by someone on each side of the frame. The work was speedy and they ran up and down the loom, tightening the thread as they went. The hand weavers, all women, sat in sandpits which were deep and uncomfortable, their wooden looms above their heads. Mostly were elderly women with thick lensed spectacles to assist their failing eyesight, it was intricate work and skilful hands pulled every thread. None of them spoke English, and no one could explain anything, but they were welcoming and friendly.

Weaving a sari at Jandrapetta

At last we arrived at the pin neat factory compound in Chirala, it was my first real visit and surprising to find a huge tobacco re-drying complex and two compounds of perhaps 40 established bungalows with trees and gardens, very different from the dirty villages and worse towns we had passed through, a haven of sorts behind high walls. The children were immediately whisked into the party, rather ill prepared and ill clad for the occasion, but they soon got into the swing of things eating curry puffs, pop corn and sticky jalebis. A dark brown Father Christmas in red robes distributed gifts some, thoughtfully, with the name Wheatley on them, then the exhausted children flopped into Bonnie and we drove another 50 miles to Guntur following the Pritchards and their three girls, so it was a chaotic arrival at Helvetia. The house, originally the home of a Swiss trader, was set well back from the dust and noise of the Calcutta highway; at night it seemed quite romantic but by day it looked dusty and old, having been patched together through too many monsoons.

Dragging pyjamas, nappies, toothbrushes out of suitcases, we got our four weary children to bed, assuring them that Father Christmas would again come through the air conditioner, before sitting down to a formal dinner in the high ceilinged dining room. Christmas Day started about 5-30am when Julie, Ting and Alla Pritchard jumped out of bed and immediately started ripping open packages and, by 6-30am, it was all over and the parents sat bleary eyed in rumpled nightclothes whilst seven children rushed around, treading on toys screaming with excitement. As always the Pritchards were hospitable and the whole festive season was social and exhausting. There was a small swimming pool so everyone was leaping in and out, and we were careful to watch our children. It was a boozy time with plenty of cold beer and gin lime sodas tinkling with ice, and dinners enhanced with glasses of our red wine.

Many of our Mysore and Bangalore friends, both Indian and expatriate, had not really taken on board that we were to move to Andhra for several months.

"You're going where? Andhra Pradesh! Are you mad?

"We have to," we moaned, "It's where the tobacco is grown and handled."

"You simply cannot, a terrible place" they were horrified, "No one shifts to Andhra Pradesh, no Indians will go there, it's a filthy place!"

After Christmas we stayed for a few days at the beach in Vadarevu and then moved to Chirala for two months and were joined by Nanny. She was very small and thin with a flat, yellow expressionless face and spaces between her teeth. She wore sarongs and little white cotton blouses, covering her bald head with a home-made black cotton cap. Snatching it off was a constant source of fun for our mischievous children and it made her angry, so they were warned that they were cruel and she felt very unhappy without her head covered. We did not know how old she was, perhaps in her late forties, but she looked considerably older. She was very Burmese with a clipped oriental accent and an inscrutable demeanour and never relaxed into carefree giggles; but she was a kindly, efficient and trustworthy ayah. She turned her hand to anything such as washing, sewing, cleaning, cooking, serving at table, shopping and, above all, children.

Her name was Margaret Coleman because, she said bluntly, "I married Coleman," and that was that. Much later we discovered that Nanny was Burmese born, and fled overland to Calcutta when the Japanese invaded Burma in 1942. The horror and fear of the invasion caused the complete loss of her hair. In the 1930s cheap labour was recruited and shipped from Andhra villages by Burmese rice mill barons from the north of the country. When the Japanese invaded, the Andhras and some Burmese fled and made their way to India; the journey from Burma to Calcutta was terrible, across the swampy deltas of East Bengal. Thousands were swallowed up by thick mudslides, and others died from pestilence caused by rotting bodies and bad drinking water. Nanny somehow survived, arrived in Andhra and got a job in a hospital in the large town of Vishakhapatnam where she met *Coleman* who was a patient. He was an Anglo-Indian mechanic at the ILTD factory in Anaparti and they married in church *but not properly* and she gave birth to a son, Richard Coleman. He was a handsome lad with pale skin and almond shaped eyes. Nanny's subsequent life was centred around the company, working for various employers and she eased herself into our family and travelled everywhere with us. Being so small she took up very little room and we looked after her until she died in Guntur in 1976.

In the New Year of 1969 we moved into Palm Villa West, a 1924 unwieldy residence. It was one of a collection of ten bungalows on the other side of the railway line from the factory. Living *on the other side* was a definite demarcation between management and non-management and, in the olden days, between British and Indian. Through the two compounds, trains ran frequently back and forth along the main line from Madras Calcutta with long heavy wagons and carriages pulled by powerful diesel locomotives. In addition there were overloaded local steam engines, with people riding on the roofs and hanging out of the windows and doors.

The compound was pleasant, everything was grown on sand and fertilised by tobacco waste, the bungalows were well spread out and had been planted with orchards rather than gardens. A decade or so before, a nine hole golf course was created at the far end of the compound but, when we arrived, it was not used, apart from as a lavatory by neighbouring villagers.

Palm Villa West had an open veranda with no security or privacy and looked onto the sandy park land with its many trees. Opening out onto the veranda were three lots of double doors, two of which belonged to high ceilinged old fashioned bedrooms with antiquated bathrooms; the other to a large, dingy sitting room leading to the kitchen and back door. None of the rooms adjoined which made the house impossible for family living, we could not lock all four children into one room, so we separated and each of us slept with two of them. It was a long low building with mud green and tomato coloured walls set off by Cardinal polished floors and cumbersome rosewood furniture. The kitchen was archaic, certainly better than the Mission House but with few mod cons. Someone had whisked around with a broom and swabbed the floors with a smelly mop and, although our stay was to be short, I could not stand the dirt and employed a sweeper plus a girl to help Chinnathambi and, between us, we cleaned the place and washed all the curtains. A tailor came with his treadle machine and made bright new cushion covers, and I collected dried grasses and arranged them in sand filled earthenware jars.

A company mali worked at each bungalow and was provided with two water pots and a rake made of bamboo. He spent all day, when not asleep under a tree, wandering up and down his patch making rows of zig-zagged herring bone patterns in the sand, up and down, up and down. There were wells sunk all over the place with only one ring of cement above ground and easy to fall down. They were full of brackish water and this was pulled out in a metal pot on a rope and scattered on anything that might grow. For the malis it was an indolent life, unless they were dragged into the kitchens and made to do all the sweeping and shopping.

Christopher and Sally Harding

What we did have in our particular garden was a huge sandy hole left from a dead tree. The mali removed the roots and made a perfect cavern for children to play. The only other expatriates on the compound were Sally and Christopher Harding. They had two children; Richard already at boarding school in the hills at Kotagiri, and Victoria, still at home and much mothered by her bespectacled ayah, Estheramma. Victoria was a constant visitor.

"Can I play in your hole?" she appeared every afternoon, blonde and pink, wearing neatly smocked dresses and pretty shoes and socks, Estheramma close on her heels. Simon instantly called her *Mitoria* and the two became firm friends and played for hours, her little voice piercing and determined above his sonorous tones. Meanwhile Nanny sat on the sand with the twins playing around her, trying to join in with the bigger ones.

The factory was regimented by regular whistles, which indicated when to wake, go to work, eat tiffin, have lunch, eat tiffin and go home. In the season the whistle sounded regularly all night to get the workers to attend their shifts. That and the trains roaring by made for a very noisy regimented life.

Mike got used to a new routine, he was no longer his own boss in a huge territory but a tiny ant in a massive organisation. The factory re-dried tobacco leaf after purchase, the central stems were removed from the leaves by thousands of women, all sitting cross legged in a shed, and the lamina was put into large re-drying machines where the moisture was removed by heat and then pressed into bales. At that time there were over 7,000 labour and the buildings and warehouses covered several acres. He learnt about grading and was often away visiting tobacco buying stations and depots all over Andhra Pradesh.

When he was at home we packed a picnic lunch, and collected him in the Chevrolet as soon as the 12 noon whistle blew. Then we all went to Vadarevu and ate a leisurely lunch on the beach, we used a Thermos food container with three covered saucepans inside, and enjoyed curry, rice and dall. This, with fresh fruit, started our healthier diet after struggling to be buffalo eating *Yewro-peans* in Hassan. The children flopped in the water and paddled, and it was a wonderful respite, but Mike was due in the factory at two in the afternoon, lateness was not tolerated.

It was soon Chirala's turn for another Triangular cricket match, an invasion of visitors from Bangalore and Hyderabad and tons of food to cook. In Chirala we had no mess or hotel facilities, the factory canteen produced only *idlis, vadais* and *rasam*, so everything was cooked in the bungalow kitchens. It was a trial for all the cooks who possessed different skills, methods, languages and confidence, ditto their Madams. Our first task was to prepare 14 chickens (delivered alive in two squashed baskets) and concoct eight desserts. Never inventive with food my suggestion was chicken casserole and banana custard, but Chinnathambi had better ideas. Finding ingredients needed resources almost beyond me, in Hassan we got good fresh vegetables but Chirala's choice was poor and mostly of the Indian kind; gourds, bitter leaves, aubergines, okra, red onions, potatoes and green bananas. In season there were papaya, mangos, cashew nut fruits, sapotas, custard apples, oranges and tiny yellow plantains.

The visitors arrived from Hyderabad and Bangalore for the cricket match and were put up here and there. We welcomed a couple and begged and borrowed sheets and towels as these were not supplied. The matches were played on Chamiers Field at the end of the management compound, where they put up benches and a scoreboard and the rough grass was cut by hand repeatedly. Bats, balls, stumps and bales were dug out of the stores, a tea urn was produced and the cricket began. I proved a sharp eyed scorer and moved the rings on the board, the match was getting heated and Christopher Harding, never a loser, was batting a particularly vicious 50mph ball. Anyone else would have ducked but not Christopher, he got it straight in the mouth. It was an appalling accident for such a young man and he was badly injured, amazingly only two teeth were shattered, but he suffered a heavily lacerated mouth which needed seventeen stitches. The company medic, Dr Sadananda Rao, came into his own; already a trained dentist he dealt with the teeth and managed to do an impeccable embroidery job on Christopher's mouth. The resulting scars were tiny, the pain was almost unbearable and Christopher sucked his drinks and lived on *pish pash* (a mixture of rice and mince) for several weeks before he was able to chew.

Life was complicated as Simon's tonsils were swollen with sacs of pus and he was miserable. I took him to Dr Sadananda Rao, a rotund bespectacled orthodox Telugu.

"Too much infection," he squinted down Simon's throat with a pencil torch, "We'll treat with anti-biotics." Strong anti-biotics could be purchased without prescription and were overused in India and the doctors, eager to cure, did not have enough knowledge to understand the side effects. He wrote out a note and I requested transport and went to town, about two miles away, to get the medicine. After two days we noticed that Simon was having trouble walking, he was limping and wavering from side to side, when usually he was running and jumping. Now he was thin, mopey and hollow eyed. I took him to the doctor.

"Too much anti-biotic," the doc was philosophical, "I forgot to prescribe Vitamin B Complex to counteract the weakness in his body." He was not apologetic but wrote another note and, after a few days, Simon recovered and was brighter. My Dr Benjamin Spock did not cover the complexities of modern drugs and, it was many years later, when an American anthropologist in West Africa, Bob Harding, gave me a book, *Where There is No Doctor.* How useful it would have been *where there was a doctor.*

Andrea and David with the Mehdi children at Vadarevu

Susina was ready to return to school by train, the other three children could not be left, so we asked if Manni Mehdi, one of the Muslim wives, could take her. Manni was travelling with her own two children to join St Hilda's in Ooty for the first time. Susina was very excited at the prospect of travelling by train, not a bit sad at saying goodbye and couldn't wait for the train to leave. We felt differently when we got to Guntur station and were horrified at the first class carriage expecting clean bedding and a blanket, but there was none and it was cold. Manni produced a warm shawl and Susina's teddy was used as a little pillow. It was awful watching the train chuff out of the station, I knew I should be on it too, but the truth was that I was afraid of train travel and had not ventured into its complicated uncomfortable intricacies. The idea of embarking on a three-day journey via Madras made me very nervous. Manni returned to Guntur after about a week and sent me a note through the company *tapal* (post) saying that Susina got off at Coonoor cheerfully, and ran to meet her matron. She said it really helped her own two children to have such a positive and happy companion, but we couldn't help feeling we had abandoned her.

I missed speaking the local language, and picked up the odd word of Telugu known as the Italian of the East. It was certainly easier to hear than the rolling tones of Kanarese, but I was not there long enough to have any use from it. After the relatively clean and organised state of Mysore we discovered that Andhra Pradesh was, as our friends predicted, very unpleasant. Sanitation seemed not to exist at any level, apart from wealthy residences. We were told that it was *unclean to 'go' in the same place twice* so there were no latrines or long drops, and good Brahmin doctrine stated that each person should use an open air site and a fresh one each time; difficult in an area of dense population. The villagers, who exercised very regular habits, wandered to the fields either morning or evening carrying their *lotas* (small brass water pots) and squatted among the crops eagerly followed by scavenging pigs. When my mother came to stay and asked what everyone was doing, I told her they were picking flowers, "How nice," she said vaguely, but this was less believable on the beach when I substituted flowers for sea shells. Fortunately our company beach area was considered private and kept clean.

Chirala was ramshackle, undeveloped, muddy, full of drains and pigs, buffaloes and straw. I needed wellies and a stick to keep off the animals, rather than flip flops and bare legs. The medicine shop was owned by the only English speaking retailer, a polite man with a fridge and Amul butter nudging the medicines. Chinnathambi came home from market, "Dirty place Madam," he mumbled, washing his hands vigorously with Lifebuoy soap. Already his spirits were drooping and he was homesick.

Our knowledge of living amongst Indians of all types was limited. In Hassan we met only domestic and field staff and a collection of varied outsiders, but living in Andhra meant being in the midst of orthodox Hindus, many of whom spoke little English. They lacked empathy and, although spiritual, they seemed unable to share their spirituality with those who did not understand their own particular brand. Orthodoxy cannot be dabbled with, the word has a Greek derivation; *ortho* or *right* and *doxa* or *thought* and refers to the correct worship and doctrinal observation of religion by some overseeing body. Generations of Hindus have absorbed this doctrine and passed it on, and many of the orthodox are unshakeable in their beliefs. For the women life was full of ritual and puja, and a very firm devotion to their own particular god. Each morning they cooked while the day was still cool, after which they bathed and oiled their hair. Each tiny house had a *puja* room, or a small space for *puja* (prayer), an oil lamp was lit and flowers arranged before the images of the deities, recitation of religious scripts, meditation and, perhaps, a chanting of *mantras* and it was all very serious and obligatory. I tried to make friends with the ladies when we visited the club as none invited me to their homes, but failed dismally. They simply could not relate to me and talked amongst themselves. For Mike it was easier; in the factory there was a male camaraderie and a universal respect for each other, men are far less complicated in their relationships than are women.

Club parties usually happened on a Saturday night, and this was the day for women to fast, so were not allowed to eat dinner. Dinner was usually appetising as we organised a *pool-in* and everyone made dishes to share at the big table. I questioned the ladies about the dilemma of not eating having slaved over a hot stove, some were stern and assured me, "I will fast." One or two others were less strict, "We will bargain with God," they giggled, "We'll fast on Tuesday." When we were all sharing the food it was noted that many of the vegetarian husbands surreptitiously dug into the thick gravied, full of bones, mutton curry, hoping their wives did not notice, and the *pool-ins* were difficult for young, shy brides, having to produce something out of a new home.

The status of a woman in India at that time was not strong, and for a widow or someone divorced almost impossible, they simply were not rated or acknowledged. My mother, a regular correspondent, had been seriously ill in hospital and we did not hear for several weeks, and had no telephone link with anywhere and I was getting worried. Mike was often away and could not pull strings to get news, eventually we received a letter forwarded from Hassan by registered post, requiring a signature. Mike was again away and the postman refused to give me the letter because I was a woman, although it was addressed to *me*. When Mike returned he collected it from the Post Office but, after that, I snatched any letter off the postman and ripped it open so he dared not go back with a mutilated envelope.

Eventually I worked it out that the Indians we lived amongst did not have the natural culture of *social life;* it was an imported custom. They were different and clannish, they did not like to be alone, so the women huddled together and the men huddled together but got no value from *being* together. There was no spiritual affinity, no closeness, it was an animal need to cluster often in silence staring into space, perhaps a form of defence? It was undemanding, low key, effortless and most of the time achieved nothing apart from social intercourse coloured by nervous giggling and awkward body language. It drove me mad, it was such a waste of time as no conversation reached any conclusion. Already a fish out of water, local habits alienated me almost completely.

One of the supervisors, a kindly man, involved me in conversation and could see I was struggling. Mike worked very late and was often still in his office until 10pm so Mr Krishna Rao visited sometimes in the evenings, and we sat on the veranda and talked of religion, Hinduism, temples, pujas and traditional worship. He loaned me the *Bhagavad Gita* originally written in Sanskrit and known as the *Song of God*. I diligently read the book from cover to cover but got lost in the long conversation between Krishna and Arjuna on a battlefield just before a war, the outcome of which relied on philosophies to resolve the moral dilemma of war. The Hindus see this important document as a sensible Guide to Life, but it gave me no such uplifting comfort. I also read several books by Sathya Sai Baba, a world renowned *avatar* or teacher, a small baby faced man with a mop of black Jimmi Hendrix hair. He quite fascinated me, mainly because of his large following, but again provided no comfort. Amongst millions it is possible to be very lonely indeed.

The Hindu culture it seems is more dependent on what happened to the ninth century god rather than what happened in a battle a hundred years previously or what happened yesterday. During discussions with various people I found it amazing that knowledge of their great-grandparents was non-existent, whereas they could spout off details of their particular religion going back to the year dot. The past was accepted but the effect of war and pestilence was perhaps not considered as part of history or how it might change the pattern of life. It seemed to have no leaning on *why* things occurred. I knew many women who accepted their religion without question and gained a great deal of peace from it, but am not sure that they gained as independent thinkers and doers. Life ticked along in the monotony of ritual, it was difficult to understand and difficult to get a meeting of the minds. Religion was serious, as was their dress, their diet and unbudgeability. It was a whole new ball game of social relationships and I had to be careful what I said. Some of them were very smart indeed, too smart perhaps, but they were held back by their lack of spontaneity and fun. Life for them was not fun, it was heat and drudge with a terrible sense of responsibility to achieve. The children were taught by rote at school and, if parents could afford it, they were privately tutored in the evenings. It was all slog slog slog, and that seemed the ethos of the company, work until you drop (dead) and some of the men did, their high cholesterol diets led to early heart attacks and vapours of tears from the bereaved.

Chinnathambi became seriously ill with bronchitis and when the anti-biotics did not work, Dr Sadananda Rao resorted to penicillin, to which Chinnathambi was allergic and suffered the most dreadful reaction. We nearly lost him but the normally shambling doctor quickly injected him with the antidote. After a while I became used to this man and learned to respect him, basically he had good medical ability but his methods were unorthodox. Visiting him in his role as dentist was an experience not to be repeated, his drill was hand operated by a weak old woman, and he fished around my mouth with an old probe and then drilled with a blunt head imploring the woman to turn the wheel, "Fastly, fastly," as the sparrows above us flapped away, frightened by his shrill voice.

Chinnathambi was laid off for several days until he was well enough to go home to Mysore by train. He wept and was so sad to say goodbye to the children, he was a dear old man and very faithful. I hated preparing food so much, especially in such disgusting kitchens, that we were soon searching for another cook.

Chirala Town

Chapter 15 – Shimoga 1969

We started from Chirala at 4am in thick mist. It was a gruelling 14-hour drive to Bangalore, with a puncture on the way and very hard on three young children who needed constant amusement with songs, nursery rhymes and snacks in their hungry tummies. The week before we left, a telegram was sent reserving a large room in a comfortable hotel in Bangalore, and we were longing for a hot bath and a good rest. The receptionist (or so he said) did not receive our booking and was unhelpful, and we were forced to stay in a vegetarian doss house with the children sleeping on the floor.

"Don't like this floor," Simon was exhausted and gruff, "It's hard under my *bott-omm*," and he laughed because he'd said a naughty word.

Andrea wandered around twisting her hair and sucking her thumb, "How far Hassan?" she demanded imperiously, "I want to go *home*!" She had the most penetrating cry of all our children and was very tired, so we blocked our ears until she lay down on the thin mattress and went to sleep.

David, who had matured a lot in the last couple of months, was too intent on playing with his cars on the shiny floor having been released from the hot, stuffy car.

Brmm, brmm - I like Bang-lore. I'm hung-y. Brmm, brmm.

Next evening we turned into the gates and up the dry and droughty drive of the Mission House. Nanny was relieved to get out of the car and and move into her small quarter; the journey had made her very tired and her mood was unusually sour. We had arranged for a Madras cook to start work and sent money for his fare, but he failed to report for duty. So, while Mike unpacked the car, I set to and cleaned the filter, boiled drinking water, made the beds and got everyone settled in. India was a trial in a situation like this when everyone was hungry and there were no edible canned goods or instant food, and nowhere to buy anything cooked and wholesome, so we resorted to porridge and the inevitable bananas.

Next day Chinnathambi turned up looking slightly better, but thin and weak.

"I'm *wery wokay,*" his deep set wise eyes reassured me, "Doctor said I'm *wokay* but not to work *wery, wery* hard. Please Madam," he pleaded.

He was anxious, so we put him on light duties and insisted he took plenty of rest. It was a relief to have him back but we did not want him to get sick again. He said the children had grown a lot since he last saw them in Chirala, and he was really missing *Missy Sujeena* who was at Hebron.

The word *Shimoga* was becoming more frequent in Mike's vocabulary and it was obvious that he was going to have to manage both the Hassan and Shimoga areas. John Maclean had been posted to Andhra and his area needed a lot of attention and expansion. Reluctant to vacate Hassan, it was agreed that the children and I should spend part of each week in Shimoga. To make the house comfortable we packed bed linen, cooking utensils and a couple of pictures for the walls. We expected endless guests who would have to be grateful for a roof over their heads and a meal at our table, like Hassan, there was no suitable hotel accommodation for visitors.

"I want my pedal car, my bike, my cars and my books," Simon was determined his world was not going to be upset, and stood worriedly as I sorted through the miserable toy box. "And that!" pointing at a soft toy not touched for months, "And that!" And so it went on.

Shimoga was a big, hot sprawly town full of industry with a huge population. The name is derived from Lord Shiva - basically *Shiva Mukhu* - face of Shiva, fined down to the Lord's nose or *mogu* - hence *Shimoga.* Another idea was that centuries ago, a famous sage kept a boiling pot of sweet herbs to calm his sharp temper. One day some passing cowherds took a sip and called the location *Sihi Moge* or Sweet Pot. To my mind there was nothing sweet about Shimoga and I didn't want to be there.

Mike, who always locates good properties had, several years earlier during his survey, found a quaint little house in the residential area of town, quite an old bungalow with one top floor room. There was a central porch leading into a sitting room and out to an open grilled passageway ending at the bathroom, kitchen and dining room. The single bathroom was primitive but functional, provided with a proper loo and basin and, in addition, a huge copper tank insulated with cement which had a tap at the bottom. It was continually filled by a pipe and heated with firewood from the outside. All that was needed was a bucket and a dipper and endless baths could be taken with lovely warm water. The three dark, hot, poky bedrooms were all on the right entered by nasty little double doors. The passageway looked out onto the garden and was always airy and sunny or swamped with rain in the monsoon.

The garden was the best bit, a walled in orchard, the Indian owner was obviously keen on fruit as there were mangoes, sapotas, figs and cashew nuts, avocado pears and, unusually, celery. The *mali* was an elderly lady called Chinnamma who liked her own company. Chinnathambi agreed to move and become the cook and caretaker of the house and we employed a sweeper to help him. Chinnamma was happy to carry on with her work and keep the copper tank in the bathroom filled and the fire alight. Compared to Hassan, life in Shimoga was more isolated and lonely, we did not get to know anyone, or familiarise ourselves with shopping, as we carried all our supplies from Hassan in boxes and baskets.

The twins and Simon enjoyed the small house and compound because it was so safe; there was a big locked gate and no back entrance and they played freely. The only scary thing was the prospect of invisible snakes, but the children made up little picnics, or played with tin cans and a bucket of water.

Sometimes Chinnamma filled up her metal pots and drenched them, "More! More!" they cried. *Ila. Saku.* she said, "No – enough", and lay down under a shady tree to have a little rest. Mostly the compound was peaceful with little movement in it, the walls were high and we could not see people passing on the road. The two elderly *Chinnas* and Nanny were quiet, cooking up their food in our horrid little kitchen, and we were all panting for the mango showers. The weather was blisteringly hot and the twins were covered in prickly heat. My only solution to this problem was to soak them in warm water until their skin got wrinkled which eased the itching and wild red rashes. In Hassan there was a home-made bath tub which allowed enough room for the two of them to splash and soak, but in Shimoga there were only buckets and dippers.

We had promised to take Susina out of school for Easter and had booked five nights at St Margaret's, but Mike was sowing seedbeds so he cancelled, which made me furious and frustrated. She was away for such long spells and I had no say in how life was organised, I was a pawn in the game of over worked men and a greedy, grasping company. I wrote and carefully explained why Daddy was so busy and why we could not come; her little face must have fallen and she will have cried. After Easter her letter was cheerful, though we were not sure how much pressure was put upon her to *be happy,* there was always someone leaning over her shoulder whilst she wrote. However in May 1969 we were due a week's leave in Ooty, which coincided with her end of term play. It was fun, full of singing and dancing and, as usual, she giggled throughout.

Simon could no longer attend the Muslim school regularly but, as he learnt nothing, it didn't matter except that he enjoyed the other children and the *fighting*. It was important that he was kept occupied and he was adept with crayons and paper, although the wax crayons melted in his hot little hands and frustrated his desires for clean lines.

"That *air-flane* is too splodgy," he cried in despair, trying to rub it out with his sweaty fist making the drawing far worse. There was nowhere that we could purchase decent stationery and teaching aids, and Mike brought home big pieces of brown wrapping paper off cartons of cigarettes, and the kids drew on the back of them. He and I talked at length and decided, definitely, that Simon must start at Hebron on his 5th birthday in August.

The lack of a cook continued in Hassan and was made worse by our comings and goings but, eventually, we got a rather posh lady called Kamala who was competent and knew her rights. Her cooking was good and she was pleasant, but our upsy-downsy lifestyle was difficult for her to cope with and she did not last long. For a while Chinnathambi came up and down with us, but it was not good for him so we took on yet another cook, David, recommended by ILTD people who had retired. But he became clever, cocky and insolent; Mike propelled him out of the house by the scruff of his neck when he refused to prepare vegetables or wash up. We were coming to the conclusion that our low key life in Hassan did not suit their exalted ways, we were not good enough.

In Shimoga I was so bored that I took my little sewing machine and started to make a patchwork quilt, using the luridly patterned cotton material from my maternity clothes. I sewed in the top room which was like an oven, and painstakingly cut diagonal shapes with big scissors almost getting down to the bone on the middle finger of my right hand. The material piled up and was machine stitched into wonky strips and joined in a herringbone pattern. The idea was to make four single quilts but, after completing about 20 strips, I changed my mind and decided to make one double quilt instead. The warps and wefts got out of alignment and it became a wretched thing as it grew and grew; it was heavy, unwieldy and definitely ugly with so many conflicting patterns. Eventually it was finished and, a couple of years later, a virtuous tailor struggled to line it, an almost impossible task as the cloth went every which way. The result was a warm colourful bedspread which brought back memories of uncomfortable pregnancies and steaming in Shimoga.

Chinnamma outside the gate in Shimoga

One day, whilst we were in Hassan, Simon asked gravely, "Mummy, when are you going to get this stone out of my nose?"

"What stone?" I asked vaguely, rubbing his back and sloshing him with muddy looking water.

He leant backwards and pointed up one nostril, "There," he said firmly, but I could not see anything and was too busy heaving him out of the waist high tub, and then drying and smothering him with Johnson's scratchy prickly heat powder.

A couple of days later he was more insistent, "When are you going to get this stone out of my nose?" he shouted.

There *must* be a stone in his nose, "Just blow out, blow hard," I urged. He did and out popped a stone about the size of a pea, I was horrified, and he was highly relieved.

"You see! I told you!" and he splashed me all over with water.

We made a visit to Bangalore, the first for eight months. My shopping list was long including bed linen and underwear for the children, with the usual shortage of cash. It was a brief sojourn but we ate out and saw two films. For a change we managed to look at each other without someone crying or yelling, "Mummy he hit me." But it was not enough, we had reached the stage when all the pressures were invading our relationship. At this time Mike was travelling 2,000 miles a week and we were exhausted trying to cope with so many people and so many facets of the complicated crop and growing conditions

When we got back Frances O'Brien was staying at the Redfern Hospital eagerly awaiting the birth of her fourth child. She waddled down the road to see me each morning groaning that waiting for babies was the most tedious past time.

"It had better be a boy," she laughed, "Gerald won't be able to hold his head up at

Goorghully Estate if it's another girl. It was - a beauty called Deborah. I rang Gerald, who was in Bangalore.

"Oh good," he said, " We won't have to buy another London house with an extra bedroom.

Susina came down from the hills to Mysore on the chartered school bus where I met her. She had grown and lost some teeth and her hair was longer, thick and blonde. She was more peaceful and enjoying her new hobby, knitting. Her report was excellent and she could now read upside down and sideways as well as the right way round. We did not have enough books and longed for a library or a bookshop. With Nanny's help we repaired and replaced lots of her clothes, and Simon's clothes list started building up on the spare bed. Luckily we could order name tapes which came by post and were so wide they could be machine stitched.

Injections were due again. Simon was a devil and fought, bit and scratched anyone in the vicinity who held a hypodermic. He roared with anger and fear and we were forced to hold him down. We stood in line for TAB injections and the needle got stuck in Susina, the syringe broke and she bellowed her heart out. Ice creams were promised but there were none when we got to the shop - *no current* they said dispassionately.

Soon it was time to take Susina back to Coonoor. Our driver, William, drove us in the Ambassador and we stopped every so often for snacks and drinks. It was a 200 mile journey from Hassan to Hebron and another 120 miles back to Mysore where we spent the night. We reached Coonoor at 3pm, which was too early as none of the other children had arrived, Susina was devastated and sobbed pitifully as her dormitory was horribly empty. She did not mind going back but she *did* mind having no friends to play with when she got there. So we waited until more arrived and it was safe to leave her, and this gave me a chance to talk to some of the staff and they said that she was a model child. The Chaubes kindly put me up when we reached Mysore, very tired, and William stayed with some relations, driving us back to Hassan next day.

That year there was a dreadful cyclone in Andhra Pradesh, which swept away villages and people, babies and toddlers, cattle and pigs, dogs and ducks and shattered the lives of thousands ruining many of the tobacco areas. The situation alerted a Belgian Jesuit priest, Father Michael Windy, who rushed around the area in a rickety jeep, long fair beard streaming in the wind, scattering children and chickens as he careered down the narrow muddy village streets. He was a mover and a shaker and soon got things going to provide help and funds. Cyclones, typhoons, hurricanes are all extremely turbulent, with differing names owing to their geographical position. The storms are a system of winds blowing in spirally towards an area of low pressure and often occur without much warning.

Sally Harding wrote graphically from Chirala of this devastating event. Helicopters flew over and Sally and Christopher, and many other families, were cut off for five days on the factory compound, surrounded by damaged property and fallen trees. The noise of the storm was deafening and it raged for three solid days causing much flooding throughout the area. They needed a boat to reach Parchoor where ILTD staff lived in a large bungalow with the ridiculous name of Paradise. The noise did not abate and 50% of the trees fell, gardens were stripped and roads washed away, with four feet depth of water everywhere. As always, looters lurked and the Hardings abandoned their house and climbed on to the roof. There was a terrible stench from 300 dead bodies swirling around from the next village. The eastern seaboard of India is very cyclonic and there was a fearful loss of life both inland and out at sea.

Three years later, when we were living in Chirala, the Village Reconstruction Organisation

(VRO) was initiated by Father Michael Windy, who never took time to stop and discuss anything. However he did vaguely mention that there were two Belgians nearby and drove off in a cloud of dust. They turned up at our house soon after, bedraggled and sunburnt. Robert Ceulemans, 29, was a Professor of Classical Languages at Antwerp University and also secretary of a charitable organisation, which sent people to India to work in Father Windy's villages. He and his wife had come to investigate the living conditions before sending volunteers. Windy who worked in India for 25 years, lived and slept anywhere (and with anyone) had left them in our neighbouring village instructing the villagers to feed them. The Ceulemans spent four days of hell, before getting blistered and swollen after working in the paddy fields. They were desperate and ill and the villagers brought them to us, much to their relief – they described our house as *a small bit of heaven*. In the village they were given a room, two short wooden charpois with rope bottoms and without mattresses, pillows or bedding. As there were no latrines they were obliged to squat in the fields along with the other 500 villagers, and there was nowhere to wash except beside the public well. Marie, aged 27, was a history teacher and crumpled quickly under these conditions. They stayed with us several days and were treated by Dr Sadananda Rao for heat stroke.

Cyclone damage

We met up with another couple, Ann and Jim Smith, who also worked for the VRO. By then, Father Windy's idea was to teach villagers how to construct houses using sturdy materials, in contrast to their traditional precarious dwellings of mud and straw. The Smith's were driving in a motor home overland to Australia when they met Father Windy in Delhi. He so impressed them that they changed their plans and detoured to Andhra Pradesh, and their smart home on wheels caught the attention of every hamlet they passed through. They stayed four hot months and helped to build a new village, the mud and sand getting into their hair, under their nails and deep into their feet. Ann often played her harmonica and soon all the little children were singing and dancing, "Well you must have a bit of fun dear," said Ann seriously, "Or else you'd go barmy wouldn't you?"

When they left, the whole village turned out and gave them a grand farewell party. The poorest provide the best entertainment and they were festooned with garlands and left with tears in their eyes. After some months they returned and lived above the VRO office in Guntur helping improve the already built villages by constructing schools and small health centres. As a retired RAF couple, their energy and stamina was amazing and we spent many happy hours with them when they could spare time to relax in the comfort of our home. They surveyed Orissa after another cyclone, travelling by 3rd class train and sleeping on a station bench when the train was delayed. They went up a river in a flat bottomed boat and disembarked on to low lying mud. The young Indian volunteers accompanying them showed Ann how to suspend herself on a bamboo pole and *swing out.* Jim waited helpfully at the bottom to catch her and, as she was swinging erratically on the pole, he laughed heartily and said he had seen baboons before, but nothing like this.

"I got him nicely splashed with mud as I landed," retorted the sparky Ann. They were an inspiring couple and completed a whole project in Orissa before heading home to England.

Despite a quieter time, Chinnathambi was not good and, whilst coming home from the market, collapsed in the street in Shimoga with severe bronchitis. We went to the hospital and were told, after thorough tests and an ECG, that his heart valve was faulty and that he could have a heart attack at any time. So he was retired again. He desperately wanted to work and needed the money. At that time in India, male life expectancy was 40 years and Chinnathambi was already 66 years, he was such a dear old man, but past it. Months later he sent a letter from Mysore *Respected Sir & Madam I am went the Hospital two times. Doctor examined my body clearly also tested my body by Electric Mission. And Doctor gave some tablets and Doctor told me to take rest till end of this month. After this month I am coming to Hassan. Doctor told me that I shall write everything to Madam about my health. I hope I may see Sujeena before she going to school and please tell my Namaskar to Nani and children. P C Chinnathambi.*

Without him our lives in Hassan and Shimoga continued relentlessly. There were continuous visitors of different castes and diets who needed bowls of fresh *curds* (yoghurt), picnics, early starts, late arrivals and general nurturing. At one stage we were expecting an invasion of all the expatriate nobs from ILTD Guntur and Calcutta, tall men with large appetites who wished to visit both areas. A bazaar trip to Mysore was planned to enable me to buy the meat and vegetables, to prepare as much as possible in advance as our fridge was inadequate and freezers did not exist. At the last minute we got a message that only Ray was coming, I was speechless and bit back the tears of total frustration. It had been a gargantuan task to prepare food in two hell holes and keep it fresh.

On this visit, Ray agreed we extend our two year tour until May 1970, and afterwards take UK leave for 5½ months, which included Mike attending a senior management course at BAT's Chelwood Vachery in Sussex. We were due to stay in Hassan and Shimoga for one more year and then move permanently to Andhra Pradesh. In one way the news was good; as Mike had taken winter leaves for fifteen years and looked forward to the idea of seeing an English spring.

We were busy easing Simon into the idea of *sleeping* school and he was quite cocky about it although he had no experience of being away from us overnight. Next time we saw Vera Windus (still soldiering on in Hunsur), we asked if they would have him to stay. She was delighted, "He will be good company for Sarah," she said, "We'll probably send her after Christmas as she is so bored here." Simon spent four nights in Hunsur; the first night was unhappy but after that he was fine.

Susina came home again on the school bus to Mysore and, after the holidays, we all went up to St Margaret's to take both children to school. The twins watched the packing of trunks, polishing new shoes, collecting toys and preparing tuck with a certain amount of aplomb. They seemed to have no yearnings to join the fun, Andrea stomped around noisily and David, as usual, did his own thing. We left early one morning with two school trunks, four children, Nanny and ourselves; we needed a lorry rather than a gracious 1934 Chevrolet sedan.

The school term started on 25 August and Simon celebrated his fifth birthday on 24

August. Mike and I felt dreadful but Simon was cheerful, probably helped by his confident sister who told him lots of good things about school. We prepared a tea party in the St Margaret's garden and made all their favourite things as well as a chocolate cake with five candles on it.

David, Simon and Andrea playing in Ooty

Everything was *last time* so they enjoyed *last time* ice creams, chocolates, boat rides, pony walks and all three boys went for haircuts at the Ooty barber. Normally their hair was cut by Mummy so this was a new experience. David appeared from the scruffy barbershop, shorn of all his blonde curls, and said, "That man put polish on my head."

We packed the car and drove down the mountain to Coonoor and under the Deo Supremo archway. Miss White, Simon's new matron, greeted us with, "Do you think he's really ready for school?" our hearts dropped, he was the youngest entrant.

Susina was in a new dorm, Sunshine, with none of her friends so she was upset and Simon became anxious. He bit Miss White on the arm and battled with her, showing his occasional awful temper that he would not give up easily, and it was another harrowing farewell. The twins stayed firmly in the car sucking their thumbs, gone were the usual giggles.

We came back feeling flat and worried but heard from dear Miss Hall that they were both fine and well settled. We were beginning to disbelieve this pillar of the Plymouth Brethren society that they were *both fine* but took her word for it. Putting a child into boarding school is one thing, but having put two tots into boarding school, we both began to wonder the reasoning behind it, and felt complete and utter traitors.

When we got back there was a company headed letter, our posting had come through. Mike was destined to be Depot Manager Guntur. It was a lousy job, lousy place, lousy house and no garden.

Chapter 16 – Nanny and Mariamma

Nanny realised that our domestic life was pretty chaotic, and asked if she could bring her family, as they had no home. Without really thinking we agreed, as there were enough quarters, which she said would be adequate.

We had not expected a whole family, which included her son Richard, his wife Mariamma and a one-year old granddaughter Monica, plus a little shy dark boy called Ardiya who, we discovered later, was Mariamma's son by a different father. Their journey from Vizianagaram in Andhra Pradesh took two days by steam train, and they rattled into our compound on a bullock cart with tin trunks and bedrolls. They settled into the quarters whilst Nanny busied herself efficiently with our children. It was not long before Richard Coleman departed, he was a smooth, unstable, well spoken Anglo-Indian-Burmese with itchy feet. Mariamma and Monica cried copiously when he disappeared and Nanny was stoically sad.

Mariamma asked me for work, she was quiet and appealing and we brought her into the house. She was older than Richard, very South Indian and dark, a Telugu from the east, with an open face and friendly smile. There was no one to consult about her background, but Nanny was from honest stock and recommended. Our neighbours were Kanarese and kept to themselves, and the missionaries lived in a hospital world of their own.

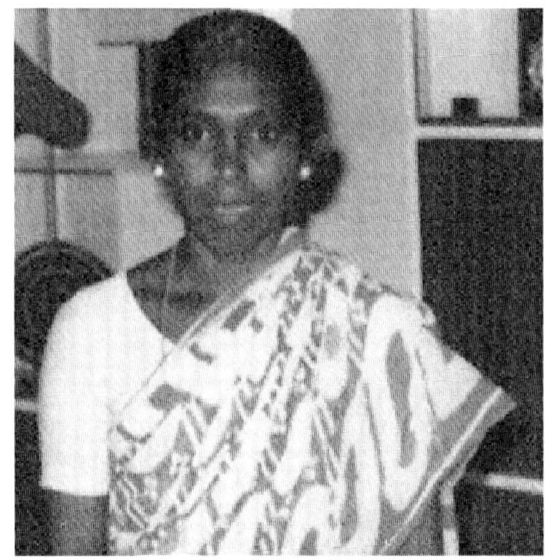

Mariamma

"I'll help you Madams," she encouraged. She didn't mind what she did, particularly when she realised that I would do anything too. She started off helping in the kitchen, chopping vegetables and washing up. She was a clean, quick worker and learned new duties fast, singing snatches of Hindi film songs as she washed the plates, her glass bangles jingling, and her poor English soon improved. Her father had worked in the rice mills in Burma and after fleeing the Japanese, carrying Mariamma in his arms as she was very small; he then became a watchman at a block of flats in Calcutta. In the evenings Mariamma played with the expatriate children in the yard and quickly picked up both English and Hindi, although Telugu was her mother tongue. She was soon doing the majority of the cooking and, although she could not read or write, her memory was phenomenal. The children liked her banana pancakes and Mike adored her mulligatawny soup.

She was familiar with making chilli hot Andhra food using tamarind and heavy spices so English food was an eye-opener to her, "I'll try Madams," she said cheerily and remembered every recipe by heart. She made shepherds pie from goat, rissoles from illicit beef and custard from buffalo milk. Her menus became adventurous and we could leave her to serve up a good lunch for an endless trail of company visitors, and dining room dinners for overnight guests.

In the quarters it took our servants hours to boil rice on three stones. They laid damp wood on charcoal, lit matches – often half a box was used before the first match ignited - blew and fanned the weak flames with a piece of cardboard whilst using up *working* time and not getting much done in either home. We talked it over with them and it was agreed they could cook on our gas, and that our food shopping would be done at the same time. We adjusted their wages, and Mike helped by bringing home bags of rice from the villages. The system worked well, their quality of food and health improved immediately, and there was more time to help me. It also stopped any thieving, as no one was hungry and Ardiya and Monica began to thrive. Contrary to speculation we didn't actually sit together round the dining room table, or even eat at the same time, but some of our visitors were entirely disapproving of this communal lifestyle and, under their breath, mouthed *Tut, Tut* at the children playing in the garden together. I tried to explain that we were all strangers in a friendless town, and that we needed to support each other. Personal space was respected and privilege was not abused, but they did not understand. We were up against the dreaded caste system. Mariamma's positive help enabled me to refine our household staff to the few dependable ones, and quietly get rid of the hangers on. She was a godsend and we have remained close friends to this day.

At last we got letters from our two little ones at Hebron, *Dear Mummy and Daddy I hope you are all well and happy tell Daddy I send a big hug and big kiss and I send all of you a big hug and a kiss I am very happy at school with Simon it is nearly my Birthday and I will be able to give some cake to Simon and I will be happy when it is my Birthday. On Saturday I had to stay down from the playground because it was raining but after tea the bell went to go to playground and when Simon came up to the playground I had to go to the dorm. Love from Susina XOXOXOX*

Simon wrote (or dictated)*: Dear Mummy and Daddy a baby is sleeping in this house. We went for a picnic on Saturday Love from SIMNO (*sic*).*

Although Simon was the youngest, his best friend Stephen Erikson was the biggest. As the baby of the school he wrote his name himself but the other words were silhouetted. The letters were sweet and comforting and a lifeline, and we knew that Susina looked out for Simon and read my letters each week. He probably enjoyed the silly drawings more than anything. For Susina's seventh birthday we packed up lots of salty crispy things to eat and sent an apple green embroidered dress, plus a couple of things for Simon. Mike was busy and exhausted but, for me, there was too much time to think and I was missing them both dreadfully. Failure was a strong feeling, not being able to hold and hug my children and to comfort them when they felt ill and sad. It was difficult in low moments to come to terms with such a terrible separation.

Not long after we made a very quick trip up to the hills and managed to take them out for a brief 24 hours. St Margaret's was full so we stayed at the Wellington Club, in the valley below Coonoor, and enjoyed good food and comfortable surroundings. We had not seen them for two months and Simon went very red and clutched my hand and said not a word until safely in the car.

Susie was well settled and enjoying her lessons, or so she said. We went up to Ooty and took Lyndy O'Brien out from her stark Roman Catholic convent, which gave Hebron the appearance of a homely paradise. It was very hard to say goodbye to all of them; they looked so small and vulnerable.

When we got back to Hassan I started writing Christmas cards to send by sea, and wanted to enclose a photo of the twins, so we went to the Star Studio in town. It was a fusty black curtained closet over a drain; the photographer barely spoke English and was extremely nervous. His camera must have been fifty years old, on a tripod with big bellows and a string to pull when he was ready. There were powerful lights which, when turned on attracted every passer-by, and soon there was a crowd of noisy, curious bystanders, all making comments and laughing at us. The Indian stare is a force to be reckoned with, it lacks curiosity but is penetrating, unflinching and unforgiving. Andrea and David hated this attention, it was bad enough to be caught in the car in a traffic jam in Bangalore with all the windows open; this was like being on a stage and waiting for the bad eggs to be thrown. So their mood was not good as they posed, his light flashed and we beat a hasty retreat. Several days later the proofs were collected and were awful, Andrea looked like a junior footballer with a sullen face, and David, although two inches taller, took on the persona of an emaciated shrimp.

The rains stopped and we enjoyed some rare sunshine. Our move to Andhra was creeping up, it was early October and time to prepare the Mission House for the next occupants. We washed all the curtains, mosquito nets, mattress covers and soft furnishings and lay them on the grass to dry. Our garden was bright with cannas, gerberas, marigolds and oleander bushes. At the front near the veranda was my precious geranium collection planted in hand thrown terracotta pots. Geraniums were so easy to grow and cuttings were gathered, well wrapped in wet newspaper, from every garden we visited. The common red variety was avoided but we ended up with a paintbox of shades including cyclamen, pink, coral, white and a deep maroon.

The farewell parties were beginning, we were not so sure that anyone was sad to see us go, but it was important to attend, first to Hunsur and then Shimoga for a difficult gathering with farmers and field staff. Ray accompanied us for a final inspection but uttered no words of appreciation. For the last time I cooked dinner and breakfast on the one gas ring that worked, waved goodbye to Chinnamma and flopped into the car with all our bags and belongings, for the all too familiar three hour bumpy journey back to Hassan.

Later we went to Bangalore for shopping and to purchase meat at the market for our Hassan staff party. Standing amongst 150 dripping bloody carcasses was a gruesome business, the floor covered in blood, the goat heads waving at me at eye level and the little muddy hooves dangling in my hair. Nevertheless the deal was done and the sloppy meat and sinewy mutton was wrapped with big green leaves, tied with coconut fibre and flopped into flimsy hand-made baskets. On the day of the party we expected the clerks and supervisors to arrive awkwardly and sit nervously around the garden on hired metal chairs. But it wasn't difficult, it was good natured and pleasant. We were garlanded with beautiful flowers, and treated to cups of First Class coffee and presented with a sandal wood elephant pulling a log. Photographs were taken and the party was a comforting, sweet and sincere gesture. The Gowda farmers also gave us a dinner and produced a bottle of rum for the occasion. We sat on the ground and ate curry and rice off big green washed banana leaves whilst they regaled us with voluble speeches in both Kanarese and English.

Farewell party at Hassan

We also gave a party for as many surrounding friends as could come, and prepared our own form of a Hassan banquet of various meats, curries, noodles and salads with grape fool to follow. All this in our murky kitchen the size of a wardrobe. Next day a crowd of us drove to the Foster's stud farm and took vegetarian food with fried rice and chapatis, followed by jam tarts and brownies. Shelagh and Fred, and the O'Brien's, were very sad that we were leaving Hassan. We all got on so well and there was a severe shortage of expatriates amongst the coffee estates.

Guntur was a blot on the horizon, a posting we dreaded. Previous visits were brief and made enjoyable by plenty of parties, but this was for real. We were told that the depot was right on the main trunk road, that the house was semi-detached and that there was a small garden, but we did not know that there were over a hundred labour in the workforce, that the warehouses and buying courts were close to our property and that there were vast acres of burningly hot concrete and corrugated iron sheds. We were also told that there was only one *reporting trip* a year to Madras, unlike Hassan where, if we could fit it in, we could go to Mysore or Bangalore several times.

After five years of struggling to settle, packing the Mission House was like a stab through the heart and we certainly did not want to leave. The children were unsettled and David hid every available toy in sight and waited patiently for his own transport to collect his boxes. A five ton lorry was stuffed with our *saman* (belongings), which included over a hundred bottles of wine and many pots of geraniums. The whole experience of living and working in Hassan and Shimoga had been difficult but, after all the slog, we were beginning to enjoy our home and had adjusted to the difficulties of living in a small Indian town. Andhra Pradesh was not considered a plum posting and Guntur was definitely bottom of the list. The expatriate staff had spent almost all their careers there and, in the absence of any experience elsewhere, the company had become a complete backwater. Living conditions were not up to standard, and there was a lack of concern for the staff and their families. The only ethos was just hard work similar to a Victorian sweat shop in a very primitive environment.

Thank goodness Nanny, Mariamma and family were all coming with us, and Nanny came up to Ooty when we collected the children from school and we enjoyed a few days holiday at St Margaret's. When we finally left the Mission House the car was so loaded we were pushed out of the driveway, it was such an awful way to leave I could have wept. Half way up the *ghat* Bonnie conked out and it was nearly dark. Mike thought it was the condenser so, with great difficulty, we pushed the cumbersome vehicle around and *free-wheeled* thirteen miles down the steep winding road to the small town of Gudalur. By the light of a kerosene lamp a mechanic took everything to bits until, finally, he conceded it *was* the condenser and replaced it. Ah India! By now Mike was totally finished and he let me drive, not something he encouraged.

"Don't forget to double de-clutch," he said as he dozed off.

"Double what?" I shouted, "What does that mean?"

"Foot in, gear out, gear in, foot out, it's easy," he yawned and his head fell forward.

With only three floppy gears and a mountain to climb, it was scary. The night was black, the massive lorries raced towards me and I behaved like a ballet dancer with foot in, gear out, gear in, foot out, but not pirouetting on my navel at the same time. Long after midnight we rolled into St Margaret's driveway, all sleepy but safe and sound and absolutely starving. It was arctic and the mountain air was pervaded with eucalyptus.

"Ah! we're here," Mike woke up, stretched and clambered out shuffling around with things. One of the dozy servants appeared and soon we were all inside with the kettle on for hot water bottles in the cold beds. All our food was finished leaving squashed bananas, crumbled biscuits and old peanuts.

Next day we went to the Hebron carol service, full of joy and squeaky voices. Now that Susina was getting older her feelings were more evident and she was quite emotional and tearful when she saw us. Simon was distant and far away and it was not until he was reunited with his pedal car in Guntur that he felt at home again.

Previously we met some jolly Germans, Ruth and Rudo Wynands, and joined them at a fantastic dance at Wellington Club, ending up in their house up the mountain drinking champagne and eating frankfurters. We all laughed until we ached. Eric and Zohra Chaube and their children were with us too and, next day we went trout fishing on the steep and muddy edge of one of the barren, grey lakes. It was damp and uncomfortable and the children looked like mudlarks and, needless to say, no fish were caught. The weather was crisp, dry and sunny and we trekked over to Kotagiri hospital to have our eyes checked. We faced up to the journey to Guntur, at least it was the cooler season, but the endless dusty, pot holed miles were the same. We completed 200 miles in one day and 400 the next. Andrea suffered a very bad tummy and we stopped frequently; it was difficult keeping her hydrated during the journey and she became quite weak. Bonnie was superb and sailed along the roads like a queen, not even a puncture.

Shelagh and Alec Barby kindly welcomed all of us to stay for a couple of days before we moved into the depot house. They had been with ILTD a long time, always in hot and torrid Andhra, with a large family of five children, one of whom, Andrew, tragically died of a liver infection in his late teens. We were absolutely exhausted after all the upheaval of moving and travelling and I had severe stomach gripes and went to bed for a day.

Chapter 17 – Guntur Depot 1970

Arriving in Antarctica on 17th January 1912 the explorer, Robert Falcon Scott, wrote in his journal, *Great God! This is an awful place!* Had he visited Guntur in 1969, his journal may well have carried a similar message, *Great God! Another awful place!* Although the final Nizam of Hyderabad was reputed to be the richest man in the world, Andhra Pradesh was then one of the poorest and least developed states in India.

It must have been more *awful* for the men of ILTD who pioneered the area in the early 1930s. Many were bachelors who were not allowed to marry until they had completed a couple of tours, others were grass widowers whose wives were in UK with children. For many, solace came in a bottle, hence the joke that ILTD stood for *In Liquor Till Dawn.* Basic foodstuffs, such as bread, came from Madras, water by bowser and there was no electricity or decent sanitation. Mosquitoes and snakes were daily guests, and panthers were hunted in nearby forests. The men were steadfast and, despite appalling heat and conditions, they established the SILA - South India Leaf Area - but we found little archival evidence of their contribution during our eight years in Andhra Pradesh.

Drinking water from the drain

Guntur is in the north-eastern sector of the state in the Krishna River delta and east of the low lying Kondaveedu hills where, occasionally, we took the children for little picnics on cool evenings. A district headquarters and taluk, it is one of the oldest (and notably the filthiest in the early 1970s) municipalities constituted in 1866, although originally founded by the French and ceded permanently to the British in 1788. Prior to the colonial era it came under the rule of the Nizam of Hyderabad, then again the French and British until India reached its Independence in 1947. It is an important railway junction 40 miles from the coast and, commercially and agriculturally, has always been a rich place with tobacco, rice, cotton and oil mills. Most residents are orthodox wearing traditional dhotis, long shirts and saris, all sharing the language, a particularly ancient and pure form of Telugu. The population during our time was about 800,000, always rising with new housing and industrial developments burgeoning around the city limits. Occasionally determined foreign tourists visited Amaravarthi to see the Lord Amareswara temple, housing the earliest and world famous Buddhist relics and sculptures. Because there was no respectable hotel accommodation in Guntur, most covered the 500-mile round trip from Hyderabad.

The oldest part of Guntur has a haphazard bazaar system, narrow streets and tumbling buildings, sprinkled with silver and copper shops. The pavements need careful navigation, the slabs unevenly laid, kerbs damaged with piles of dumped sand, wet rubbish and repairs half done. The shops and stalls, guarded by metal shutters, were just narrow little boxes open to the lanes and stretching across the drains.

With no room to go inside, the shopkeeper sat on a sort of tray surrounded by goods. Most were Hindu traders and moneylenders whilst artisans tended to be Muslim. Despite the poverty and deprivation there were vivid flashes of pink, scarlet, acid yellow and magenta of swaying saris as women walked, baskets balanced on their heads. Away from the old bazaar were lines of glass fronted cloth shops, frame shops, electrical goods, pharmacies, Bombay Dyeing bed linen and various others. Holy cows ambled, lorries, cars, motorbikes, buses and rickshaws tinkled, hooted and clanged circumnavigating the town, rounding a roundabout here and a circle there. Standing on raised platforms, khaki-clad policemen haphazardly controlled the traffic. Some wore fancy turban type headgear with cockades and others sported boy scout hats, and all wore extraordinarily revealing shorts. These were stiffly starched and stretched widely over their bony brown knees, like extra large women's skirts. We all feared to look up, they were certainly voluminous and draughty and must have stood up alone when removed.

Guntur policeman

Our first sight of the depot house was of a squat semi-detached bungalow, with an open veranda and a tiny neglected garden with a low wall. The drive into the depot proper led from the main Grand Trunk road carrying dust shrouded vehicles and a constant stream of chattering passers-by allowing no privacy. The building was whitewashed in and out, so it was clean, and the window frames were painted black; it looked mean.

The building was designed to be cool on the inside so it was very dark. There was no burglar proofing and our sitting room was at the end of the outside veranda with no door or any security. The house proper was entered through the windowless central dining area, a natural passageway into the kitchen and a welcome entry for stray dogs to laze and scratch on our chairs and then hunt for food. On our first day one mongrel scoffed six eggs and shells from the kitchen counter. There were two and a half bedrooms, one so dark the lights were left on all day. Our en-suite room shared an adjoining dressing room for the twins. It was a hot house, bang on the depot buying courts, where tobacco was purchased from the farmers, with all the accompanying noise and clatter. Mike's stuffy depot office had no air-conditioning and was across the buying courts which suffered summer temperatures of up to 130°F (54°C). The servants' quarters were a dingy line beyond the kitchen, populated by a mix of staff and hangers-on with accompanying livestock. The depot could be accessed from the town through a back lane, known as Shit Alley, which was exactly that with squatting people and herds of gobbling, black hairy pigs.

Mariamma and her children travelled from Hassan on smoky steam trains. Monica was jumping up and down, "Coming on train Madams, Ardiya, me sleeping on train." Richard reappeared and they all moved into the miserable quarters at the back. Mariamma was happy, she was fascinated with Richard and they sat every evening once work was done, chatting and smoking *beedies* together. There was so much housework that Richard was invited in to help, but he was too smart by half and very irritating. Eventually he departed again for Hyderabad, leaving Mariamma pregnant.

Andhra Pradesh is in a cyclone area and our arrival coincided with unprecedented rain and accompanying mud, with no sweeper to clear up the mess. It was difficult to unpack and keep the children occupied, so Simon resorted to riding his precious pedal car on the veranda littered with half opened crates. His school report was good but he was not finding it easy to express himself which made him very argumentative. He *went off* the twins and kept asking if they could be given away; school gave him new dimensions and he was very fussy with his appearance. He learned to ride Susina's two wheeler which made her absolutely mad, particularly when he went pedalling off down towards the main road at high speed. Susina was told of the Christmas myth of gift giving, stockings and chimneys aka *air con-dish-on-ers*. She found it a complete joke that we had been pretending the whole time. She was more concerned about books she might receive, not who brought them. An avid reader it was distressing to have no access to good children's books, nor any library facilities and we begged and borrowed as many as we could

She read many a piece about Lord Krishna and Ganesh, the elephant god, amongst the cheap badly printed missives that were available, including Noor Jahan, the most powerful Mughal Queen in comic form. She needed lots of attention, and didn't feel very pretty having lost her front teeth. She loved Mike particularly, but he so often was not there for her. David had grown tall and was developing well with lots of new words. Because we crossed the railway line so frequently he became very interested in engines and asked wise questions about the bell, the light, the fire, the driver and *how does it go under the bridge.* He was beginning to tell tall stories with a slightly wicked nature and a lot of curiosity, his little fingers into everything. Andrea was more gullible and down to earth, very cuddly, bestowing kisses liberally and calling everybody *oddyboddy.* One evening the twins were so bored that they pulled down all my imported make-up in the bathroom and spread it around, drawing on the walls with precious lipsticks, and then flooding the floor mopping it up with imported soft toilet paper. Furious and frustrated they were told they should go to bed without supper. Mariamma was distraught at such cruelty and was weeping and begging, "Please Madams, they are only little children, please Madams." They got their supper but it was annoying as my special English lipsticks and creams were ruined.

Mike was in charge of millions of pounds of tobacco, and also of the organisation of the tobacco markets due to open on 2 February 1970. He was responsible for the standard of grading and the employment of over 1,000 labour. Although a new challenge, he found it a mundane job in extreme dirt and heat and confining after his large Hassan and Shimoga areas. The weather became so hot that he walked around with a piece of card in his hand and swiped the sweat off his forehead, it was the only way to stop the salt getting in his eyes. Once the markets opened foreign tobacco merchants arrived from UK, America, Russia, Japan and other places to purchase the processed crop. Tobacco was bought on a worldwide scale and buying was very competitive. There were many markets beside ILTD; National Tobacco Co, Golden Tobacco Co, East India Tobacco, Nava Bharat Enterprises and many Telugu barons such as Maddi Lakshmaiah, Chebrole Hanumaiah and Polisetty Somasundaram.

Visiting overseas merchants became good friends and cheered our lives. There were a lot of parties with an over indulgence of men, but the ILTD Indian management coped well with these foreigners, and the wives worked hard preparing semi-European food. The local pattern of parties was to drink until it was considered the correct time to serve food, often not until after 10pm, by which time most of the guests were pretty drunk. After dinner everyone made a quick getaway. It was a tiring and unhealthy way of entertaining, but this was the unchangeable custom. So many times we were asked by the British visitors to persuade their Indian hosts to produce less booze and provide an early dinner, but this fell on deaf ears.

"Sorry," we said, "We can't change them."

"Oh God," sighed one, "I could kill for shepherds pie and an early night."

The complete lack of hotels forced many of the company families to accommodate foreign guests particularly those from Imperial Tobacco Bristol and the Japanese Monopoly. Several merchants stayed in guest houses, some with swimming pools, which we all enjoyed. It was also customary to go to the beach at Vadarevu on Sundays and play various games of *rum punch* rounders. Mike hated the beach parties; he did not feel sociable and often worked on a Sunday morning to catch up. The children absolutely loved them and became very good at enjoying the company of adults, having always gained full value from the fun-loving characters they met. Sundays at the beach were a high spot of the school holidays.

We purchased our beer and *gauli* sodas at the Guntur Club. The sodas were in very thick glass bottles and the bubbles sealed in with a marble which, when pressed down with a strong thumb, went off with a sharp squeaky gassy *pop.* We joined the club, but it was mostly Andhra men, sniffing and snorting, wandering around in their fine cotton shirts and see-through dhotis drinking gin and playing rummy. Some played tennis in the cool of the evening, and snooker was a popular past-time, we visited quite often and soon got to know lots of the expatriate tobacco visitors and enjoyed their company.

NP and Geetha Kumar were our ILTD neighbours; we met him in Tanganyika but he seemed to have forgotten the friendship formed there and it was two months before we were invited into their home. Later, Geetha and I became good friends, and she was very kind to our children providing them with their favourite South Indian idlis and dosais. Sometimes she invited us for breakfast, a lovely treat. Like all Hindu wives she served us herself, dressed in a crisp, fresh sari, gold bangles jangling with a powder buttu carefully arranged on her forehead. If one of us said that we enjoyed a particular dish, she remembered and it formed part of the next offering sent to our home on a tray with her bearer. My favourite was upma; Andrea's was spicy rasam.

1969 Christmas at Vadarevu – Mike, Shelagh, Natalie, Christopher and Sally Harding

I was not too well and needed a small operation, and talked it over with Shelagh Barby who recommended the Roman Catholic St Joseph's Hospital. It seemed sensible to take advantage of Nanny's childcare in Guntur, rather than having surgery in Suffolk. This was a big mistake as the lady surgeon was not experienced in the procedure, but that was only discovered later. She was obviously nervous and imported an anaesthetist from Vijayawada, "He'll know how to do better," she reassured me, meaning he would knock me out properly. There was no pre-med on offer, so I climbed up on to the couch in the operating theatre and watched them sharpening their knives, feeling very nervous. The anaesthetist who was called something like Dr Hari Ramachandrasetty, was quiet and grey-haired, and put the mask over my face and said gently, "Just breathe in and count to ten, and then you'll be gone." Having counted to 160 he said, "She's gone," so I wiggled my fingers furiously, worried that he may turn on too many taps and Mrs Vitley may *expire.* Next thing I was being resuscitated and still very much alive. It was a near miss.

David was a tot and brought to visit. Large crucifixes and pictures of Our Lady were on all the walls. He looked quizzically at the realistic bleeding Christ hanging above the bed, "Who dat Maharajah?" he asked in his little four-year old voice.

Shelagh and Alec Barby were very supportive; they were in ILTD for most of Alec's career, and had lived in particularly unpleasant parts of the state. They were to be transferred to Nigeria, a place perhaps financially more agreeable but potentially a hazardous living and working experience. Alan and Barbara Rands were to transfer directly from Lagos to replace the Barbys.

Shelagh and I became good friends and helped each other with our respective children. Before she left she gave me 25 books, solving a desperate need and, shortly after, a departing missionary sold me 30 more. It was Christmas holiday time and the Barby children welcomed ours, and we enjoyed many visits to their shady pool at Shorthorns. To reach their house we drove in Bonnie two miles up the Ring Road, over the rusty railway line, along the crowded roads with large, wobbly rickshaws, huge bullocks and bulls and fat pigs waiting while people squatted over the drains oblivious of passers-by. Big buses honked, turbaned men pinged the bells on their rusty cycle rickshaws, ponies trotted pulling tongas and cars pushed past. It was risky to use our wide car for town shopping and there was not much luck in getting a depot vehicle. Relying on busy Mike was hopeless, so one of the servants was sent to the bazaar, disappearing for hours on end and often not understanding what was wanted.

One thing we did get was good TB free milk. A wild looking man came with a black hairy buffalo cow followed by her tiny month old calf. We bought four *seers* a day (about eight pints) and after boiling we skimmed off a great bowl of thick cream and this made super ice cream which we stored in the tiny ice compartment of the fridge. We missed the English vegetables we had bought in Hassan; in Guntur there were gourds and leaves, lots of bitter and sour varieties of a type of marrow, stringy beans and yam tubers. Fruit was not bad and mangoes, in season, were the best. Bread was sweet and doughy, there were no cold stores apart from butter at Goodwill Stores, which also sold bikes and motor cycle parts. There was an efficient United Nations sponsored government pork factory about 30 miles away, near the local airport, Gannavaram, and fish came from the sea.

Christmas came rather rapidly leaving me in the usual state of disorganisation. It was agreed that we share with the Barbys and the Hardings at the beach. There were eleven children, six adults, all needing personalised gifts, and four cooks who required supervising, and there was absolutely nothing in the shops. It was agony, but everyone else, used to this communal living, seemed well in control and a turkey and ham were ordered from Madras. We trekked down to Vadarevu with boxes, bags, gifts, sweets and snacks and tons of food, and settled ourselves in. The kids had a great time and the parents enjoyed the little holiday. Gift distribution was a dreadful one-by-one affair, and there wasn't a single parcel under the decorated casuarina tree with my name on it. Having made so much effort to purchase gifts for every member of each family, I was left picking up bits of paper and smoothing them out, helping children construct games, reading a few stories, and straightening out more paper. I wandered out to the chaotic kitchens to see what was going on; the usual muddle of onion and potato skins all over the floor, the sinks full of greasy *dekshies* and the cooks all shouting at each other. Out on the back steps, amongst the sniffing dogs, a sweeper girl was hulling prawns and another mixing up fruit salads with her hands. Oblivious of all the preparations the children gambolled in the water and waves and were happy playing on the beach all day, whilst the parents shared the life guarding duties. We were looked after by Ghouse the bearer, he was an elderly small Muslim, a wonderful man who was very conscientious and courteous and worked all hours to keep us happy. His tall assistant was Peter, dour and humourless, who we all called The Colonel. These two were remnants of the past, and new employees never matched up to their high standards of service.

Once back at the depot, the children were bored, there was nothing to do and Nanny and I were busy getting their clothes ready and sending the trunks off early by TVS (Transport Vehicle

Services) lorry. They faced a three day journey by steam train, the Circars Express followed by the Nilgiri Express, with a day in Madras between the two, and they were taken by missionaries from the Rajahmundry area. They left on 27 January and we received a postcard on 3 February informing us of their safe arrival. We were all sad and the servants were particularly droopy.

Ghouse

After learning Kanarese I tried to pick up Telugu. French came back into my head followed by dribbles of my Mother's Spanish and Italian which she was learning passionately when I was at college, also Swahili after our six months in Tanganyika overtoned by Latin. I bought a book *Learn Telugu in 30 Days by K Srinivasachara.* I knew I must pick it up fast and, after some months, was prattling away with huge confidence without grammar or script. Managing servants and shopping was almost impossible without this skill and it gave me a real sense of belonging, unfortunately in a place where I did not wish to belong. The market traders liked me for trying, and it made all communication so much easier. The book was complicated; after the first few pages it got onto the nominative, vocative, objective, instrumental, dative, ablative, possessive and locative cases, bringing back horrible memories of my Latin lessons at school. Telugu declension defied me and it was easier to pursue the language in my own sweet way. Out of politeness my Indian lady friends never laughed at me, never corrected me and never helped me, they seemed to think that an English woman knew best, whilst I longed for some tuition. How little they comprehended us foreigners. The book was morally and politically correct in that I should always *respect the National Flag* and *health is wealth, everyone must have physical exercise*, and *we can happily spend Sakranti holidays here.* It was a nice language, easy to hear and the words articulated well. One thing that amused me was that our servants referred to Mike as *Ayagaru* and I copied them, unaware I was exalting him with the honourable term *Lord.* Eventually I became ungrammatically fluent in Telugu picking it up here there and everywhere.

Before we went on UK leave with a stopover in Moscow, we gave a big party and decorated the house with garlands of sweet smelling jasmine, interspersed with twinkly lights. A surprising 28 guests arrived, 13 English and 15 Indian, in high spirits. The radiogram played full blast and Mariamma excelled herself with inspired and delicious cooking, "I can do it Madams," she assured me with confidence. She served thinly sliced cold venison, sweet and sour pork, fried fish and tartar sauce, fried rice, Chinese noodles, salads and home made potato crisps. We also marinated some chickens but they were tough, Mike called it *racing chicken,* as it was just carcase and drumsticks. He said the left leg was the best as the right one did all the scratching, but it was hard to tell the difference. There was a huge fruit jelly and a large scooped out pineapple, the chunks mixed with cream and sugar and put back, accompanied by platters of meringues. Mariamma was grand and our last guest left at 4am.

Not long before our departure Alan and Barbara Rands arrived in Guntur from Nigeria and were in a state of shock horror, I felt rotten abandoning Barbara who had to settle in and find her way around at such a hot time of the year and under such difficult circumstances.

It was mid-April and a mad dash to get away. Mike was working until the last minute, and it was necessary to crate up all our belongings. The depot staff gave him a really good send off, over 700 of them gathered and he was garlanded, presented with fruit and we all patiently listened to several Telugu speeches. We raced the 20 miles to Vijayawada, and it was a miracle that we all got onto the Howrah Mail for Madras. It left rapidly and the twins had so eagerly anticipated their first train journey that, after we had been rolling along for half an hour, they asked, "Mummy! Mummy! Where's the train? I want to get on the train *now!*" It was hard to convince them that our journey was well under way as it was too dark to see the passing countryside and we made up rhymes about the *clickety clack of the wheels on the track.*

Chapter 18 – Dilemma

We flew to Bangalore and drove up to Ooty to collect Susina and Simon. They were jumping with excitement, particularly as we were to fly to Delhi and take advantage of an Air India stopover in Moscow. Simon greeted us gruffly with, "I have found Russia on my map, look, see," pointing agitatedly with his little forefinger. We stayed in a super hotel in Delhi and the children enjoyed room service, all rolled in on a big trolley with white damask napkins and delicious food under huge covers. The bearers fussed over them with great care. Delhi was an oven and it was a relief to board the first class compartment of the plane, a well deserved treat after an arduous two year tour. The cabin was roomy and cool and we drank champagne. The other passengers were startled to see four small children galloping around, all needing a good haircut. Much trouble was taken with their clothes but we were so out of touch with English fashion that they looked like refugees. David did not help the situation by plonking himself on the lap of a large man in a brown suit who was not amused. We landed at Moscow with some trepidation; we did not know what to expect.

The temperature was a fresh 40°F (4°C) when we arrived bang in the middle of the Cold War, a period of great tension between the United States and the Soviet Union and their respective allies. Although on the same side during WWII, they became rivals with terrifying threatening overtones of military engagement and political battles. Stalin saw the world divided as *capitalist* and *communist*, President Truman saw it as *freedom* and *complete subjugation*. Unfortunately, following the Cuban missile crisis in 1962 and the invasion of Czechoslovakia in 1968, this pattern of on/off unease lasted from the mid-1940s to the late 1980s, and our short stay in Moscow occurred during the *period of stagnation* of President Brezhnev.

Beautiful girls with lovely complexions, wearing big fur hats and grey overcoats, welcomed us warmly at Moscow airport, and were sweet with the children. We drove through forests and past little *dachas* surrounded by fir trees. There was not much traffic and, as we entered the city, we saw it was clean with very little litter. We were booked into the gracious shabbiness of the Metropole Hotel, strategically placed opposite the Bolshoi Theatre; children were not allowed to attend performances but we went inside to see the gilded boxes and red plush velvet seats.

On each floor of the hotel sat a fierce receptionist who handed out a little bar of sudless soap, a roll of stiff toilet paper and no smile. The rooms were sparse with a couple of beds, a table, a chair, and a cheerless bathroom without a plug, a rough towel and only just warm water. The hotel produced awful food and the children survived mostly on bread and jam. After dinner there was dancing, jolly jiving and rock. An over active woman lost the heel of her shoe, and this was flashed around the floor like a puck in an ice hockey match, but the woman continued to spin frantically, heel or no heel.

The reception staff were helpful and all spoke good English. We booked a sight seeing bus and travelled with two prim English schoolteachers, a large family of Germans and a silent black priest. Our lady guide was strict and bossy, and told us that 800 years ago Moscow was once a small village on the banks of the river. She took us to the impressive University campus to enjoy a fine view of the city from the Lenin Hills and Gorki Park. Although April, the weather was chilly and we were surprised to see a huge heated swimming pool steaming away. We wandered about in the enormous Red Square which was being prepared for the May Day parade. It was crowded and there were queues of people waiting to see Lenin's tomb guarded by soldiers of the Russian Army in high boots and stiff collared long grey coats. Despite the crowds the atmosphere was dull and quiet and our children, with their squeaky enthusiastic English voices, became a focal point of interest. We saw the Kremlin with its ancient belfries and church towers which had been standing since the days of Ivan the Terrible, also the pretty onion shaped domes of St Basil's Cathedral, nine churches in one connected by passages and vaults. In contrast was the brutal architecture of Hotel Rossia, the size of an American block with 6,000 bedrooms. We drove down Gorki Street, the main thoroughfare, with typical bustling shoppers and went into large department stores selling a few poor quality goods.

Curious and friendly people were fascinated with our four lively children skipping about, as all theirs were tucked away in nurseries. Whilst we sat on a bench licking pink ice creams, we noticed many people continually quaffing beer, feeding coins into slot machines and drinking from throwaway cups. We descended into the Metro with its completely confusing signs, and were amazed at the grandeur of such a public transport system with panels of carved marble and mosaic lit by glass chandeliers.

The Moscow State Circus was a real treat for all of us. The Big Top was full of little children, their faces glowing with anticipation, and the precision of the acts was quite incredible. Daring trapeze artistes swooped above whilst sleek horses, acrobats, happy little dogs and famous Russian bears were all around us. Just one clown kept us amused between acts, relying more on humour and funny situations than weird costume and slapstick comedy. A uniformed orchestra played lovely music, and there were twinkling costumes and lights. Our hearts stopped as we watched a well rehearsed plate balancing act on spinning poles; the whole tent was quiet as the young man raced backwards and forwards and kept all the wobbling china on the move. It was a far cry from the scary circus we had experienced in Hassan. Afterwards we caught a bus back to our hotel and were literally almost squashed to death by well meaning Muscovites, who pushed us into an overcrowded vehicle in their enthusiasm that we should not miss it. Our small children were nearly trampled by heavy shoes and big knees. It was very frightening but, with force, we got out at the next stop and walked the rest of the way through quiet city streets.

Mike, David and Simon

Our short stay ended, we drove to the airport and met up with the Sparrows with their three children, who had boarded Air India at Delhi, also travelling first class. The seven children greeted each other with shrieks of joy and played between the wide double glazing of the terminal lounge, squashing their noses against the glass. The other passengers reeled with horror when we all trouped on to the plane and, although we tried to keep everyone quiet, the cabin became riotous particularly as Jeremy Sparrow spoke only Hindi and waved a knife around. In the end Mo and I lodged ourselves in the bulkhead seats quaffing champagne, talking our heads off and ignoring our unruly families, whilst our respective husbands snored.

Our leave was busy with too many guests, masses of DIY and lots of dust in the house plus a trip to visit the Kennedy's in Ireland. Mike was on a management course at Chelwood for a month involving serious studying, whilst all the children caught measles so it was impossible for me to get out and buy a loaf of bread. I was not well after my experience in the Guntur hospital, and was on the list for further surgery. Mike took Susina and Simon back to India and, after a long flight, they flew from Bombay to Bangalore, and then drove the 200 miles up into the hills to Coonoor. Mike hugged the exhausted children goodbye and then drove back to Bangalore totally shattered. He was already back into the ILTD mode suffering a ridiculous arduous journey with no stops, and next day travelled on to Guntur.

Meanwhile it was a job to get Ivy Lodge ready for rental and to carry all our heavy belongings to the top floor. The twins were uneasy with the disappearance of their toys and Mummy constantly sitting down and sighing. Money was tight, as we had spent a lot on the improvements, we did not share a joint account and it was necessary to rely on cheques being posted from India. Feeling weak and tired, I had another operation in Ipswich Hospital, whilst my sister-in-law kindly took the twins, and then me to recuperate for six weeks.

Mike sent sad and lonely letters from Guntur; he was not used to me being away. Nothing came from the children in Coonoor as their mail was obviously going to Guntur. Mike completed a survey of Tamil Nadu state and managed a quick trip to Coonoor to see Susina and Simon. Simon did not recognise him after only six weeks separation, and Mike was very upset.

Still feeling ill, the twins and I flew to Calcutta where Mike was attending another management course. We stayed in one of the best hotels but I soon spotted cockroaches creeping across the bathroom floor. The twins were fractious and jet lagged and we were unable to enjoy a reunion dinner together. Next day we flew to Vijayawada and drove back to Guntur, to the depot house. Always comforting was Mariamma, with her new baby in her arms, smiling and saluting in her own way, and Nanny ready for another assault course looking after Andrea and David. We had been away six and a half months.

Mariamma waited for my return before she named her baby boy. Richard, true to type, had done another bunk and she was coping alone, but equably.

I want Denzil, her brown eyes searched my face.

"Denzil!" I squeaked, "Wherever did you get that name from?" Mariamma was a good Hindu woman, and all names in her community were of a traditional nature. First they took the initial of the father, which in this baby's case was R for Richard, and then a chosen name. But Denzil was going a bit far in the confines of Guntur and its unsophisticated society; perhaps it was Nanny's choice? She was a Catholic with strong ideas, but was as enigmatic as usual. In the end we compromised on D Raju. Mariamma's prefix was Deepalli, the name of her own father and, at the last minute, she seemed more inclined to give the baby her own initial rather than that of the wandering Richard. So D Raju was named, but the sweet and delightful baby boy has always been known as Bujie to us all. Indians are very fond of pet names such as Sweetie, Pinky and Bubbles for girls and Tiger, Bunny and Rajah for boys. Many men are known only by their initials, it was odd but we soon got used to AC, VN, NP, AK - and Uncle. Three of my close friends in Guntur were called Iti, Bitty and Prithi, and another two called Veena and Meena. Lots of siblings were given alliterative names like Prio and Pravina, Gowri and Girish, Kowshik and Kartik and Dhian and Devika. Children respectfully called unrelated men and women *Uncle* and *Auntie,* my preference was to be called Natalie, but that was considered impolite so it was *Natalie Auntie* which, when addressed by someone only a couple of years younger, was irritating.

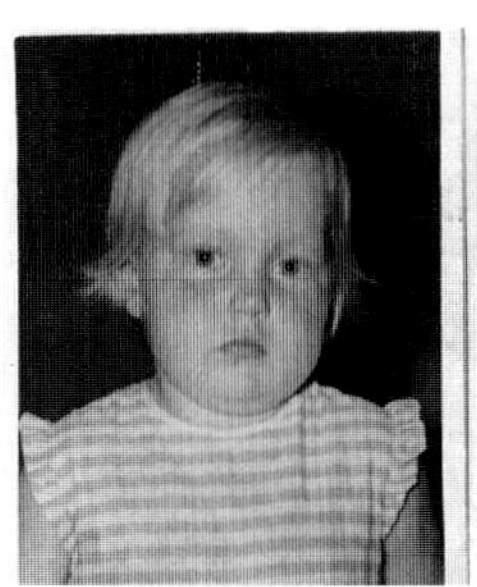
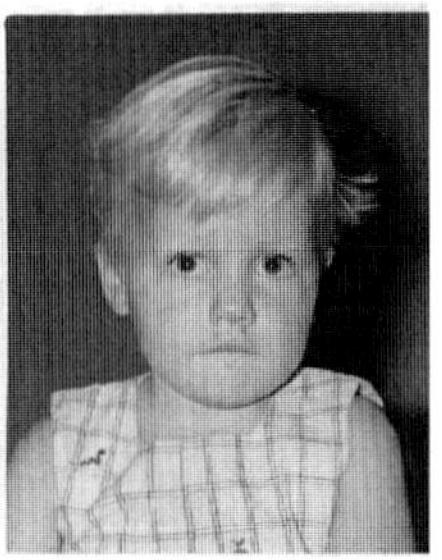

Andrea and David

By the time I got to Guntur, dates and days had become a muddle and I was very disorganised. Mike had been so busy, the unpacking still needed doing and my energy was at rock bottom. Then came the horror story. I had firmly set in my mind that Susina and Simon were travelling home with the chaperoned Andhra Pradesh party on the 21st November, a Saturday, arriving at Vijayawada station in the evening. We sat at home on the Friday evening, looking forward to meeting them and discussing what time we should leave next day. But I had made a horrible mistake and, as we talked about them, they actually *were* arriving at Vijayawada station and we were not there. Mrs German, who escorted them back and forth, was frantic and did not know what to do. The train stopped at Vijayawada for only a short time and, in desperation, she left the children with the station master (a known Christian) and gave him some money. He in turn entrusted a porter who took the children about three miles by cycle rickshaw over a long and very windy bridge, and then hired a taxi to drive the 20 miles to Guntur. Susina and Simon aged 8 and 6, were totally exhausted and absolutely terrified. It was dark, cold and they had been travelling for nearly three days. Somehow they remembered the smelly back entrance into the depot and found our bungalow. Everything was dark but they climbed onto the veranda and tapped hard on our window. It was 2am.

"Mummy! Daddy! We're here. Mummy!" Their voices quavered with fear. We were fast asleep and awoke absolutely horrified and they cried with relief, while guilt shrouded my whole self at the realisation of this unforgivable mistake. The well meaning Mrs German should have kept them with her, fortunately her judgement of the Christian stationmaster, and his choice of porter was very reliable, but it was irresponsible to have put such small children at risk. We were so shocked by what happened that the porter was not given enough reimbursement for his responsible actions, and we were unable to locate him later but sent Mrs German a telegram, 'Children safe' and a very apologetic letter. Susina and Simon did not dwell on their horrid experience, but the memory always creates a sick feeling in my stomach.

Dear Granny and Grandaddy *9.12.70*
I hope you are having a lovely time at England. It is very hot in Guntur. I am sitting in the dining room writing this letter for you. I have come home from school for the Christmas holidays.

Andrea and Daivd (sic) and Simon are very happy. I hope both are very happy. Mummy and Daddy are very happy with lots and lots of LOVE SUSINA.

India was a sub-continent of dust, desert and drought, rich and poor, life and death, good and bad, weak and strong. The drama sat firmly on our shoulders as we continued our difficult life in Guntur. It was time to seriously discuss whether there was any future for us in India. We were living under such appalling conditions in an unhealthy alien climate; from March to May the temperature was often as high as 130F (54°C) in the shade, the mercury almost bursting the glass in the thermometer. Two of our very small children were separated from us and miles away at school, and our two youngest were soon to join them as there were no suitable schools locally.

When we arrived in India in 1964 there were about 20 expatriate families in ILTD, but by 1971 the numbers dwindled to two. The company was previously a subsidiary of BAT, registered in the Isle of Man, but became a Division of ITC which itself had become an Indian company. The atmosphere had changed and the new Telugu General Manager, spitefully known as Mr I, was aggressive and megalomaniac. There were many hirings and firings, resignations and much ill feeling. We were sitting on the fence as an expatriate member of BAT management working for an Indian company in which BAT only had a minority stake.

1971 Staff photo Guntur depot – centre Natalie and twins, Geetha, Vinay and NP Kumar, Mike

The ITC Chairman came from Calcutta for meetings and there was the usual party. We always amused him so he sought us out, and he knew me as forthright, "How are you getting on?" he asked idly, quietly sipping his Scotch.

"You have no idea how awful it is here," I replied.

"Oh - I think I do," he said carefully, "If I was here, I'd shoot myself."

"Well," I said, "Next time you come down, bring your gun." He moved away laughing and nodding with a sympathetic smile as if to comment, *I know what you're saying, but I'm not going to do anything about it.*

After a lot of heart searching, considering all the options, UK school fees, the good BAT pension and the alternatives of other employment, we decided to stay. It was with heavy hearts that we faced the prospect of several more years in this hell hole, with no indication of any future posting elsewhere. Within a couple of years all the children were due to start UK schooling, and I knew I must stay with Mike in India, it would be unfair to leave him in such unpleasant surroundings causing a great deal of unhappiness and strain on our relationship. This decision would be hard for the children to face, months of separation and thousands of miles of travel.

Meanwhile life continued and each season was dreaded by all for its long hours and high temperatures. The local harvest festival, Pongal, was celebrated with gaudy enthusiasm, by the mainly Hindu society but Christmas was a dream. Turkeys and plum puddings were a forgotten remnant of the Raj. Our children instead gorged on idlis and coconut chutney, potato stuffed dosais, sambar and snake gourd, peppery rasam followed by gulab jamuns and sticky jalebis. They were in heaven. There was the usual Christmas party at Chirala factory and fancy dress was a challenge. Somehow we managed to dress them up as a cowboy, an accident victim, a Hickory Dickory Dock Clock and Miss Marigold. They loved the games and the races and the tea, lots of sweet and sickly Indian sweetmeats. Mike was an embarrassed Father Christmas turning up on a trailer pulled by a tractor. Susina recognised him immediately but Simon, always in a dream, did not and said, "He's a funny Santa Claus, he's got a talk like my Daddy." and Andrea said "And a sort of face like Daddy, but not really like Daddy".

Dear Granny and Grandaddy *6 Janewry 1971*
I hope you are well and happy. Thank you very munch for the bicycle and for the doll in the cot and for the yellow car and little blocks and simons presents. I hope you had a very happy chirstmas in England. We all had a very chirstmas down at the beach. One day Mummy had a coffee party And I had to give out all the food and plats and the others went for a picnic to Guntur club. It is nigth time here I am sitting in the sitting room and mummy and Daddy are having supper.
With love from Susina xxoxxoxxoxo

1971 at the beach photo taken by Susina

We drove to Vadarevu for New Year in Bonnie, putting her under unfair strain, as she had not been on the road for a year. She broke down at 8pm in pitch dark. The children were fractious, tired, hungry, bored, thirsty and fed up while Nanny conked out and snored. Mike left us and hopped on a passing bus to Bapatla and brought back a mechanic who diagnosed wiring problems, probably caused by a rat, and it took two hours to fix by torchlight. No lorries stopped and helped as they thought we were *dacoits* (robbers). We took the kids to the beach, got them to bed and whizzed back to Chirala Club for the party at which we arrived just before midnight. All this was a lot more fun than life in Guntur.

Chapter 19 – Move to Chirala

While Mariamma was busy with baby Bujie, we employed a cook called Timothy and his untidy daughter, Violet, as a sweeper girl. Timothy became very ill, so I was dashing in and out of his filthy quarter with a thermometer, his fever was 104°F (40°C), which finally came down with Codeine. Sharing his poor house was the newest member of his family, a baby boy weighing just four pounds, a little raggy bundle of skin and bone, the son of Timothy's mute unmarried younger daughter, aged 15. Timothy was caught stealing and dismissed, and Mariamma returned, somehow juggling the feeding of a tiny baby and looking after us.

Susina and Simon returned to school with the missionaries, Dr and Mrs Short, and they all travelled second class, in a dingy carriage crammed with passengers, mostly farming folk, but it was easier for the chaperone parents to keep their party together. The Shorts had travelled home for Christmas with their three children and were returning to school with just two. During the holidays their six-year old daughter, Catherine, died suddenly of bacillary dysentery. The tragic news was relayed by telegram and sent shock waves through the small and scattered British community of Andhra Pradesh. Susina and Simon were speechless, Catherine had been their happy, lively companion on the journey home and now she was gone. Death was not part of their lives, certainly not the death of a fellow child.

Dr Short was in charge of a West Godavri leprosarium, 150 miles north and a true Christian missionary. We met him on Guntur platform and gave our condolences, we felt so deeply for them, but he said it was *God's will,* Catherine had not responded to any of the available drugs, it was a rare and shocking occurrence. Dr Short's acceptance of the loss of his little girl, seemed the ultimate in sacrifice for the missionary path he and his family were following in this disease ridden alien area of India. We never came to terms with the tragedy.

Guntur Depot *Tuesday 3rd March 1971*
Dear Susina and Simon
What lovely letters we had from you last week. Simon wrote a super letter all by himself and we think it was very good indeed. Now you will be able to write to us every week without Miss Tallett doing the writing for you, and soon you will be writing like Susina. Day Day liked the picture of the big black car going down the side of the hill. It must have been fun when you went to Brooklands stream and made a dam and got all dirty. Did Miss White mind that you were all muddy?

Last Saturday we went to a big party on Ring Road. It was a goodbye party given by British India Tobacco for our friend Ernie Jenkinson who comes out every year to see the tobacco. There were 100 people at the party, what a lot! It was in a big garden by a swimming pool. All the trees and bushes were covered in tiny little coloured lights and it looked just like fairyland. They had fireworks too and rockets and things. We had chicken and rice and ham and salads and peaches out of tins for pudding.

Daddy is working very hard, he does not come in until late at night and then he is very tired. It is just as well that you are at school because if you were here you would be asleep when he leaves in the morning and asleep when he comes home at night and he even works on Sundays too so you wouldn't see much of him would you?

Baby Bujie is growing very nicely. He is rolling over and sitting up a bit. He is being a very good baby. Mariamma is cooking and is more peaceful now that Timothy has gone. We are trying to make a little garden but the naughty squirrels have munched all the seeds up.

It is getting hotter here now and we had to start using the fan at night. I find it very hot when I have to go out and do the shopping. We send you lots of love and hugs. We are always thinking about you. Mummy, Daddy, Andrea and Day Day x0x0x0x0x0

A Guntur tobacco party

Meanwhile, in the hills, Vera Windus kindly took Simon out whilst she and her husband, Mike, were in Ooty. Simon wrote: *Dear Mummy and Dadd, We went out for the week end. We went horse rideing and we saw tod-stoles. they were red and white spots. A tree has fallen down where the swings are and it has fallen on the hej and brocken the hej. I am looking forwed to see you. I fowed a big tod-stole. We went horse-rideing two tims. I galept with out the man holding eight times. We made the frunt steps full of moss it was a long time to get it dun But it is still there I have five horse* (house) *ponts. We were going to a film But we were to lat Becos we went to the lake. We had a lovely ride in the Bout it is very very cold in autey. wen We went on the Bout We saw a black and white and brown pony. we sent shoping and I bote stikcing fun and Little Cotton tail and a witing pad and a pencel and some swits and two battrees. Love from Simon.*

Some weeks later another letter arrived: *dear Mummy and Daddy. Thank you for your letter. It was Hebron's birthday on Friday. We had a lovelley supper the tables were decratid with flowers. Danil* (a servant) *has been in Hebron for 48 years. The mony for the refugees has gone right up to Rs 1100. When we went out of the dining room we got some sweets. On Saturday we went to Shalem. We made a fire to make our lunch we had tomatos and sosgis and bread and apples and a Frid-egg to. After lunch we went down to the point and looked down at the plains. I tryed to see Anrea and David* (about 400 miles to the east) *but I was looking in the rong direction. Danil had a watch because he has been hear so long. I only had one House point this week. I am shapning a stone it is or ready quite shap. Love from Simon.*

Susina wrote: *I have not got a best friend because Alison Ringrose has gone off me and because Sherryn Bruesman has gone on furlough for six months. Next term I am going up to std. four. My hair has grown much longer. Love from Susina xxxxx*

The amount of joy we gained from these funny missives is unfathomable.

Martyn Bougourd, a Guernsey man who previously worked in both Nigeria and Ghana, was an amusing character who constantly turned up as a tobacco buyer with various companies. Martyn always managed to find a good house, usually with a swimming pool, and he created wonderful tropical gardens despite the heat. He was an extrovert, over-the-top host and very entertaining. He spent much more time in Guntur than the other buyers and we saw him frequently. He was clumsy, always knocking things over, "Whoops!" he cried scrabbling around on the floor trying to mop things up, and burning himself whilst lighting a cigarette. He was fun, larger than life, frolicsome and a devout Roman Catholic. He employed an amiable maid called Chithi, who put up with all forms of abuse and worked like a trojan to help Martyn have fun, whilst always keeping him under her complete control

Martyn with Andrea in his Guntur pool

He wrote us a letter:

Tel: *21738 officu* -office
20310 giddah - residence

P O Box 216,
Arundelpet
Guntur – 2

Thought for the day (in Latin)
NON EXCRETA TIMBA GEGE
GUNTURENSIS

8th July 1971

Dear Nat and Mike
Many thanks for your letter, I'm glad that you did not have any after effects of drinking 'Chateau Patabipuram 1971'. I have found however, that I have a distinct list to starboard after drinking a glass or two and I'm sure it is about 80° proof. It shows you what a Pressure cooker can do to a batch of 'Plonk'!

Thank you both very much indeed for your kind invitation to the beach for the weekend of the 24th. I have just had a word with my social secretary (probably Chithi) *and it appears that I have nothing on that weekend needless to say I shall be delighted to come.*

In fact my chaps will be having a little 'scheme' on. I've just had PBK on from Cal. and he suggests that his chaps sort of make a pincer attack on the Chirala factory from somewhere south of Choudrypalem a sort of picknick (as in knickers) lunch at Tangatur and finish the scheme off by evening with GOC Chirala District Maj-General Sir Michael Wheatley C.B M.C. K.M.A. etc at the club. Entertainment by Sri Bishu Tankha (there is an UNK missing) and his Ginza Geishas

First Class idea.
This is all the drivel for now all the best - Yours Martyn
CARDINAL ARCHBISHOP OF GUNTUR (C of E) & EXPERT IN ALL SORTS OF TOBACCOS INDIAN AND OTHERWISE (INDUSTRIAL SABOTAGE A SPECIALITY).

Mike was at the height of the hottest season, buying thousands of sticky bales on the tobacco courts, bending over each as they were cut twice. He was surviving on pints of lime juice, suffering problems with his eyes and becoming very allergic to tobacco dust. The temperature was 110°F (43°C) and the humidity was at 98%. If West Africa was white man's grave, Andhra Pradesh was black man's grave. There was no let up for the men, no acceptance that their working conditions were unhealthy, no provision for women and children to get away to cooler climes, no sympathy – we were incarcerated in the Dark Ages. We were all feeling fairly groggy, both Mike and Susina were ill with amoebic dysentery, and the twins and I with giardiasis. Simon was adamant that there was nothing wrong with his guts, and tests proved him right, but he did have boils in his ears and was not allowed to swim if anybody offered us an invitation to their pool. The Indians avoided getting a tan at any cost and so were not keen on swimming pools and often filled them in, so opportunities were rare for a cooling dip.

Suddenly we were informed that we were to move to Chirala within two weeks. Our home leave was deferred until July 1972, when we would have completed a gruelling 22 months. Whilst tapping on my Olympia portable to my parents about all these new developments, Simon was peering at me through the window drumming his fingertips, Susina was shouting from the dining room that she did not want to eat fattening mangoes and next door's bearer was banging on the kitchen door for ice as they were having a party. Surinder Rao, our mali, standing on one leg and then the other, was asking for a few rupees to pay the dhobi, and Monica was having a giggling fit on the floor with the twins which, probably, would end in tears. Mike sent a message for a flask of coffee and David repeatedly refused to brush his teeth.

Mali Surinder Rao was one of the strangest people we employed though he stayed with us many years until, one day, he disappeared. He was thin, lanky and very unsure of himself although he spoke excellent English, rode a bike and proved helpful and honest when going to market. He was unhappy and moody and on bad terms with Mariamma who was good natured. There was a caste problem and they were always accusing each other of being *shoe stitchers* or *stone cutters* or some other equally lowly caste. When Surinder Rao came to us he was half starved, wearing a rough tunic made out of an old sack with some of the lettering washed out. He moved into one of the quarters and joined the communal feeding plan, and soon his bony cheeks filled out and he appeared more cheerful. We smartened him up with new khaki uniforms and leather sandals. Sometimes he locked himself into his quarter where he wailed and moaned, feeding himself on salt and raw rice. After some time it seemed to me that as Surinder Rao was educated at an English medium school, he might be from a higher caste than people thought. He was misunderstood and not supported by his family, who were never mentioned.

Susina and Simon were quite looking forward to returning to the cool hills, we were all absolutely exhausted by the intense heat, sharing one hot bedroom with a worn out air-conditioner which could not cope, despite water tossed on to its exterior during the night by the watchman. Our whole life style was unhealthy and unsatisfactory. This time we went by car and the three of us drove to Madras with a packet of parathas, a tiffin carrier full of tasty potato curry, and large flasks of iced lime. We were to meet a Hebron lady at Madras station who was to take them up to the hills, but we could not find her amongst the milling crowds. Frantically we pushed and shoved searching for this unknown expatriate woman, the children running behind with the porter dragging bedrolls and bags. It was dreadful, hot, sweaty and gloomily dark and she was not there but, when I got home, her apologetic letter was waiting to say she was unable to make the journey. Privately the children were delighted, it meant a few more days of *Mummy.*

There were no available seats for me to travel so, next day we continued by car, via Mysore. The Guntur driver could not speak English and my bazaar Telugu fell short when trying to discuss travel plans and directions. Somehow we got to Coonoor and back, a killing journey of 1200 miles in three days. On my return I had to set to and pack our belongings to move to Chirala, causing Andrea and David unrest seeing their little lives torn apart. Fortunately Mariamma, Nanny and the children were coming with us, also Surinder Rao and his bike. We cheered and did not look back as we left the disgusting environment of ghastly Guntur, and Mike was ready for a new challenge in the re-drying factory.

Simon, Natalie and Susina at Vadarevu – 23 miles of beach
10 miles from Chirala town.

We moved into a house called Fairways which was a great improvement on the unwieldy, colonial Palm Villa West we had previously occupied on the compound. It was a well designed family home with a big kitchen and dining room, a sitting room opening on to a shaded veranda; two good sized bedrooms and bathrooms complete with tubs and showers. The house was at the end of a row, next to the defunct nine-hole golf course, and it was enjoyable being on our own and more independent. There was a circular drive with a tree in the middle which David hung on to, teaching himself to ride a two-wheeler in a couple of hours, and a garage which became Bonnie's home. Life again was time-tabled by the trains roaring by and the regular blasts from the factory hooter. With the help of two malis, I worked on the large and uncultivated garden. They possessed only one hand hoe, a machete and two baskets between them and, with these primitive tools, they moved tons of sand and made new flower beds. We planted elephant's ears and lilies, three beds of groundnuts, one of spinach and one of lima beans. It was amazing how quickly everything grew in the hot climate on bare sand, energised by a few loads of tobacco waste. The water level was so high the malis could pot water frequently from shallow holes dug in the ground.

Apart from factory personnel, our nearest ILTD neighbours were at Parchoor depot, the new manager, sophisticated and well spoken was educated at Eton, and definitely more out of place than we were. He and his Bombay born wife lived in the house called Paradise, which was a very unhappy experience for them. It was a spooky, run down bungalow, with large dark rooms and lots of wildlife in the roof space. They came over for dinner one night quaking with fear, as they suspected the place was haunted by ghosts. It probably was; ex-ILTD expatriates riddled it with horror stories of heat stroke, typhus and tarantulas, ghouls, evil spirits and marauding monkeys. The garden was alive with scorpions and a cobra had killed their dog. It was hard to know how to comfort them and it was not long before they left. We had a cobra living in the flower bed near our front steps, Mike saw it and deemed it *friendly,* it certainly never bothered us and was there for months. One night we came home late from Guntur and went into the spare room to get some towels. Under one bed was an unidentified snake curled up and snoozing peacefully, we crept to the kitchen and got the stick broom and Mike bashed the poor reptile on the head.

Social life at the New Club, Chirala

The New Club at the factory needed cleaning up. Our orthodox Indian staff were not *clubby* people and it was the usual case of everyone grumbling and no one doing anything. I catalogued the library which was tedious and dirty work, but the spin off was a plethora of books to read, soft and worn out, they were solace to my soul. The club had a small shop run by a polite dhoti clad clerk called Mr Ramaswamy, he kept the bar supplied with beer, liquor and soft drinks. The bar boys, like all bar boys, were often gregarious and Mr Ramaswamy, in his way, kept them in order. His shop was open at certain hours and provided oil, soaps and powders, biscuits and jams, tea and coffee and a few sweets. Outside and unlocked was a huge and rusty freezer shared by all of the 24 compound bungalows. Indians weren't into frozen food; they liked everything fresh and alive, so heaven knows how old some of the pomfret fish at the bottom were, nor how the unwrapped mutton got on with the unwrapped fowl, especially after a few power cuts. After the library there was the bar, card room and the dreaded loos to deal with. There was a big hall with a dance floor, an outside terrace with tables and chairs and a little used tennis court. The main hub was the snooker table and several intrepid Indian wives became very good players.

As I became more involved with the social activities at the New Club, my life became more structured and busier. One Sunday we arranged a family day at the beach for all the company children. There was a large number of supervisory staff living on the compound, most rather shy and retiring. It took something to get them out of their rabbit holes and join in the fun. We organised races on the beach, kite flying, a film, various sports activities and tea and dinner for over 60 people.

Fairways was pleasant and our household servants and hangers-on settled into a comfortable routine. The early mornings were fresh and I sat on the veranda with a cup of coffee watching the birds in the trees swooping about flexing their coloured wings. The twins tumbled all over me, so we wandered round the garden to see all the new flowers, and to explain how they made seeds. At 6-50 Mike completed breakfast and was off with his flask to walk the half mile to the factory, and the malis arrived at 7am and were given (in my flowing Telugu) their duties for the day. Mariamma sometimes helped me with more complicated words but, on the whole, they understood. Breakfast for the children was porridge and hot, fluffy chapatis with home-made butter and grape jam and, for me, an omelette and a bowl of yoghurt which set overnight in the kitchen. Each breakfast was a battlefield with Andrea and David fighting over the sugar basin so they could sprinkle as much as possible on their porridge.

Our store cupboard was locked and rations tediously doled out on to a big tray, hopefully preventing temptation and theft. Mariamma was often trusted with my bunch of keys and she decided what to cook, took what she needed and never let me down. We enjoyed eating Indian food, so it was rice and dall, vegetables and a little meat or fish. Fruit was our usual dessert, or puddings made from milk. Our untrained staff came from the nearby village and were taught to swab the floors with *Phenyle* (disinfectant), and scrub the grinding stones, as we lived on sand it was a constant battle to keep surfaces clean

At noon a hot husband walked home, lay in a bath, quickly ate lunch and dived onto his bed in the air-conditioned bedroom. The twins took more time to bathe and eat, food was never appetising in that heat, though iced custard apples were good and took ages as all the pulp was sucked off the big brown seeds.

Going fishing off Vadarevu Beach

Chapter 20 – Tobacco Factory

In 1918 a buying point was established in Chirala behind the railway station and, every day, 100 bales from Parchoor were despatched to the Bangalore cigarette factory. The farmers liked this quick cash system so, in 1922, the company built a tobacco re-drying factory in Chirala constructed from locally quarried stones. The operations were simple and it expanded quickly. Manufacturers preferred the mid-rib to be removed from the leaf, so hundreds of people, mainly women, were employed in *stripping* operations. They sat cross legged in lines on hard floors in godowns under the supervision of a male martinet, flicking a fly whisk to keep up the tempo as they pulled the leaves one by one through a V-shaped metal cutter. The first intake was 500 workers but they rapidly built up to 6,000. Many came from the original *village of criminals* of Stuartpuram, a 2,000 acre grant of land given them for rehabilitation. Encouraged by the Salvation Army, 90% converted to Christianity and many became doctors, lawyers and teachers. Ten per cent of the hardcore remained thieves or *dacoits,* known locally as *Yerucalas,* continuing their undercover activities whilst employed in Chirala factory. It was a perfect system, no one locked their doors and many of the men were company watchmen but, if an outsider policeman took up duties, someone could be wrongly arrested and a tragedy occur, as in the death of Tiger Nageswara Rao who was shot dead in 1980. He was a *dacoit* turned Robin Hood and gave all his ill gotten gains away. Ten thousand attended his funeral causing such deep sorrow, the factory was shut down for the day. The tradition has persisted and many of our garden boys and watchmen were *Yerucalas* but did not trouble us.

The Beach House at Chirala. An Oasis of tranquillity despite dacoits.

In the 1920s and 1930s, pioneers of the South India Leaf Area needed to increase tobacco production and experimented with Virginia seed, normally grown on light soils. The black cotton soils of Chirala and Guntur District proved successful and the farmers, traditional in their methods, realised the potential of a big cash crop. They needed assistance and a small invasion of

UK experts were shipped out to help the *ryots* (farmers) how to top and sucker, to harvest correctly and to combat disease. They learned how to stitch individual leaves on to strings and constructed miles of bamboo and metal racks on which the leaf was air-cured, then bulked, baled and sent to Chirala factory. The process took a good five weeks, but rain often produced rot and fungus. Eventually flue (or barn) curing was introduced using wood fuel to dry the leaves. This was more reliable taking only five days giving a richer, yellow colour forming the beginnings of the boom time to come.

The expatriates found Andhra unpleasant, but suffered the heat and filth and the local people welcomed them, particularly when they learned Telugu. They travelled to the villages on motorcycles, and were paid two annas a mile. The roads were rough and often impassable, so motor bikes became essential transport and an opportunity to have some fun. A Reliability Trial was held in Guntur in 1927, as well as organised competitions and rallies. There were BSA's, Triumphs, Scott Squirrels and Douglas's; some of the more intrepid wives joined in and side cars were built to carry them on a 24-mile course through villages, along the dry river beds, scattering dogs, goats and chickens. At the end of the trial there was a banquet breakfast and bottles of beer. We never discovered any records or photographs of these pioneers, office walls only displayed Hindu gods and goddesses. The only archival evidence we found of their existence were names on the snooker board in the New Club, and those only as far back as the 1950s. These men and their wives suffered health problems in an area that was hardly civilised and it was not easy to purchase stores. The railway line from Madras to Calcutta was a lifeline and Spencers, a department store of long standing on Mount Road in Madras, provided foodstuffs and drinks on receipt of telegrams with guarantee of payment through the bank or post office. Guntur was a trading post with very little provided for an expatriate and, if Chirala was as backward as it was in 1970, heaven knows what was available in 1930. Conditions of housing, hospitals and education were almost non-existent and the great god Ganesh could not succour the expatriate need for comfort and joy in this alien part of the world.

Once a growing and buying system was established, bungalows for expatriates were constructed on the northern side of the railway line, designed to be cool and dark inside with wide verandas and low eaves. The rooms were spacious and furnished with heavy rosewood chairs and tables, wooden beds and a few rugs and the bungalows had names like Durham Lodge, Sandridge and Palm Villa. They also built The Retreat at Vadarevu beach, ten miles away on the coast. This was ILTD expatriate life in Andhra Pradesh from the start, and little had changed when we came into it at the end, as we were the last expatriates to leave the company in 1978.

In 1972 the huge, efficient factory was re-drying 154 million pounds (70 million kilos) of leaf each year and was the largest tobacco re-drying factory in south east Asia and one of the largest in the world. Mike worked in an air-conditioned office, and the spacious compound we lived on was a huge improvement to life on Guntur depot. Mike rose to the challenge as AFM and then Factory Manager with a workforce of 10,000, and created a good rapport between management, staff and labour, particularly with communist unions, many of which were Marxist.

Malcolm Pereira was an Anglo-Indian supervisor and, in his spare time, a talented ballroom dancer. His enterprising wife, Olive, opened Pereira School where Andrea and David started their educational life. It was situated in an old missionary house on the other side of town and there was a large intake, many of the children coming from outlying farms, their feudal Telugu fathers realising that a good English education was a necessity of life. Olive opened an extensive boarding unit and eventually moved to the original ILTD compound, renting Durham Lodge. She stayed there many years, long after Malcolm's death and her own retirement. She was a dedicated and talented teacher and the twins stayed at Pereira's for a year, before we decided to move them to Hebron in January 1972 to benefit from a UK curriculum.

Chirala's level crossing children

Each weekday at 8am Andrea and David were the first pupils to be picked up by the factory jeep which did the rounds collecting all the other children and taking them to school. On arrival their boredom disappeared and they had a happy time, Olive was diligent and fun with primary pupils. They were the last to be dropped off at 12-30 noon and were hot, bad tempered and hungry. First they had a cool bath, the water having been run early in the morning as the pipes were laid under a shallow layer of sand and only *hot* water came out of the cold tap. They splashed around until there was enough energy for lunch and, afterwards, a siesta under the fan. In the evening Nanny took them over the railway line to the club where lots of their school friends were playing, it was a high spot of the day, and after supper they went to bed when it was cooler and dark.

There was a permanent gatekeeper at the level crossing and he was permanently drunk. His wife was beautiful but in rags, as were their four delightful, friendly children. They all manned the big heavy gate whilst their father was comatose, it was heavy and dangerous work as the trains were frequent and fast. We became fond of this family, even the smallest girl attended her gate duties and we gave them fruit and food and all our cast-off clothing.

The next time Mrs German brought Susina and Simon to Vijayawada with the school party, they arrived at 4-30am and, after our horrifying mistake, we never again failed to meet them, our sooty and weary children. Fairways was a new home for them and they liked the more modern house with a garden full of flowers, and quickly made friends with the Arulappan children who lived in Sandridge East. Joe Arulappan was the factory engineer, a dark-skinned Roman Catholic and Dolores, his wife, was Mangalorean. They had collected a wide selection of records and loved western pop music and dancing. Dolores was pretty and wore incredibly psychedelic saris, dangly jewelled earrings and lots of make-up; she was a sort of plump princess and rather lazy. There were four children; Mary, Carolyn who was handicapped, Melissa and a little boy called Sean. They were a great family and very friendly. Holiday times were fun as they played endlessly together, made up games, rode bikes, went to the beach and created lots of activities.

We were both suffering from acute amoebic dysentery and every doctor told us something different so, with the twins and Nanny, we went for tests at Vellore, about 200 miles away. We were due for local leave so left early in Bonnie, our ultimate destination was Ooty where Susina wrote, *It is so cold and miserable here I don't know what to write about,* whilst we sweltered in 100ºF (37ºC) heat. Vellore was a bustling, noisy, dirty town with a huge fort, lying on an arid plain between Madras and Bangalore, surrounded by granite mountains filled with basking snakes on hot rocks. The town attracted a floating population of at least 5,000 people a day, all anxious to be treated at the Christian Medical College, a world famous teaching hospital with 1,200 beds and an overflowing outpatient department. Founded in the early part of the 1900s by Dr Ida Scudder, a dedicated American medical missionary, it was well known for its cancer and neurological wards, tropical diseases with a renowned college of nursing.

The hospital was like a factory and we hired two rooms on the third floor of the visitor's block. Children were not allowed but somehow we managed to hide our two and Nanny and keep them quiet. We put up with unpleasant tests with tubes poked into us from all directions, performed with a total absence of bedside manner. Mike was upset by a bulging eyed Tamilian medical student wearing a wide plastic belt and an *007* buckle, wielding a probe looking like a torpedo with a light on the end.

"You're not coming near me with that thing," he exploded, and the young intern ran away.

The outcome was that Mike and I had been overdosed on Flagyl, the bitter anti-dysentery drug and, after stopping it, we felt a lot better almost instantly. The twins were diagnosed with giardiasis, which caused deep stomach cramps due to the little worms which were eradicated with an unpalatable medicine. Nanny was all clear but was given an eye test diagnosing cataracts, so we purchased a pair of spectacles to help her sewing activities.

St Margaret's, Ooty – gardeners showing off their loyalty

After a a couple of weeks in Ooty, the end of term carol concert and other functions, we made our way home to Chirala with all four children and Nanny on board. We were always happier in Mysore State with its undulating countryside, craggy outbursts of rock, sparkling rivers and the brilliant green paddy shooting through shimmering ponds of water. It was pastoral with a medieval ambience, the villagers performing almost biblical tasks such as threshing with sticks and winnowing grain in flat baskets, and the squashing of sugar cane through primitive presses. When we arrived in 1964, poverty was obvious in the demeanour and dress of the people, skinny and worried, walking barefoot on bad roads leading bony cattle. Now there was an air of expectation and village houses were neat with plastered walls and red tiled roofs. It was becoming prosperous as heavy lorries lurched along overloaded with hessian bundles of cotton, the fluff breaking through the sacking and scattering along the road sides and catching in the trees. We passed one awful accident where the prettily painted truck overturned showing its rusty underside and it's smooth worn out tyres.

We stayed in the Foster's rooms at the Bangalore Club and, that day. 3rd December 1971, the Pakistan Air Force attacked a number of airfields in the north and started the Indo-Pakistan war. We went shopping and left Nanny with the children and the air raid sirens sounded almost immediately, because Bangalore was the centre of Hindustan Aeronautics Ltd. The noise of the sirens brought back bad memories to Nanny, and she told the children dreadful stories of her time in Burma fleeing from the Japanese. When we returned they were all shivering with fear and David was buried under the blankets. We told them not to worry and that Pakistan was several thousand miles away. The bearers brought them supper and they all had a warm bath, once settled we went out again and watched the population of Bangalore scurrying around with a new found agitation as the sirens blew ceaselessly. We went to the Blue Fox for our last evening of civilised dining and dancing; we wanted to feel young and carefree for a few hours, before the incarceration of life in Andhra Pradesh.

Nellore village kids

Next morning we left at 4am on the long and hot trek home. The children were fractious, their sore eyed co-driving parents exhausted and Nanny snoring. The temple town of Tirupathi meant respite and lunch of delicious masala dosais at the Hotel Brahmin. The town was a mass of devotees visiting their idol, Lord Venkateshwara. On some days there were as many as 30,000 male and female pilgrims, the majority of whom, in an act of penance, had their heads shaved. They made fervent requests, ending their devotions by rolling around the stone floors. It was burningly hot and we were anxious to move on.

After Cuddapah we continued east and turned on to the busy Madras-Calcutta trunk road. Shortly, after a sharp bend, we spotted a crashed camper van, but we drove on to fill up with petrol in the town of Nellore. A small ragged boy anxiously ran up to our car. I was driving and

Mike was half asleep.

"Amma! Amma!" he called.

Ignoring him I shuffled through a wad of filthy rupees to pay the petrol boy.

"Amma!" he shouted urgently.

"Yes," I answered abruptly.

"Two American, bad accident," he was breathless. I waved him away like a buzzing mosquito, but then hesitated.

"American? Where?" I asked.

He stuttered, his tiny knowledge of English disappearing with fear, his mouth dry and his eyes scared and unsure.

Ekkada? - where? I asked quietly in Telugu, and he relaxed.

Akkada! - there, he pointed back, "Very danger," and disappeared.

The VW camper van had GB plates and had been in a head on collision. A man sat beside the vehicle and pointed backwards, a*spatri* - hospital, he said without expression, p*edda vee-hay-icle lorry,*- big vehicle, and clapped his hands together violently, explaining the impact. The lorry was long gone leaving crumpled metal and broken glass.

The children were peevish; "I want to go home." "Let me out." "My legs hurt." "I'm starving." We gave them drinks and biscuits and explained the urgency of the situation.

Nellore General Hospital was no more than a health centre, unhygienic and teeming with sickly people. The two British crash boys were on metal tables wrapped in a buzz of flies. William Taylor had suffered a severely broken neck and looked at us with such fear, "I can't feel anything," he breathed, "Only the ends of my fingers." Mark Hatt's ankle was almost severed and falling off the edge of the table, and an inexperienced doctor was twisting it back into place as Mark screamed in agony.

"Are you English?" murmured William. We nodded. "Thank God," he said and passed out.

The doctor was angry at our intrusion, "Impossible to operate here, I am having to despatch these men tonight to Madras on the town fire engine," and was unwilling to discuss alternatives. Madras was 250 bumpy miles south, and Chirala a good five hours north. Mike told him that he was the British High Commissioner's representative in Andhra Pradesh and, since the accident victims were British, he was accountable to the High Commission for their evacuation, and we left to find help.

We knew we must locate the local missionaries, if any, and passed a garage where an imported four wheel drive wagon was parked with *Nellore Baptist Mission Ambulance* painted in red on both sides. We stopped, found the driver and were directed to the Mission. We met two grey haired Swedish nurses, and a jolly American called Dorothy Wiley. They gave the children and Nanny juice and cake, whilst we explained the tricky problem and immediately they offered help as they were so familiar with Indian drama and bureaucracy.

"Vellore," they said, "The CMC at Vellore is the *only* place where they can be treated, we will take them." Vellore, as we knew, was about a hundred miles to the west, and the roads were rough and bumpy.

Politely and forcefully the two boys were taken from the Government Hospital, carefully loaded into the ambulance and driven twelve hours to Vellore. Immediately William was put into traction and saved from quadriplegia by a whisker, Mark was operated on several times until he could walk and they spent months in the hospital. Mike, with permission, recovered their belongings and the van was left with the police. William and Mark had taken out insurance in Kabul before crossing the border into India, and the Afghan company paid up in full covering their medical expenses.

Nellore had no hotels so Dorothy Wiley put us up overnight. Exhausted we slept on charpois in her cobwebby attic and, next day, continued our journey. We turned off at Ongole, driving across salt flats on to sandy roads through the sari weaving villages and, at last, we were home.

Four weeks later Dorothy Wiley wrote, *I still wonder at the series of unusual circumstances which brought all of us together that Sunday in December. If you had not happened along the road just at the time that the two boys needed special help, what might have happened? And if that Ongole wagoneer had not been in Nellore on the Monday noon, how would we have gotten them to Vellore? So many things just fit together very miraculously. I don't see anything which could not be called divine intervention. Doris Conney* one of the Swedish nurses *had a letter from Mark that he had gone by wheelchair to visit William and put a pencil in his right hand and with difficulty he had written a 'W'. Their minibus is resting in the mission hospital compound and everyone who looks at it marvels that both men survived the crash.*

Chapter 21 – Steam Trains

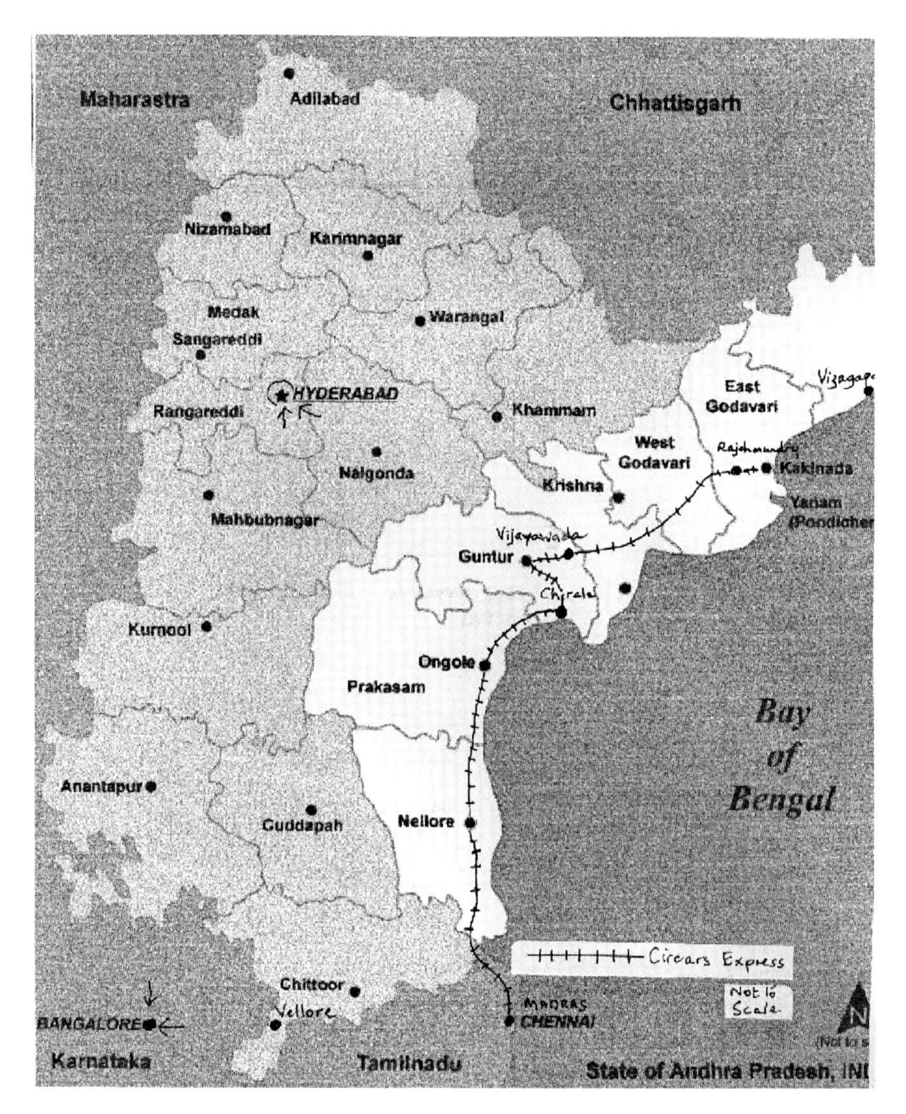

The Circars Express from Kakinada Port (north) to Madras (south)

Our next Christmas was a great improvement on most others. There were 14 round our table including our volunteer friends Jim and Ann Smith, and the entire Arulappan family. A massive leg of pork was roasted accompanied by all the trimmings; and everything was so much more normal.

"This is a happy day, Madams," Mariamma was laughing as she prepared all the food. Monica was playing with Nanny, and Bujie was burbling in a sari sling under a shady tree. Their own special meal of chilli chicken and special fried rice, to be shared with all the helpers, was bubbling in dekshies on cast iron charcoal burners.

There was a grand party for the children at the Club, a merry-go-round, side show, lucky dip and a huge tea. Simon pulled the sleeve of the Ongole based Father Christmas to remind him firmly, "Don't forget my house, it's the one at the end." He didn't, the stockings were much improved and everyone was happy.

Christmas party at the New Club
L-R back – Mary Arulappan, Susina, Victoria Harding, Simon, Carolyn Arulappan
L-R front – Melissa and Sean Arulappan, Kartik Malladi, Andrea and David

The Christmas holidays were cooler and the children bicycled, made up plays and took advantage of the 23 miles of isolated beach on which to build castles. We used Bonnie and took picnics to Vadarevu where we bought prawns and barracuda netted by the fisherman in their dug out canoes. There were a lot of foreign customers to look after and a new cook at the beach who did not speak English. He was a good cook especially after he was given a four burner gas stove with an oven, but shared the difficulties of buying limited supplies of fresh ingredients which ranged from chillis and coconuts in the market, jack fruit and plantains on the roadside, and home made papadums drying in the village gutters. There was no flour, no sugar, no butter and no reasonable ingredient for anything.

Pongal (harvest) entailed another cricket match and lunch for 50. The food was supposed to be prepared by the wives in their own kitchens, but most were reluctant to cook and many did not make very good food. It was a struggle to get past the cultural barrier of goodwill to all men, as their lives were so narrow and pre-arranged. We organised a dance and hired a band from Madras; there was a lot to organise and very few active helpers.

The twins, aged 5 years and 4 months, looked too small for boarding school. David did not want to go, Andrea, unsure, might make the best of it, Simon seemed keen about it and, we suspected, the structure of school was sometimes preferable to the muddle of home, where everyone pinched his toys. Susina was cross and did not want to go back at all, and I was not looking forward to my maiden voyage of four nights on second class steam trains. Each year Coonoor had heavy monsoons and the school had inadequate drying facilities, so the clothes list for four children included 16 pairs of pyjamas, 24 vests, 24 pants and endless pairs of socks, and this did not include their uniforms, known as *check rags* which were made by the school tailor. We supplied four blankets each, eight sheets and towels and tuck boxes filled with Bombay mixture, banana jam, peanut brittle, tamarind and hot pickle. The trunks went off by lorry on 20 January and term started in the first week of February. A poem I wrote called School Trunks was published in the Monthly Review in Calcutta:

My nerves are so fraught, the young are depressed
My time is so occupied, I hardly get dressed
My eyes are quite red with the strain of it all
As, struggling, I ink an old cricket ball.
Nine khaki shorts and ten pairs of socks
My dreams are all fuddled with sizes of frocks,
Fourteen play shirts and twenty sheets,
Sixteen blankets and tins of eats.
At last they are finished, the job is quite done
The lids are closed and I feel I have won,
The padlocks are clicked and the trunks depart
I sigh with relief, and then I start
Thinking of what went in where?
Mistakenly, did I put those vests in there?
My mind's so confused and so are my thoughts
Did I put in eight or nine pairs of shorts?

As a family our simple treat before the children went back to school was a *dinner party*. We made everything as grand as we could, and all dressed in our best clothes. Susina swept up her hair and there were candles on the table and a buffet style dinner. The Arulappan children came and drank juice from wine glasses and we showed movie films. At 10pm, we all went for a *midnight* walk around the factory and they were at the height of excitement as they ran up and down the floodlit concrete runways. Next day we took our lot for a final picnic lunch to the beach.

Early next morning the Circars Express departed from the port of Kakinada and meandered down the east coast stopping frequently before steaming into Chirala late at night, to arrive next day at 6am in Madras. The unreserved carriages were over crowded with agricultural Telugus and their piles of belongings, and rowdy marriage parties with people spitting, smoking beedies, eating and snoring, their noise interspersed by many fractious babies. The train had a couple of first class carriages with Rexine seats but were no cleaner than second, and the cost beyond the rupee budget of most. They were also unsafe as each compartment took four people and was locked between stations, meaning that a lone woman could get locked in with three strange men or, worse, a man with three strange women. Second class, three tier allowed scant personal space, six to a small compartment, with a couple of clanking fans revolving slowly but not enough to displace blood hungry mosquitoes. The toilets at the end of each carriage were waterless and filthy, just holes in the floor with the wooden sleepers very visible beating beneath. The train jolted in all directions and the toilets were hard to navigate with little to hold on to, it was a good place to lose a sandal forever. For a child, the squealing of wheels meeting steel rails was frightening and, for a mother, suspending a heavy seven-year old by its knees, dangerous in such a slippery area.

Catching the train was a horrible experience. The children were all freshly bathed with clean clothes and shining blonde hair. We were loaded with five bulky bedrolls, food and water, plus our clothes and special toys. Chirala station was dimly lit with particularly long platforms, and we did not know where the carriage with our reservations would stop. The train steamed in like a great dragon, its chimney puffing clouds of smoke, the stokers shovelling coal into it's belly, the engine driver leaning out and shouting instructions. The stationmaster was on the alert with his green flag and whistle in his mouth. The train stopped for only two minutes, and the carriages were locked so we were reliant on the guard to be awake to open the doors. It was a mad rush to read the crumpled paper glued on the side pinpointing our badly spelt names - *Madams Vitley, Miss Sujeen, Master Simeon, Miss Adra and Mr Daveed.*

"Here we are, here we are," we could barely see dear Mrs German waving at the carriage window. She had boarded with her party that afternoon at Rajahmundry, "Come on, you're all in here with us." The guard unlocked the heavy door and we clambered up the high steps, our luggage stuffed behind us, the whistle already blown.

"Bye, bye Daddy. Bye, bye," the children cried, pushing to catch a last glance. They really cried, for they would not see him for three months, and he cried too going home to rumpled beds and left behind toys.

The carriage was packed with too many passengers sharing the same still air collected through the day. In our small space was a cross legged grandmother, wrapped in a smoke smelling sari, staring myopically through pebble lensed spectacles held together with rusty wire. She grunted and moved her cracked feet so we could sit down, before preparing the bedrolls on the top tiers. The train gathered speed, soon to stop again at Ongole and Nellore and numerous small halts.

We were a group of fifteen, including two Plymouth Brethren mothers, one husband, and their seven children, plus me with our four. It was a really hard journey and difficult to be so squashed in with so many grunting, snoring, turning over people. Our children soon fell asleep as they were exhausted, having waited up so late and coped with the whole emotionalism of leaving home, Mariamma and Nanny, Daddy and going to school. We slithered into Madras station at first light to the sight of people, many squatting on the banks, smoking the first beedie of the day, their metal water pots picking up the weak rays of early sunlight. I was the only one who complained of sore bones and sleeplessness, Mrs German, aged 51, stretched and yawned and woke up with missionary zeal. Dozens of khaki-clad, red turbaned coolies, brass plates dangling round their necks with numbers on, raced along as the train came to a halt anxious to be spotted, grabbing luggage indiscriminately and shouting, *Me Ma! Me! Ma come with Me!* and running off with bedrolls under each arm and a pile of suitcases on each head.

We parted with the missionaries for the day and arranged to meet them at the station in the evening to catch the Nilgiri Express. We were lucky and used the company transit flat where we all showered and enjoyed a good breakfast. Afterwards we went to a cinema and watched a morning cartoon show, followed by lunch at a restaurant and a visit to the zoo. Susina and Simon were impressed as usually, when travelling with the missionary party, they spent hours in the station rest rooms and were taken to the nearby smutty bazaar for shopping. It was not easy working for a large company, but an awful lot harder to be an impoverished missionary.

The Nilgiri Express was a monster of a train, the steam and roar exploding from its mighty boiler, the noise of the whistle ripping the ears. We were told that steam trains were much safer than diesel. Often the driver of a steam train stayed with his engine for twenty years, loving the power in his hands and the familiarity of the hissing and puffing, and always busy and alert adjusting gauges, torquing gears and releasing pressure, not to mention brewing mugs of coffee. From Madras to Mettupalayum the train sped across the plains, gobbling six tons of coal every 120 miles. It was a long night for me, waking at every station, peering through the bars but, as the name was only at the beginning or the end of the platform, it was hard to know where we were.

By Coimbatore my cotton pillow was speckled with soot and I felt stiff after sleeping on the wooden slats, and it was 30 hours since we boarded the Circars Express at Chirala station. Now we were nearing a small junction in the foothills of the Nilgiri Hills, the train slowed and the misty letters of M-E-T-T-U-P-A-L-A-Y-U-M showed on the big sign.

"Mettupalayum, Mettupalayum," shouted the guard, as the train bellowed to its last steaming sigh, and the mothers shuffled around, whispering, and waking the children. Susina was deeply asleep, her long delicious golden hair everywhere, Simon was grumpy, David giggly and Andrea, her little nose pushed up into the air said, "Can we have dosais Mummy?"

There were few coolies, so we struggled with our bedrolls and bags, tiffin carriers, dolls and teddies, the children all crumpled and rubbing their eyes.

Mrs German was always cheerful, "Let's get breakfast," she said firmly, and strode into the greasy station restaurant, her mousy hair escaping from its cage of pins. We straggled behind her, finding places on metal chairs at oily tables. She looked at the cobwebby menu board, which offered Mutton Biriyani, Chaps or Rost, Piece or Masala. The rest was in Tamil.

Yeggs? she enquired politely of the unshaven, dhoti clad cook, waggling her head in the Indian way, *Fried yeggs*? She counted us for the umpteenth time, "Fifteen plates *fried yeggs* please," and he waggled his head in assent, smiling with a few brownish teeth. We were all hungry and eggs were a treat after vadais and coconut chutney for our picnic supper on the train.

There was much frying and clattering and bursts of smoke coming from his wood furnace. We were busy sorting ourselves out, ordering steel mugs of hot milky coffee from a boy in a worn out check shirt, the children ranging from 15 to five were anxious for their food.

The cook must have trained at a Malayalee circus for, suddenly, he appeared from behind the galvanised covered counter tottering along, legs bent, with fourteen plates of fried eggs, one on top of another. The children produced a universal *Ugh*, and Mrs German almost lost her Plymouth Brethren training, as forgotten expletives found their way into her mouth but were quickly sucked back.

The cook was upset as he had fried 30 eggs in record time. *No worry, no worry,* he said as he unstuck them, wiping the bottom of each yolky plate with a dirty piece of rag and plonking them firmly on the table. *Good yeggs, very good yeggs, not fertilised, good for wegetarians,* he was encouraging and went back to his over heated pan, wiping the sweat away leaving streaks of yellow on his forehead.

Hebron School buildings

We boarded the little push-and-pull train, the onward journey to Coonoor was to take another five hours. The carriages were small and painted yellow and blue, and the train was unique because of the toothed central rail onto which the locomotives locked on the steeper slopes, the little engine at the back pushing upwards, and a brake man in each carriage. Passing through 14 tunnels, the train chugged up into the mountains with spectacular views of banana plantations, teak and eucalyptus forests until coming to the tea bushes honeycombed across the rolling valley. Women tea pickers dressed in brightly coloured saris pulled over their heads, wandered with baskets on their backs carefully plucking the tender buds and two leaves. The fresh smells after the oven like atmosphere of the plains lifted our spirits.

Susina and Simon's spirits dropped as we passed through the dreaded Deo Supremo archway, they were truly back at school again. Andrea and David were unsure of themselves as we arrived at the same time as several other parties, and mingled on the driveway. There was a welcome lunch, we were all exhausted and starving and David and I sat with the grown-ups, whilst the other three joined the children. Susina was in a new dorm, which upset her; it was like a strange home. She did not like her house mistress, Miss Sargent, but gradually found her to be better than expected. Andrea was in the Nest with a really nice matron called Miss Jones, who was motherly and understanding and prepared Andrea a little cosy bed near her own room. The boys were in Sunshine, two of seven boys and next to each other, and Miss Reanny was their young and cheery matron. David was OK and Simon positively enjoying being back in the routine. Finally, with a sinking heart, I said I was going and Susina sweetly hurried them up to the playground forcing back her tears, and I went feeling like a rat. It did not strike me at the time but this was the end of my role as a full time mother, from now on our children would always be away and only come home for holidays. It was a dreadful milestone, and initiated a bad bout of depression, I was just 34 years old.

I went up the mountain to stay with the Rawlleys. Several years before we met Meena and Nickoo in Coorg, they were good friends of Jane and David Hughes. Nickoo was a planter and worked for Bombay Burmah, a conglomerate company dealing with tea, coffee and oil palm. They had recently been moved to Dunsandle Tea Estate, which was on the Mysore side of Ootacamund, and had two daughters, Binita and Deepika, who were still too little to go to school. Nickoo's mother was English and came from Essex. She met and married her *Indian Prince* in 1918, totally shocking her parochial family, and she and her husband settled in India in 1920. She happened to be visiting Dunsandle at this time and was good company, telling me that her own family had severed all connections with her and she had not been back to England, yet she had married into a good class Indian family and led a successful life, producing sons who became high ranking Army officers. She talked of *us* and *our,* meaning *us Indians*. It was a delight to be with such a dignified person who had assimilated so well into what must have been a strange culture, especially in those days when acceptance of a *foreigner* was very difficult for Indian parents. She wore the sari gracefully and her grey hair was in a tidy bun. After 52 years her skin was yellowed, but she retained her cultured English accent, and raised seven children in the north in Dehra Dun, spending time doing charitable work for the Cheshire Homes. Like most Indian widows she stayed each year with her scattered children and helped with darning and reading to the grandchildren. Nickoo was like a highly strung racehorse and came from a strong military family. Meena was beautiful with pale skin and almond shaped eyes, the daughter of a Nepalese mother. She and Nickoo were always kind to me and the children, offering rest and refreshment to break our long journeys, Meena and I became close friends and I followed them from estate to estate on my journeys to the hills.

Ooty was absolutely freezing, even icicles, and I did not have enough warm clothes and developed a horrid cold. I phoned Miss Hall next day and she assured me the children were well settled and only David wept a little. I tried to believe her, but wondered how many parents she placated so gently that morning. I travelled to Madras with a Baptist lady from Wimbledon, mother of two boys studying at Lushington in Ooty. She was jolly, not too holy and good company. She faced a horrendous journey to Calcutta taking more than double the time mine did; she must have felt that her children were a lifetime away from her. In Madras I met up with Mrs German, finally discovering her name was Irene, and was lucky to have company all the way to Chirala. The journey was an eye opener of discomfort and challenge, but paved the way for six years of constant forays to and from the hills. Once home I stayed in bed for 48 hours with flu' and laryngitis and utter, utter loneliness.

On 14 February we got Valentine's cards with *I love you* and big red hearts from Hebron, my first ever Valentine cards. Susina wrote, *Miss Jones has said that Andrea is very happy. Andrea has got a best friend now. David is very happy as well. I think his best friend is Christopher. Thank you very much for both your letters. I like them very much. On Saturday we did not go swimming because the pool was not full but we got into our swimming costumes and we had a water fight. Love from Susina*

Simon was busy with his own things; *We are doing Willie Worms. We have made a cubie on the playground. We have started a play called the Shoemaker with the standard 4's. We have started records now. We acted a show with the nest yesterday about king herod. Miss Hinkley came to visit Hebron yesterday. Love from Simon* and David was practical, *My picture shows 2 ladders and a slide. There are two bunk beds. On Sunday we went to church. We played soldiers at Sunday school. On Saturday we had a picnic tea outside our dorm. Love from David* and Andrea was light hearted, *We laughed in Sunday school. It was very funny. Miss Jones read a story about a king and a soldier and a boy called Peter. Then we acted it out. On Saturday for tea we went to Brooklands playground. Love from Andrea.*

1st row Andrea 5th from right

2nd row Simon 2nd from left Susina 10th David 7th from right

Chapter 22 – Leprosy Hospital

There was a lot of upheaval in ILTD and a big change of management. Mr I was waving his new broom and generally upsetting everyone, valuable people resigned relinquishing their pension prospects, they could not bear the tyranny any longer. Several suffered nervous breakdowns and there were two deaths from premature heart attacks. There was intrigue, suspicion and threat. Many of the wives were packing in readiness to move, finding new schools, persuading servants to follow and generally having a disquieting time. NP and Geetha came to Chirala and settled into Acree House, we stayed put in Fairways and the Hardings came from Rajahmundry to Guntur to replace the Rands who were moved to Hyderabad. Christopher Harding did not get on with Mr I and, after some time, they were posted to Bangalore and then Nigeria. Meanwhile Sally was in Helvetia and, as always, put her heart and soul into yet another new home, finding curtain materials, often in blue, and coping with tailors, electricians and painters. Sally was an old India hand, her father had worked for Parry's, and almost all her young life was spent in the nether regions of Andhra Pradesh. As a small child she was sent to St Hilda's in Ooty and afterwards to the Presentation Convent at Kodaikanal, a beautiful hill station in Madras State, but she and her sister, Holly, saw little of their parents. Later she completed a nursing course in London before returning to Andhra Pradesh where she met Christopher, and they married when she was young. Sally looked quintessentially English, but was deeply Indian with all its facets of strength and survival.

Andrea in Ooty

Before they were all settled at school in the hills, the children had taken up so much of my time, filling the house with chatter and unstoppable energy. The last few days of the holidays were busy with clothes, cutting hair and nails and preparing them, both mentally and physically. At night one of them often crept into our bed, sometimes we woke up with two or three. On my return, only Mariamma was aware of my feelings and came out on to the veranda in the evenings, quietly sitting at my feet. She was comforting and wise, "Madams got nothing now," she said, "Only writing letters for children."

Home making in Chirala bored me and writing articles for publication was slow especially with no reference material, but some Indian periodicals such as *Femina*, *Madras Mail* and *Eve's Weekly* accepted and paid for my work. Our radio did not pick up BBC World service so I resorted to All India Radio and enjoyed classical *sitar* music made famous by Ravi Shankar. The sitar is a large stringed instrument with a gourd resonating chamber and played whilst sitting cross legged on the floor. One of our company wives, Mala Tankha, was a talented player who diligently practised with her *tabla* (drum) player and performed in public. She was giggly, plump, fair and a rather beautiful Kashmiri, spiritually as far away from home as we were. She explained how the music developed into a general theme harmonised by a group of accompanying musicians. Perhaps it could be compared to impromptu jazz, always with a strong central core and discipline amongst the musically bonded players. I liked to be with Mala, to talk and share and to sense her real musical talent, wasted in the wilds of Anaparti where she and her husband, Bishu, were posted.

Geetha and I sometimes went to Guntur to see Hindi films, she was a devoted translator and kept me up to date with the complicated story. One film, *Geetha aur Seetha,* was about twins played by the same actress. It was a love story of babies parted at birth, one brought up as a peasant, one as a princess, and their subsequent meeting and passionate relationships with the same hero. One wore satin, the other rags, both had voluptuous hair and the inevitable sweaty armpits. The film was full of singing, dancing and fighting and, during the interval, we drank milky tea from a flask and ate potato bondas.

Captain Edna Rowley, Salvation Army

Mangala Changappa, was the wife of the Personnel Manager, and a social worker before marriage. She visited the factory crèche and taught the women about family planning. The crèche was crowded with toddlers and bare bottomed babies suspended in canvas sling cots, scrupulously clean but unbearably noisy. There were 200 under fives and they were fed and given vitamins as well as necessary prophylactics such as polio drops and triple antigen. None of the staff could understand my kitchen Telugu, there was no point in trying to help them, although I was desperate to do something.

Edna Rowley, a Salvation Army nurse who worked 12 miles away at the leprosy hospital telephoned out of the blue and suggested a visit, "Maybe you could help us?" she half asked. Help? I was ready to grow wings and fly there. It took me time to pluck up courage and ask Mike for transport, he was not keen on me getting involved with disease and was unaware of my depression or the need to use my caring abilities. Reluctantly he let me have a car and driver and off we went to Bapatla.

The hospital was managed by Edna and another Captain, Mahari Campbell, both Salvation Army nurses. Edna had been there for several years leading a lonely and dedicated life. Mahari was young and impetuous and, recently, had been elected Scotswoman of the Year. She played the guitar, loved Neil Diamond as well as her new terrier puppy, Haggis.

The old red-tiled, whitewashed buildings were set in 30 acres, shaded by big trees and surrounded by high walls. A guard, with only half a nose hobbled up with a stick, opened the iron gates, but the driver kept the engine running, "Madam please walk, I will not go to this place, I am staying outside," he said nervously, polite but adamant.

The silence, after the confusion of the busy road noisy with traffic, was ominous with no movement, a place to hide away and die. The guard waved a stumpy hand indicating the location of Edna's bungalow surrounded by zinnias popping their colourful heads through the sand. The girls gave me a warm welcome and offered coffee and biscuits. It was hot, very hot.

The buildings had long arched verandas and were separated by expanses of soft sand, burning the feet and torturing the ankles. Mobile patients looked after bedridden patients and there were 250 in total, as well as a large outpatients clinic. Three Indian officers did administrative work, and a surgeon came to perform operations when required. That was it. India was full of leprosy, heavily populated areas spread all diseases, and the bacillus *Mycobacterium leprae* was carried through the air and encouraged by a lack of living space, the sharing of mats, pillows and clothes.

Many of the patients were depressed and physically ill and needed a lot of morale boosting. Lack of feeling in hands and feet damages peripheral nerves and they accidentally cut themselves, or walked on sharp objects ulcerating the flesh which becomes infected. And there were constant dramas, that morning a boy fell down a deep well and someone tossed him a bucket to hang on to. Captain Mahari was called and threw a rope for the boy to put around his waist, then chose three patients with hands and feet still intact and, together, they pulled him out.

The sick wards were full, and silence fell as we walked in. The men had tidied the *charpois* (cots), straightened and folded the blankets. Fingerless salutes greeted us followed by shouted and exuberant *salaams*. A little boy painstakingly knitted a striped scarf from scraps of wool, using a pair of bent bicycle spokes as needles. An elderly blind man with a lumpy face sat upright on his bed, mangled legs tucked carefully under him and *salaamed* in the direction of our footsteps. Above him was an old print of Stanley Livingstone tending a sick African boy in the jungle, and I wondered what the old man was thinking, but knew he could not see how nervous I was, conscious of not wanting to breathe in his dreaded bacillus.

Children clustered excitedly round the schoolroom dressed in their best clothes, red shirts for boys and long flowered skirts for girls. Only the dropped arches peeping beneath the folds told of their disease, the pale patches on their innocent faces, the changing of features and thickening of young limbs, the scaly skin on juvenile bodies. But eyes were bright and smiles cheerful and my courage returned.

We passed on to the *village*, where the unwanted patients spent their lives. It reminded me of the film *Ben Hur* starring Charlton Heston, when his mother and sister became infected with leprosy and were ostracised into a deep cave. At Bapatla each inmate had a tiny room, a bed and a regular supply of cooked food. They nervously clustered together, feeling unclean but we *salaamed,* looked into their rooms, smiled and gradually they relaxed. A fair skinned man in a clean white dhoti joined hands in *namaste* and, in beautiful English, said, "Good morning, how kind of you to come and visit us here." He was the abandoned son of a prominent government official now living with outcasts from the beggar villages. He smiled as he lifted his stumps in respect, and indicated his little blackened room saying "Home Sweet Home" in cheerful tones. An older inmate, much mutilated, stood with the backdrop of a tattered dhoti drying on a line, and sang with a beautiful voice, his eyes lighting with pleasure. Singing, music and percussion was an important part of life in this Salvation Army leprosarium. Another, with no hands at all, demonstrated how he drew water from the well, looping the rope over his arms and criss-crossing it until the bucket reached the top and was swung, on thin tendons straining under dried skin, without spilling a drop.

Back Row left – Mangala Changappa, 3rd right Natalie
Front Row centre Captains Mahari Campbell and Edna Rowley

It was tiring walking through the hot sand and, after three hours, we went back through the cashew trees to the little bungalows, shared a simple lunch and discussed books and music and a life different from this one. But it was difficult to avoid the subject of the leprosy patients, and of my feeling for these two British women who spent endless hours caring for them with no thought of contagion or self pity. They said my visit provided a tremendous boost for the morale of their patients, as so few people had any interest in them. The visit for me opened a new door of understanding and insight into an entirely different life, and made me feel acute shame. "I'll be back to help you," I said as they waved me goodbye.

When Mike got home late that evening he looked at me searchingly, "Have you been?" he asked abruptly.

"Yes," I said.

"Oh. Have you had a bath?"

"Yes," I said.

After telling him about my day, he was more sympathetic and I was able to visit once a week, but the Captains thought it unwise for me to work with the patients, so I made hundreds of dressings of cut gauze and cotton wool which, when hung on the line in the blistering sun, fluffed up with a snowy softness. As soon as Mangala Changappa's two children started full time school, she came with me. She was sensible and supportive and, between us, we organised an ILTD Ladies Association, and dragged the shy wives out of their kitchens encouraging them to do handwork. Some were talented and we had a sociable time, finally having a sale of work and donating all the proceeds to the leprosarium. Sometime later the hospital planned an *Open Day* and sent 50 invitations to people in the local community preparing lots of eats and hiring a tea urn from a canteen in town. The only people who turned up were Mike and I. Edna was in tears and the stigma of leprosy lay heavy above us that day.

Mike was appointed British High Commission representative in Andhra Pradesh, and had been sent a list of addresses of various poverty stricken missionaries and Anglo-Indians with British passports. One of these was a retired Salvation Army Brigadier, Hilda Plummer, living in Bapatla in a mud house with a palmyra leaf roof. She came from Nottingham and joined the Army as a young girl and, in 1927, worked as a nurse in a 700 patient leprosarium in Kerala. There she handled the most damaged and infected cases, it was stern stuff and she lost all fear of the disease and devoted herself to patients for 52 years. Hilda adopted an orphan Telugu girl, who later married and produced three daughters, so she settled in Bapatla and set up a mini-clinic on her veranda, where she delivered babies of the beggar women from the Untouchables Village. She lived a simple life dealing with her patients, bathing babies and chatting with her neighbours. She listened to her radio, read old books, drew water from the well and cooked rice and vegetables on her kerosene stove. It was always enjoyable to visit and I took bunches of grapes in season, and the village children shouted d*raksha auntie* (grape auntie) as they ran to greet me with their big smiles.

Level crossing at Chirala

In Chirala the factory was running at full tilt and we continued to have assorted visitors despite the heat. One was a Mr Postlethwaite from Alliance Insurance in Madras, who came to inspect fire appliances. All the relevant staff were alerted and each piece of equipment was examined beforehand. Mr Postlethwaite decided there should be a practice alarm on Shed No 69, so Mike sent a *peon* (messenger) on a bike to sound the hooter. Off he went at great speed, got to the correct area but forgot the number of the shed and pedalled all the way back to find out which it was. By that time the worker who was supposed to start the hooter had disappeared, the fire engine driver had gone for tiffin and there was no water in the hydrant. Mike was totally mortified as he had organised everything beforehand and it all went very wrong. Mr Postlethwaite was not amused, but more tolerant by the time the rest of the factory was successfully inspected, and he had come to our house and been liberally wined, dined before we saw him onto the Circars express to return to Madras.

Our accident boys, Mark and William, came to stay once they were fit enough to travel and we met them at the station. Two cheerful faces, sporting bushy beards, peered from the smeary third class windows and out they hopped covered in smuts and full of hugs. William was in a neck brace and Mark plastered from hip to toe and on crutches. Mariamma was pleased to have some life in the house and cooked up lots of meals, and we all had a very social time with trips to Guntur and a couple of weekends on the beach. They were such funny boys, full of jokes, awful songs and rhymes and cheered the whole community up. As well they repaired and cleaned all our music making equipment improving our sound quality enormously. It was a fun visit and they have remained close family friends, and are forever grateful to that worried little boy who alerted us to their accident in Nellore. A couple of years later William returned from New Zealand and brought his bride, Alison to meet us.

ILTD Chirala Factory Staff – Mike centre 2nd row

In contrast, one lunchtime Mike brought home two travellers who were outside the factory gates, having travelled on the top of a tobacco lorry through the night planning to hitch to Calcutta 1,500 miles north. They were filthy, smelly and dull witted probably due to marijuana. She was an American anthropologist and he a Parisian design engineer. They had lived in an ashram in Madras State and meditated until reaching their present impoverished lethargic state. Mariamma quickly made parathas and tomato salad to boost the lunch already prepared, and they sipped water and ate slowly. I was determined not to invite them to stay fearing they may be with us for weeks, but offered the use of the bathroom, and both took advantage of a good scrub and hair wash before putting on their dirty clothes. He dug a splinter out of his foot with my darning needle and she picked her teeth with the same needle and, at last, they left, "Merci, it's been nice meeting you, au revoir," kicking the dust with their sore feet, heaving up raggy rucksacks and a guitar, they wandered down the drive holding hands without looking back. Why we took them in I do not know. Kindness? Moral conscience? These young people were travelling aimlessly in a poverty stricken country, begging from beggars. On another occasion two Peace Corps boys turned up, and we arranged that they stay at the beach as it was a quiet time. They were so grateful they sent us a note via the water lorry and invited us down for dinner. A few months later a Dutch couple, Ëno and Sacha Berentsen, cycling round India turned up on their lightweight bikes. She was an air hostess and he an economist and were good company, having completed 3,000 miles with plans to go onwards to Malaya, Indonesia and Australia. How they survived and looked so well on street food and staying in government rest houses is a miracle.

Just before the end of term we received our first invitation from the Deputy British High Commission in Madras to the Queen's Birthday. But what to wear? Feeling less than confident with my appearance, in the end I settled on a black pin tucked top, a long black and white skirt and, of all things, false eyelashes, I must have looked like Minnie Mouse with my home-made clothes and hand-cut hair. Mike was more appropriately dressed in a dark suit, pink shirt and flowery tie. We recognised only one of the 500 guests and felt like country bumpkins.

Mike returned from Madras to Chirala and I travelled onwards to Mysore to catch up with Zöe after a year, it was fun to chat and share news and enjoy two parties. The Windus marriage had been on the wobble for a long time, which was not surprising as they had been moved to Shimoga and were more isolated. Vera, who was a sturdy girl and a good mother, tried hard but she needed other women, fun and bright lights, and was constantly staying with the Bedi family in Mysore. Things got very strained and she went off to Bombay to be a model. Mike Windus was in Mysore and we travelled to Ooty together to collect our children. A big bloke, he was totally broken, and I found it devastating when he cried copiously on my shoulder, beside himself with anguish. Afterwards he resigned and they all went home, but the damage had been done.

The Parents Day performance at Hebron was lovely to watch. Andrea and David were in a sweet little play called Mumps, all in pyjamas with pink padded cheeks with a sick teddy. Susina acted a big part in her class play and was the shoemaker's wife, and Simon solemnly recited poetry. What joy to hug and cuddle them, and take them home for a short, month long holiday. It was blistering and our train journey was almost unbearable. Mike met us at Chirala station and, as we crossed the railway line, Andrea said "Daddy looks different." He did, we had spent weeks without power, the season was in full swing and he was working all hours. He had also been nipped by the Changappa's Pomeranian which had not been injected for rabies. The doctor prescribed a course of seven injections in the stomach, these were debilitating and each injection reminded the last sore lump to swell up again.

The holidays went in a flash and we were all sleeping in one room, hot and cramped. The children soon acclimatised and were overjoyed to be with their old friends the Arulappans, going around in a great gang and eating their respective mothers out of house and home. We spent days at the beach, enjoyed evening parties and little shows. At the end of the holiday it was 112°F (44°C) when we left on a torrid Sunday night. The train was packed and stifling, Susina became unwell, and the journey was difficult. On arrival at Hebron we realised it was mumps and she went straight into the sickroom. It was dreadful leaving her alone, just the worst thing, but I had reservations to get back. How can you tear yourself in half? I did not seem to be fulfilling any of my roles, but just struggling to survive, failing as a wife due to the appalling conditions of our work situation, and certainly a sub-standard mother, never there when needed and always departing in a crisis.

Susina wrote in June: *I am going out of the sick room on Sunday. Miss Neuendorf lent us a record player and a few records, which was kind of her. Have you had some rain yet down in Chirala. We have had a little rain here up in the hills. Fiona Duff has had mumps so she comes to see me nearly every meal. I am reading lots of books here in the sick room love Susina.*

Briefly from Andrea: *I won in the sports I came third I have the card. I sleep next to Lynne* and David: *We saw a monkey with a chopped of tail. We painted at the dorm. I pained a little clown. We had tea on the lawn on Sunday. We had Sunday school in the forest.* Simon's talent for writing was fast developing: *Thank you for your nice letter. We made some nice creepy crawlys and we have put them on the wall and maybe we will make an insect village. But I don't think we will because there is not enough space. On Saturday we went swimming and I swam the length for my first time. We have got our loccers painted. On Thursday it was sports and I was in the sack race and running race. When it was the sack race it started to rain and we had to go hopping through the rain. We had staff race, babys race, ladies race, mens race and servants and the Lights won. Miss Shrag has come back to Hebron to teach on Sunday we had Sunday school in the woods and after that we played and I made a tent with peter and David. On Saturday we found 4 marble pouches. On Saturday morning there was a littel fire. But it was put out quikly. I am going to write my bug stoie now. My storie ...... One bright morning I went for a walk in the woods. And I met a funny little insect that ran across the road. I said Stop! Stop! Stop! so the insect stoped. He looked at me and said. Who are you? I said I am Simon will you come home with me. He said yes. Love from SIMON.*

Chapter 23 – Telangana Riots

The closeness in the house made me feel as if my whole body was encased in one of those dome like dryers at the hairdressers. Outside it was a furnace that swelled up in wave after wave with no remission, and my letters home focused on My Boredom and how the house was a shell with echoes of children. Mike was no company, stressed, overworked and all he wanted in the late evening was his dinner, his bath and his bed.

The airwaves improved and, with much fiddling, BBC World came through more clearly. I listened avidly to the stock market, how to breed Fresians, population explosion and football results. By the Hindu stars, rain should have fallen, but the wind still came from the land and there was a hell of a lot of Indian heat blowing our way and everything was as dry as dust. Desperate for books I was reading anything by anyone including Edna O'Brien, Malcolm Muggeridge and Mills and Boon.

Bonnie

Mike was due to attend a productivity course in Hyderabad, and was given permission to take me. By now we were sleeping on the veranda and disturbed all night by roaring trains, early dawns and cawing crows and the prospect of going *anywhere* was exciting. Bonnie was taken from her shed, and we travelled, via the Nagarjunasagar Dam, 200 miles on one of the loneliest, barest and most arid roads we had ever encountered in India, and Bonnie sailed along. We passed only eight lorries, four buses and six cars during the whole day. It was surreal and scary and, had we broken down, we would have run out of water and there were very few petrol stations. It was like a trip across the outer reaches of the Sinai desert, with ghastly flat landscape scattered with scraggy scrub and hot rough rocks, interspersed occasionally with herds of thin thirsty goats tended by gypsy tribes known as Lombardis. The women were filthy but exotically dressed in bright coloured skirts and tops beautifully embroidered with mirror work, their arms covered in ivory bangles, their matted hair weighed down with large silver ornaments. We passed over the huge and famous dam, a massive hydro-electric project with a large lake disappearing into nowhere surrounded by barren treeless hills. The water level was very low due to the long hot summer.

We stayed with Alan & Barbara for a couple of nights. Alan had been transferred to Vazir Sultan Tobacco Company, another BAT company separate from ILTD. It had none of the hard graft of the South India Leaf Area. Before she married, Barbara was with the American Foreign Service, so her first two postings to Guntur and Hyderabad were demanding.

We moved into a quaint almost Victorian hotel called the Rock Castle which was dusty and homey. The building was perched on rocks with a fantastic view of the twin cities of Hyderabad and Secunderabad. We occupied half a cottage with a veranda, sitting room, bedroom and bathroom all for very few rupees. Social life was far more than expected and my home-made clothes were inadequate, even Mike said, "We must do something about your clothes." I nearly fell over, I looked like a rag bag. Barbara, always honest, remarked that *you are the least best dressed woman I know,* which made my heart tumble, but it was obviously true. However we were having a very jolly time with meals out, films to see, we couldn't have come at a better time, but my depression was deep and did not go away that easily.

Barbara Rands and Natalie in Hyderabad

We shared precious time together and went sightseeing, Hyderabad was fascinating with ancient bazaars full of veiled women whispering around in black clothes, varnished toenails peeping beneath their burkas. The bangle bazaar was like entering fairyland; strings of glass bangles tinkled and shimmered, their frailty was their charm and they came in all sizes from newborn baby to that of a large grandmamma, in every imaginable colour, striped with gold, silver, rainbows and glitter. Early one Saturday, whilst it was still cool, we motored up to the massive Golconda Fort built on a granite hill in the 12th century surrounded by overpowering crenellated ramparts. The citadel was protected by massive gates covered in pointed iron spikes, designed to deter elephants from battering them down, wars in those days were not to be taken lightly. We explored as much as we could before it became too hot, and climbed to the Durbar Hall at the top of the hill with wide rocky views.

The Bouchers who were with ILTD and VST were retiring after 26 years and we saw them off at the airport. We were the only white faces in the milling crowds, there were now nine remaining expatriates in both ITC and ILTD and we felt like the last green bottles hanging on the wall.

Simon wrote: *Are you glad that you are having some rain instead of sitting down in Chirala reading newspapers. I have got a very wiggly tooth. In the dorm we were pileing three stools on top of a loker and we got a hokey stick and pulled the bottem stool and they came tumbling dow with a Bang! Crash! Boom!. I am longing for August to come because then I'd be longing for England. On Saturday we had a party and the boys wore pirete hats and the girls wore clowns with fishs in front. And I gave Miss Jones a bottle of glue. We had tuns of scrumy food we had buns, biscuts, cheese and we had crayons for a present and we had jelly and a ship cake witch was best of all. We played oranges and lemons and runnel ball and all sorts of games and I won four marbles and in another game I won some others. On Sunday we saw a drunkedn man and a car came took him away. In the mornings it is so cold and the afternoons its so hot. Now I have got another wiggly tooth.*

Simon and David were settled at Hebron but we planned to move them to the senior school, Lushington Hall, up the mountain in Ooty, situated on the side of a well wooded hill, great for making dinky toy tracks, overlooking the really beautiful Botanical gardens which sported fierce signs, *Plucking of Flowers Prohibited.*

We drove back from Hyderabad, packed up and soon departed on leave. The children flew by Indian Airlines with a school party and we met them in Madras. They were so excited and all in good spirits. We boarded Swissair to Geneva where we stayed two nights in a hotel. The best thing for the kids were the little bars of chocolate under each pillow and, the first morning we were totally mesmerised by a shiny vehicle washing and scrubbing the street with water and suds. The weather was crisp and fresh, the Alps towered above us, the Lake glistened in the sunshine and we gulped in great mouthfuls of fresh air.

Enjoying a picnic in Suffolk

Leave was hectic with too many visitors and the massive task of installing central heating into our medieval house with its maze of wooden floorboards and beams. Having placed the children into the local school, I stayed behind to get the job finished and Mike returned to Madras in November to find himself in the midst of Telangana riots, which had disrupted the whole state. Separatists wanted to keep their piece of Andhra Pradesh nearer to Hyderabad, and their own language, a mixture of Urdu and Telugu. We lived in the coastal area, once part of the Madras Presidency of British India. The trouble went on for months and a great deal of damage was done. There were no communications and Mike arrived in Madras to discover that the traffic clerk at Guntur had followed his instructions made in August, and he was *still* booked on the train to Chirala, though all had been cancelled for weeks and most of the stations en route wrecked. Orders were orders and it was not up to the clerk to question them. Exhausted after his flight Mike hired a taxi and endured an awful journey with detours as so many bridges were wrecked. In Chirala the railway station and the post office were burnt down, much of the town was damaged and a large tanker of diesel was flamed outside the factory gates. The trouble continued right through the Christmas holidays.

In Woodbridge the central heating took so long to install and test that we did not get back to India until 20th December. It was an exhausting scramble to pack up and lock our belongings in a room on the third floor and prepare the house for tenants. Also to cope with four children who were occupied with end of term jollifications including nativity plays, carol services, Father Christmas, never mind Christmas shopping. Many years before we had purchased two lightweight expanding suitcases from Marks and Spencers. After countless journeys they were battered, but they held so much stuff that we were reluctant to get rid of them. Before we came on leave we packed them as full as possible and sent them to the baling department where they were securely stitched in hessian. With forethought we brought a baling needle home and, whilst the kids were sleeping, I sat on the floor like the Tailor of Gloucester with a roll of twine and stitched them up. This was after staying up most of the night before to finish painting the stairway.

Travelling with four children was no joke, luckily Mike's uncle Jim kindly stuffed us in his small car and took us to Heathrow but he had to battle through heavy traffic. He suffered serious road rage and threw both hands in the air, opened the window and shouted at the next car, used his horn to excess or tried to ram the vehicle in front. No wonder his wife was in such a constant state of nervous tension. She gave each child a crispy gingerbread man *to eat on the plane*. Childless, she did not realise that they could not wait that long to start nibbling. They carried their own little bags, and the gingerbread men were already losing limbs and spreading crumbs. Andrea snapped the head off hers and spent ages hunting round the dirty floor to retrieve the Smartie eyes and currant nose. Getting through security and into departure was a mammoth task of stop, start and chasing bits of brittle gingerbread en route. Once there, our Air India was on *Last Call* and we were a long way from the gate. Simon, aged eight, was despatched along the concourse to warn them we were coming. David was busy foraging for the arms of his gingerbread man which fell off under a seat and between someone's feet, as Simon, his flaxen hair flying and his anorak acting like a sail, raced away on his mission. We were still travelling first class which was a relief, but the exhaustion before was not allayed by space and nice food, most of which the children ignored.

Bombay airport was its usual hen house of confusion, crowds, noise and copious spitting. The advantage of our hessian wrapped suitcases was that they slid across the floor pushed by small children, who were really super assisting me as there was absolutely no way I could lift them. Our entire amount of luggage weighed 180 lbs and an aggressive customs man said we should open them, "If so," I retorted "You can close them." Had he opened them he would have found a lot of old clothes, second-hand comics, Surprise Peas, Angel Delights, Tampax, Bovril, Clarke's sandals and M&S underwear. Luckily he let us through but, because we were late, we were not met and missed our onward flight to Hyderabad. There was no Left Luggage so we took everything in a rickety taxi, miles into the city, to the Taj Mahal hotel near the Gateway of India.

We had six hours at this magnificent hotel. Oh! how we could have done with a couple of days luxury and rest. It was another world, one we had not experienced, with a huge swimming pool, arcades of exotic shops and fine dining. The children bathed, got into bed and slept deeply whilst I struggled to keep awake ready to catch the next flight. It was an effort to rouse them and drag our load of luggage back to the airport. The plane to Hyderabad was small, and the one after to Vijayawada even smaller. Mike was there to meet us which was a great relief, and I told him Simon's anorak was lost which annoyed him.

"You are very lucky we did not lose Simon," I said, almost at the end of my tether with exhaustion and worry. Someone shouted from the plane, an air hostess was waving a piece of our hand baggage, and I ran across the tarmac to retrieve it as the plane was revving up for take off to Vishakhapatnam.

Our journey home was marred by more student agitation all along the way, quite frightening, but nothing like as bad as it was a month before. There was no power for days on end and the factory generator packed up under the strain. Going to the bazaar was all road blocks and police questioning, and the children were searched when they went to Pereira School. We were not in any danger, but the Telangana perpetrators and agitators who wanted separation certainly were. Every day something new happened, another strike, more burning of buildings, it was unsettling, very inconvenient and we were beginning to worry about the power supply, which came from the Nagarjunasagar Dam, being taken over by the separatists. Already we had massive power cuts and used kerosene lights, with no fridge or fans and, worse, no music. The trains were not running so how were we going to get to Ooty? Industry was grinding to a halt, labour being laid off. We could not get cooking gas, sugar or flour and there were no postal deliveries. By March 1973 Indira Gandhi intervened and took Andhra State under Union control, obviously for her own political reasons.

Premila aged 4

The first news when we got into Fairways was that Mariamma had given birth to a baby girl that morning, the result of a brief Richard visit nine months previously. So it was a question of getting supper and settling the children before I could visit her in the quarter; the baby was lovely, and both were well, but I sent them to hospital for a couple of days to ensure a quick recovery. We never saw Richard again, but this last daughter has clung to his name and is known as Premila Coleman, she is fair like her father who has never set eyes on her.

It was straight back into Club life and the children's party for 50 to organise. Geetha Kumar and I worked like slaves, it was a pleasure to see all the little ones having such a treat. Our own Christmas was enhanced by presents bought in the UK and Mike purchased locally made bicycles for everyone. In a way it was good to be back, the weather was at its best and there was help in the house.

Despite the heat our children and the Arulappans decided to put on a show in aid of the leprosy hospital. It was an ambitious undertaking and entailed a lot of work and rehearsals. All eight of them ransacked cupboards and drawers hunting for suitable apparel. They found crayons and paper and made invitations and programmes, as well as coronets and crocodile tails. I agreed to make dinner for 36 guests, and we concocted dishes out of what could be purchased in the market. The concert was a huge success with many different acts performed on our front veranda with the aid of a factory spotlight. We cooked popcorn and roasted groundnuts which they wrapped in packages and sold. Six little plays were seriously rehearsed and written into their hand-made programmes. Toy Town Wedding Song was performed by a giggling Susina dressed as a tin soldier, and a giggling Andrea dressed as a bride. They all joined in to recite an AA Milne poem about animals without tails, afterwards performing a noisy Indian war dance covered in crows feathers, war painted with my lipsticks and eye liners. Then there was a Melodrama and a Finale of Everyday Things. The originality and persistence of all eight children was commendable and they donated the cash to the leprosy hospital. Edna and Mahari were chief guests and touched by such hard work and generosity.

On the beach with Monica

Our journey to school was hampered by disruption of trains and my return to Chirala was more difficult as I took nine hours to travel to Mysore by bus (100 miles) before I caught a train to Bangalore. I stayed with Caroline and Fred Foster in their rooms in the Bangalore Club and we went out, with friends, dining and dancing at the Ashoka Hotel. Next day Fred, en route to the races, saw me off at Cantonment station, and helped me into my second class carriage with aplomb. Fred was tall and elegant, aged 54, the perfect gentleman, wearing a beautifully cut fine wool suit in Prince of Wales check with a large pair of binoculars suspended on his shoulder by a pig skin strap. In contrast I wore my tie and dye pant suit, hair in a pony tail, feet in flip flops and was loaded down with dusty bags and bedrolls. Fred respected my travelling style but, as the train chugged out of the station, he raised his trilby and smiled with a *rather you than me* look on his face. The onward journey deteriorated with no car or accommodation in Madras, nor reservation, but I sorted things out and reached home in one piece, absolutely filthy and finished.

Soon after I went to the leprosy hospital to discover that Mahari had rolled over in a Bedford van seriously damaging her back entailing several months on her stomach in hospital. Edna was away in Kashmir so I offered to take the terrier puppy, Haggis, home with me. One Sunday we gave a big curry party at the beach and took her with us. Everyone liked the little dog who showed her appreciation by licking legs and arms vigorously. The Hardings and Martyn came from Guntur and there were other visitors. A couple of days later Haggis's behaviour became strange, she was frantically digging holes in the sand looking for dark places, and was trying to catch her tail. She went off her food and looked odd so I took her to a vet, noted for his treatment of cows and chickens, his clinic was held every day under a tree.

"Worms," he said decisively.

"Not worms," I said, knowing it was something more serious.

The vet examined her, but obviously knew nothing about dogs. He said she was dehydrated and gave her a saline injection. During the day she became worse and that night she died under our bed. We were both suspicious that she may have become rabid, but there was no way of contacting Mahari to find out if Haggis had been injected against rabies. I went to see the vet.

"Where's the dog?" he asked peering into the back of the car.

"The dog is dead," I said, "Do you think it died from rabies?"

"Not rabies," he said stubbornly, "Not possible Madam." Unconvinced, I asked him if he kept veterinary books at home. He did, and we went to his small house in a narrow street where, on a dusty shelf, were several volumes. I looked up rabies and went through all the symptoms and immediately recognised that Haggis definitely died from *furious rabies,* there was no doubt. The vet told me that it was impossible to absolutely confirm the diagnosis unless the dog's brain was examined, and advised me to go to the agricultural college about five miles away. The people at the college thought I was mad, a frantic Englishwoman requesting for someone to cut off her dog's head. They gave me that usual *she doesn't know anything about life in India* look, and said, "We have no instruments Madam, you will have to go to Hyderabad," and politely showed me out of the building.

Mike and I were convinced we should all have anti-rabies jabs and Dr Sadananda Rao was consulted, "Not possible here," he said, "But if the dog has been licking and you have open sores or mosquito bites, the rabies will penetrate through the skin." This was becoming horrific as so many people were with us at the beach. The doctor said the nearest place which supplied the vaccine was the Pasteur Institute in Coonoor, "I will send runner soonest," he said blandly.

"Coonoor?" I almost shrieked, "That's three days away."

He waggled his head, "You can wait eight days before you are in danger of infection," he said with no expression, "I will send the runner. Tell your friends, they will all have to have 10 x 5cc injections in the stomach."

"Ten!" We were unlikely to have any friends after spreading that news. Mike made the calls from the factory and was greeted by horrified reactions but acquiescence, but complete disbelief by Christopher Harding who insisted that we arrange to have the dog's head removed and the brain examined. Mike offered to send him the dead, now putrefying dog, and stressed that there was absolutely no doubt that the dog was suffering rabies when it died, and quietly said goodbye, "See you when we get the vaccine," and put the phone down. Martyn got the wind up about using local vaccine and had his own supply flown out from London.

The vaccine arrived and was taken to Guntur for the initial jabs and we all met at jolly Martyn's for gin lime sodas and rabies injections, prostrating ourselves on his bed in turn whilst the doctor injected our stomachs. Apart from Christopher, we all decided it was time to laugh and make the best of it. The following days, with one day of no injections in the middle, were very painful, uncomfortable and unpleasant, and it took several weeks to get rid of the soreness.

Mahari recovered and was back at the leprosarium, so I telephoned her with the bad news. Her first reaction was, "Did you take a photograph?"

Chapter 24 – Acree House

There were rumblings in the company and several transfers. Mike was promoted to Factory Manager and we moved into Acree House, named after some long lost director. It was not as sunny and airy as Fairways, but had the advantage of a large swimming pool shaded by a beautiful cerise and white Mary Palmer bougainvillea, and also a separate guest quarter with two bedrooms and a kitchen. The best perk was a company car and driver for the first time since we left Hassan. Subba Rao, the company bearer, came with the job and the children referred to him as *your friend* because he was so irritating. His method of dusting, as with most bearers, was to hold the duster by the corner and flap and he managed to flap most of the ornaments into small pieces, or at least knock them over so they were chipped.

Acree House

We were sad to leave our Fairways garden having nurtured it from nothing, but removed the bamboo tree and trundled it down the road on a wooden cart, and planted it in a big hole full of water. After some months it recovered and continued to give pleasure until we left. The new garden was a challenge and the new job entailed a great deal of entertaining, as well as organising and socialising in the club. We dealt with export customers from all over the globe, and coped with all manner of diets and food fads. Many of the more orthodox Indians were finicky and suspicious they were being offered something that was forbidden or unpalatable. The Japanese, were terrified of being served *dynamite,* and either picked at grains of rice, or brought their own packets of noodles and seaweed. Russians were bolder, they swigged Scotch by the gallon and swallowed whole hard boiled eggs by the dozen.

We welcomed a six foot tall Nigerian, Bashiru Tukur, a Muslim from Zaria, to stay for more than a week, so we had to *halal* (cut the throats) of live chickens from the market, avoid all pork and he disliked dairy produce. He was so homesick he could hardly speak, he was a handsome warrior, but with a soft heart and no interest in tobacco, he just wanted to get back home. After he left us he travelled on to Rajahmundry and stayed at the Delta Club. There was no electricity and he nearly passed out with the heat. He wrote, *The servants here except one do not understand any English at all. The one who does understand, does so for only 10% of what I say. So if I want to say things I have to say them in ten different ways! Natalie, I find it very difficult to cry even at the death of some people, but that night I sat at the club and started to picture my wife and children and I could not stop weeping. When I was with you 12 days passed like three and I did not want to leave you both. Honestly I was at home, but it's good I've left Chirala to see real Indian conditions. Due to drinking unboiled water here I have lost the two kilograms I gained whilst staying with you!*

Three BAT London directors were expected, it was spit and polish time, all over the place, and lots of lavish catering to organise, it was a farce of illuminated trees, food brought in from Madras, vegetables from Ooty and hired cooks from the cities. Our job was to lay on a dinner for 80 at the beach, ten miles away with a bevy of untrained servants, worse was that we were threatened with an All Andhra electricity strike. A couple of days before the party I went to the market and purchased 20 pathetic ill and featherless chickens, no doubt crawling with fleas with their little beaks open, gasping for water. Choosing the fattest was difficult, none came into that category, they were all underfed and tough, bundled into a basket. stitched over with hessian and dumped into the boot of the hot car. Whoever was handy, faced the grisly task of dismembering them, the servants never flicked an eyelid at this performance, it was all part of life, and they enjoyed all the bits like claws, innards and skin. We made the chickens into curry, and two huge bekti fish were transformed into what was elegantly known as *fish fry.* Did we have bread for breadcrumbs at the time? We were all so used to shortages and lack of ingredients that the secrets of the kitchen were never divulged.

Our directors were in a feisty mood and their behaviour did not go down well with our orthodox Indian management. There was little politeness, more an arrogance to show them who was boss, causing great offence. As the last expatriates in an Indian company, they made no enquiries about our welfare or that of our children, or how we were coping with the climate or lack of normal facilities. It was not their business.

Shortly before the party began Mike came home with a bundle of directors' dirty clothes, "Can you get these washed by eight in the morning," he asked hurrying into his bath.

"Eight?" I almost screamed with fury, "This is not a Chinese laundry." Nevertheless *kow-towing* in my obedient wifely way, I dragged out the primitive washing machine, threw in all their sweaty shirts, underpants and smelly socks and tossed them into the bath for one of the boys to rinse and hang out. I should have been loading cooked food into the car, curling my hair and putting in my earrings. I persuaded a bevy of hangers-on to take the washing and somehow dry it overnight, did they run up and down waving pants in the breeze and squashing socks between their warm thighs? Everything was dry and ironed in the morning, and that's the magic of living in a place where your staff really do try and help when the chips are down.

The party was a huge success, mainly because there were ample supplies of Scotch and the food was good. The guests were polite and in a pleasant mood, there was a fresh sea breeze and Vadarevu looked quite magical with the casuarina trees twinkling with coloured lights. Next day we waved them off as they travelled onwards to Hyderabad and then to Calcutta with entertainment all the way. We were not surprised to hear several weeks later, that the youngest of the three died of a heart attack shortly after returning home. The pace they travelled, the partying and no doubt the stress was quite phenomenal.

A teacher brought the children on the Nilgiri Express to Madras and I met them at the station. I so looked forward to seeing them all but, as they got older, their need for individual attention was demanding, they were argumentative and crying out for more of my time. The holidays were short, yet all the sewing and sorting piled up so they went back as tidy as possible. Susina came home with lumps of chewing gum in her hair, the boys wanted to do outrageous things like climb high trees or jump over the railway line, and Andrea just wanted to sit on top of me the whole time. The reason for this spirited restlessness was the absence of the Arulappan children who had moved to Bangalore for their education. I coped as much as possible, but as a very part-time mother it was difficult to fill the needs of children who were craving for a hands-on, always there, always knowing what they wanted, mother. Mike was too busy at work to become involved, although in his way, he tried

Taken at a photographic studio in Ooty 1973
Andrea 7, Simon 9, Susina 11 and David 7

Two bad things happened. First David bashed his face on the handlebars of his bike and soon afterwards was bitten by a stray dog and given seven rabies injections in his stomach. Second, Simon took Bujie on the metal carrier of his bike, and Bujie's little ankle was mangled in the spokes. The intense screaming was reminiscent of injury by fire, and I ran down the road in fear. Bujie was in agony and his ankle incredibly mutilated, Simon was absolutely beside himself with mortification. Somehow we got home, the phone for once worked, Mike was in his office and sent the car so we could go to hospital. Bujie was sobbing and frightened and the nurses shouted at him. That was their way, it was cure by fear rather than compassion. He was such a good little boy and I held his hand and stroked his forehead, talking quietly, while Dr Sadananda Rao, already acclaimed as a first class embroiderer, stitched him up. "Very severe," was his only comment. The nurses wrapped his foot and ankle in mounds of dressings and bandages, "Baby not crying," they said to me, so surprised, "Our babies always cry too much in hospital," so I left them to work it out *why,* knowing that this single experience of kindness would not budge their ingrained training. Bujie stayed in the house on a mat on the freshly washed floor. The weather was hot and it was not good that the little foot may be festering under the bandages, although I was instructed to *leave dressing alone please, do not tamper, come back in one week please.* After a few days the thick bandage was stained and there was an unpleasant smell, so we removed it and realised that Bujie had gangrene, his foot was literally rotting and the stitches almost broken away from the skin. My American Dr Spock bible had no section on baby gangrene, but common sense told me to leave the wound unwrapped covered in a dry dressing after swabbing it with diluted Dettol. The Doctor showed no surprise, "Healing well now," he said drily, pushing his spectacles up his nose and wiping sweat off his forehead. Bujie recovered and full movement returned to the complicated damaged construction of his little ankle.

Soon it was time to get the bedrolls out and again plan our journey. Simon had come home with a very good report from Lushington but he absolutely hated going back. Gone was the little blonde nonchalant boy who marched bravely into school, at nine he was miserable and expressed all the dreadful things that were going to happen to him, and he stood clinging to me with silent tears rolling down his cheeks. The others were less upset, but his misery was infectious and it was heartbreaking leaving all of them in their dorms, and making the lonely journey back to Chirala.

One bright spot was the arrival of Bulbul and Benji Benjamin in Madras. Benji was a friend of Eric Chaube, and we met him years earlier whilst we were staying in the Mysore Metropole. He was a sparky little man with a resonant voice and a rather pushy manner. Bulbul was quite different, she was small with a soft voice and sweet face, highly intelligent with a lovely sense of humour. We got along immediately, and always picked up where we left off, we were two very different women from different cultures but with a common bond of interests and a natural spiritual understanding of each other. The most complimentary remark made to me during our 14 years in India was from Bulbul, "You know Natalie, what I like about you is that you are not a Memsahib."

They had three dear little girls, with eyes as black as buttons, and lovely welcoming smiling faces. Preet, the eldest, was giggly and thoughtful, Mita in the middle was a jack-in-the-box and Nayantara, the little one, was a cute baby in a high chair gurgling away. They rented an upstairs apartment in a lofty colonial house on a tree lined street, and it was there that we were welcomed to refresh ourselves on our tedious journeys and to spend wonderful days together.

Youth Times cover

The Circars booking system failed and there was no berth for the eight hour journey, instead I sat on a hard seat marked *Attendant*. In the middle of the night at Nellore station, the guard unexpectedly shouted at me to move to another carriage. The old steam trains were high off the tracks and it was difficult to climb up and down in a hurry. A coolie ran behind with my bag on his head and bedroll under his arm, but the train was already moving as I tried to jump on to the steps but, instead, fell in a heap on to the platform. By this time a few people were awake watching this wretched English woman trying to get on the train, and one of them pulled the communication cord. The train squealed to a stop and I was pushed and hauled aboard with my luggage thrown in behind, all the time trying to give the coolie his well earned tip. Mike met me at Chirala at 5am, took me home and I slept for hours.

Settling back into my *no children* mode, I was pleased to have been commissioned by an Indian publication *Youth Times* to write on *Violence and Unrest in Village Youth.* Although a complete novice I was not going to let this chance pass me by, so invited two lads from a nearby village to come and talk. We sat on the veranda and drank chilled orange fizz, with colourful birds whizzing and whistling amongst the trees. The boys were receptive, spoke quite good English and were most illuminating. They explained thoroughly how rampant the feudal system was and how villagers were completely over-ruled by the rich landowners. Later we met an Indian doctor who worked on a nutrition project for Oxfam and he confirmed what the boys said about the attitude of the people, fear, ignorance and way of life. The article was a challenge for me, accepted and paid for.

Christmas at the Ooty Club

Christmas was spent in Ooty and Mariamma, with baby Premila, travelled by train to help us there, it was a bit of an ordeal for her, but also a change of scenery. We provided her with blankets, jumpers and shawls and found her a nice warm space in the house to sleep, rather than sleep in comfortless cold quarters. The children were invited to a wonderful Christmas party at the Ooty Club with a rather posh British Santa Claus called Nigel, who arrived and departed in Bonnie. The tea was sumptuous, the games were fun and a far cry from our simple celebrations at Chirala. We spent New Year's Eve with the Hughes in Coorg and afterwards went on to the Byerly Stud to stay with the Fosters. The Stud always reminded us of the Weald of Kent and their land was accessed along the ruttiest of lanes which became almost impassable in the monsoon. By the time we reached their bungalow, rounding the paddock rails and watching the brown foals gambolling in the grass, it was incongruous to be met by tiny Shelagh, oh so English, wearing a riding hat and jodhpurs greeting us, "Oh my dears, what a journey you must have experienced, come in and have a cup of tea," and turning towards the house she bellowed at the top of her voice, "Mary, or Gopal or Kasim, which ever poor soul was in her comfortless kitchen, "*Chai!*

Chai! Jaldi, jaldi!" (tea, tea, quickly). Despite living in Mysore State for years, Shelagh never learned Kanarese, and all her orders were offered in colonial Hindi which her staff were sensible enough to learn as quickly as possible. As their guest quarters were small the children were put up in a horse box, and rolled giggling down the ramp each morning hair full of straw and sleeping bags down to their knees.

Fred and Shelagh Foster at Byerly

One day, with Fred, we went to Manzarabad Fort, an Indian treasure several kilometres west of Saklaspur, and built by the French in league with Tipu Sultan in 1792. It was a small intimate fort, shaped like a star and well set on the top of a hill 3240 feet above sea level, with a steep climb to reach it. We all loved Manzarabad, it was magic, it was empty and isolated, it resonated with history, battles, war cries and howls. All we met were a bunch of milky cows, feeding on the uncut grass and mooing gently. The views were stupendous and the sunset was the most magical of experiences. Afterwards we drove through the Saklaspur bazaar and stopped at the old fashioned coffee planters' club for a cold beer and a plate of salty groundnuts. The club veranda was our favourite beer sipping place as it provided several planters' chairs made from teak frames and rattan seating. These were a real Rajish remnant, as the sahib could recline on his lounger and pull out two wooden rests at knee level, part his legs and prop them up to relax. Not a good idea in baggy shorts, but the ultimate in decadence as the first of the cool evening breezes wafted in from the hills, and the chitter chatter of the bazaar infiltrated from the town.

We were so strapped for cash to pay the school fees that we decided to sell Bonnie. It was a dreadful decision. We left her at the Bangalore Club, forlorn but proud, and then Fred decided to buy her and sent the money straight up to the schools in the hills. The company messed up our train reservations so we travelled overnight to Madras on an extremely dangerous *luxury* bus, loud with raucous music and racing along in a wild fashion for over ten hours, with the odd disgusting stop for public toilets and street food. We caught a day train to Chirala and travelled third which was a revelation for Mike, "This is not bad," he said lolling back in an almost empty carriage and I bit my lips as this was his maiden second class journey. There were no refreshments along the way except spurious cooled water in big drums on the platforms, plus the odd smeary glass of hot milky coffee. No one met us at Chirala station, there were no rickshaws and we sat like poor relations until someone was raised at the factory and came to collect us.

Chapter 25 – Catering for all Tastes

It was only mid-January but the season was in full swing, the factory operating three shifts and Mike working all hours. The Acree House job was full-time and we wanted to put a sign on the drive *Wheatley Hotel - Catering For All Tastes.* The income tax authorities had made an error and Mike was pressured into paying off a large debt over six months, so he put me on a minimal allowance adding to the frustration of being an unpaid company cook and hostess. School bills loomed each term, and the sale of Bonnie, fortunately to the Fosters, only temporarily allayed what seemed to be a permanent state of poverty.

Bullock carts creaked along the roads loaded with harvest, it was *Pongal* and the annual cricket match between Chirala, Bangalore and Hyderabad. We organised the usual dinner and dance for 100 people and hired a more *with it* band from Madras. Soon after we held a dinner at Acree House for 40 people. Our kitchen was like a factory and, on such occasions, Papaiah the company cook at Vadarevu, came to help. He was a talented Telugu but our common language was stretched to the full. On party days he shuffled in wearing baggy khaki shorts, a sloppy shirt, his long grey hair swept around his head. He came early and, as the day progressed, the floor became a sea of onion and garlic skins, ginger shavings, potato peelings, chilli seeds, mutton bones and all the débris of food preparation. Nothing was swept away until the dishes were made.

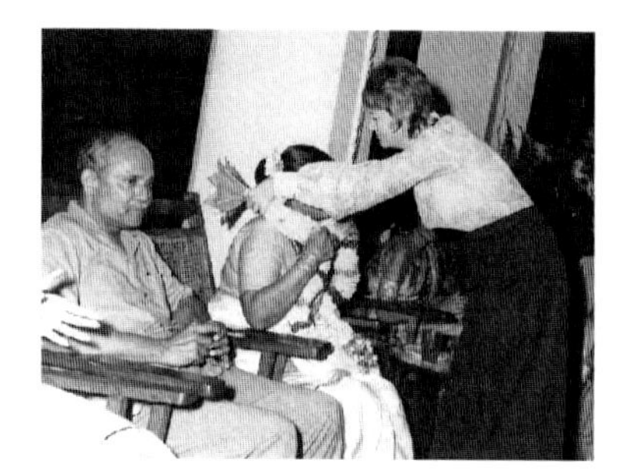

Chirala Staff Association Party – 1973 with Mr Ramananda Rao – Personnel Director

His speciality was *gulab jamuns*, a particularly gooey sweetmeat described to me by Bitty Malik as *fried condensed milk balls.* And they were. *Seers* (approx 2 pints) and *seers* of buffalo milk were poured into a large *dekshie* and Papaiah stood for what seemed hours stirring and condensing the milk. When it reached a certain thickness he added a small quantity of *maidah* (flour) and mixed it rapidly until he could make small balls, which he rolled quickly in the palms of his greased hands, dunked them into boiling oil and fried golden brown. The final stage was to soak them in thick sugar syrup for several hours. They were sickly with a particular deliciousness.

Life was all visitors and we had to get the children ready for school again, as well as preparing Susina and Simon to sit their entrance exams for Norfolk schools. One Sunday, which was never a day off, there were two house guests staying in our guest house, Sunset Cottage, and five people at the beach including an Indian Air Force Air Vice Marshal and a Salvation Army

Colonel and Commissioner with accompanying wives. They all needed looking after so we went up and down to Vadarevu and, in the evening, was the AGM of the ILTD Staff Association with Mrs M T Wheatley presenting the prizes. No one had asked me but I did.

As the children became older they got far more upset about returning to school. It was gruelling coping with their misery and knowing that what they felt was true, it wasn't made up. We reached Madras and it was 92°F (33°C), and when we arrived in the hills after a night on the train and a three hour jeep journey from Coimbatore, it was a freezing 30°F (-1°C) amongst the tea gardens. We were so late that the girls' unpacking had to be done and their beds made before the boys and I could say our sad goodbyes. Then, in the dark, our driver took us up another 1000 feet to Lushington, "Oh Mummy do I have to?" each one begged pathetically. David, who never cried when going back to school, fought the tears, broke down utterly and wept copiously, Simon was just miserable and shivering.

The kindly Rawlleys were expecting me and we sat up too late, feeling sorry for ourselves with children at boarding school, and talked as the firewood crackled with our feet up on the stone fireplace, sipping Calvados. Next day, bound for Bangalore, the jeep broke down and I thumbed a lift for 200 miles and arrived at the Draytons. Their lives were so different from ours, pleasant and sociable with golf and tennis to break the monotony. Bangalore had a big expatriate society and plenty of friendly Indians who threw parties and planned picnics. They could buy *proper* food, speak a *proper* language and live a *proper* life. It was a hectic visit and we went to a dinner party as soon as I had bathed and changed, three parties the next day, and lunch on the last day plus a mass of shopping. I got back to Chirala to find a brief letter from Simon, *You forgot to put the mango pickle in my case.*

Four days after her accident we received a telegram that Susina had fallen from the Giant Stride and broken her leg, fracturing one bone and cracking another. By the time we got this upsetting news we assumed she was back at school and sent telegrams and letters of comfort. She had a dreadful time and was very scared. At night she was taken to a Norwegian Hospital, 16 miles up and over the hills on winding roads. She was in severe pain and admitted, but no one from school stayed with her, nor did anyone take her to the bathroom or give her a hot drink. She was cold, frightened, alone and only eleven. The leg was set in plaster, someone collected her and she was soon adjusting to walking with crutches where there was hardly any flat area, it was all steps, hills and climbing.

There was a threatened All India rail strike, but I managed to reach the hills to collect the children in March. It was the first time I had seen Susina since her accident and she was still in a heavy plaster. Getting back to Chirala was difficult as the strike was a reality and there were no trains. I had promised to take three Salvation Army children to Nellore, plus our own four, so we formed a party of eight. Instead we were marooned in Ooty for two long weeks with no accommodation and very little cash. I off loaded the Nellore children on the local Salvation Army and we landed up unexpectedly on the Rawlleys for the first two nights, all five of us, and felt like Mary and Joseph finding a stable. As always they understood, though it could not have been easy to have such an invasion. Somehow hot food and beds were found and Nickoo kindly fitted rubber pads to the bottom of Susina's crutches to stop her falling all over the wooden floors. Then we moved into St Margaret's and the weather was rainy with heavy hailstorms. I sent anxious telegrams to Mike but he did not receive them and, in the end, he was so worried he jumped into his company car and drove for 20 hours to rescue us. It was such a relief to see him and, after a night's rest, we all squashed into the car and he drove back again.

It was May and fiendishly hot and Susina had a difficult 600 mile journey. Ambassador cars are fitted with front bench seats leaving no room for a plastered leg and three growing kids in the back. It was a relief to get home but for such a short time, in a week we were waiting for the Circars Express on the dark platform. We boarded to discover there were no berths reserved for us, and only four seats to share with Susina's plaster. Simon said gruffly, "Mummy when can I get away from this man's feet," struggling to find a few inches for himself whilst the grunting farmer propped up his broken toes, the skin on his heels so brittle they clacked against the floor. He snored, and sniffed and yawned and crossed his legs and offending feet time and time again. We thought we were hardened to such journeys, but we were not. After leaving them, my return was no better by van, jeep, train and rickshaw and, once at home whilst looking for something, I opened a cupboard to discover that termites had gobbled through precious photograph albums ruining all the pages. There was a pair of sparrows desperately nesting in the curtains, I called them Nirmal and Susheela and wrote a story about them, later published in England. There were also cockroaches scampering through the store, who were only worthy of death by poison. But there were good things including a garden full of coloured birds, and sitting on our oval veranda felt as if we were in our personal aviary. There were not many trees in the vicinity, but there was a collection of well established ones in our compound, old and dense, so the birds found them a haven in the dry heat.

Acree House garden in cool weather

Mike was able to get away on a trip to the Far East which was good, he desperately needed a break. Wives never accompanied husbands, unless they were very grand, so I stayed in Chirala and pined. He wrote letters which helped and travelled to Bangkok with a man from Calcutta office on a mission to sell Indian prawns, another ITC diversification. He flew to the tobacco areas of Chiang Mai in Thailand and on to Tokyo where he completed a successful sale to the Japanese Monopoly, after which he was taken on a pleasant 200 mile drive through the Japanese countryside, preferable to dining on raw beef in expensive Tokyo eateries. He enjoyed the experience away from the factory and selling his product and, as an aside wrote, *I will have to get better kitted out with some more snappy clothes.* My home-made shirts stitched from cut pieces, bought by weight in the Chirala bazaar, and the Top Tailor trousers from the Pasamuru boulevard were not standing up to the test.

My parents were in a bad way and needed my help but it was impossible to contact them by telephone so, before Mike returned, I had already left for England with Susina and Simon who were successful in passing their entrance exams and due to start new schools in September, and Mike brought the twins home about a month later. Our leave was busy, much of the time taken up by my dear father who was very forgetful, so he stayed with us for a lengthy period to give my mother a break, and he then went into a Home. Susina and Simon started their new schools with some trepidation, she to Runton Hill and he to the prep school of Greshams. The schools shared social events so they saw each other during the term and flew back and forth to India together. BAT had the most wonderful meeting and greeting service for children, compared to other companies who struggled with Universal Aunts or elderly grandparents, our children had their travel arrangements organised and were collected from the railway station and kept safely, if bored stiff, until they were on the plane.

Mike returned to Chirala in November to heavy rains, but he was happier as the planning he had done the year before was paying off. David took the entrance exam to a prep school near Woodbridge and wrote to Chirala, *Dear Daddy I have passed my exam for Brandeston Hall. Now I won't be a coolie. Love from David.* We were delighted as David would go on to Framlingham College where Mike and his two brothers were educated, and we decided to send Andrea to St Felix School in Southwold the following year. I stayed on to see Susina and Simon through their first term at school and then flew back accompanying young Guy Drayton and the twins with 400 lbs of luggage. Susina and Simon followed a day later and we were all chewing our nails until they arrived safely, it was a time of great unrest, hi-jackings and bomb blasts in the Middle East, and we were stuffed into a jumbo jet, unable to land at either Beirut or Tehran. It took us three hours to get through Santa Cruz airport in Bombay and on to a flight to Madras. India Tobacco Company had diversified into paper and hotels and we were able to stay in the Hotel Chola in Madras on our way to Andhra Pradesh, it was five star and boasted an ice rink.

At Acree House Mariamma was on the doorstep with quiet words and gentle smiles, "I am missing you Madams, missing you and children, and Masters." It was such a relief to see her and unfortunate that I went down with dreadful flu' and a crashing head which lasted for six days. The weather was at its best, sunny, breezy, not too hot and all the children were in the pool. The bougainvillea was really beautiful and the view was of cascading blossom with four different shades of bright pink. It was a lovely setting in cool weather, even the garden was sprouting and many plants had survived the drought conditions. We spent a quiet Christmas eating two stringy chickens and a Mrs Peek pudding boiled with the paper still on. Not long after, a crippled old tailor was installed on the veranda with his ancient treadle sewing machine employed to prepare clothes for school. He was paid 25 pence a day with breakfast but did not turn up for three days.

Fever Ma, he said pitifully as he hobbled up the steps, *Very fever, too much please.*

Norfolk and Indian terms did not coincide so it was necessary to make two trips up and down to see the children to the airport in Madras and to the Nilgiri Hills.

Life was exceptionally busy at the factory, and Mike was coping with visitors and making sure the 24-hour operations ran smoothly. The tobacco quality and quantity that year was poor making it more difficult to fulfil orders. There were Russian visitors from their embassy and, on 26 January 1975 - India's Republic Day - Mike raised two flags and reviewed all the factory watchmen, breakfasted with six American professors travelling under the auspices of the Rotary Club, after which there was an all day cricket match on Chamiers Field and full house for lunch. A week later the ITC Chairman and his wife came on a visit and she wrote in a note *...the* *bougainvillea was so beautifully decorated with fairy lights and everything was very pretty.* That month we produced 178 meals out of our kitchen.

Natalie, Gill Drayton, Zohra Chaube, N P Kumar, Sally Harding

Sometimes guests, with their food fads, arrived at the house unannounced and we quickly scrabbled around laying more places at the table and producing more food. Our kitchen was dark and compact with limited worktops, a sink with a cold water tap, a normal sized fridge and no freezer, but we *had* risen to the dizzy heights of a four burner gas stove. It was exhausting work running the house, doing the bazaar shopping and being pleasant to each and every person. Purchasing food was slightly easier, sometimes there were little cabbages and cauliflowers and the odd carrot, but never in the hot season. Flour and sugar were back on the market and the chemist still stocked small packs of Amul butter.

Friends came from Madras for the weekend and we were relaxing in the garden with after dinner coffee and Mike kept saying, "Are you all right sweetie?" He was not normally so concerned as to how I was feeling, and it was only when we went to bed that he told me he had received a telegram, *Daddy passed peacefully away today - Mummy.* Although expected it was a terrible shock and made me very sad, my father was a special person and our relationship very loving. Whilst still in Woodbridge, I had phoned my brother to say that if anything happened, I would not be able to leave India in a hurry because of tax regulations. As expected he failed to cope with any of the usual arrangements, including staying a night with my mother, leaving my aunt Norah and my father's brother, Hugh, to do their best. Feeling totally let down all I was able to do was to write to my mother every day, *Poor Daddy went in such a lonely way and you were told in such a lonely way. It all seems awful. I read your letter and then went for quite a long walk. The sky was darkening and was a deep rich red. A good breeze was blowing and I only met a few watchmen wending their way to their night's vigil.*

It was March but already the weather was very hot and a strong *Rohini* wind was blowing from the land. Soon it was time to collect the twins for the holidays and they were sleeping on mattresses on our bedroom floor. Not long after the two older children flew into Madras. It was a much nicer experience watching a plane fly in than watching a plane disappear into the stars.

For a couple of seasons there was a young tobacco crowd, mostly from Zimbabwe, staying 25 miles away at Chilakaluripet, and others in Guntur. We all met up and our weekends were spent with them far down the beach where we put up *shamianas* (open tents) and played rounders and cricket and silly games, taking picnics and drinks and having fun. The beach was so long and deserted, just odd fishermen wandering along with lines and nets. Often we saw giant turtles upturned and dead, teetering on their massive shells as the waves washed them back and forth. Meanwhile Mike was at Vadarevu unwillingly sipping beer with Russians, trying to keep them happy. Their alcoholic intake and endless snacking was quite phenomenal, and they were difficult, highly emotional guests.

I went on leave early to help my mother, and Mike brought the twins a month or so later. Our leave was hectic with work on the house, children's activities and the entertaining of many friends. David, aged just nine, started at his new school all dressed up in a green tweed suit with short trousers and long grey socks, and we had four children at four different schools, a pattern which continued until they completed their 'O' levels. At exeats and half terms they were kindly looked after by various relations and, when they got older, they stayed with friends. Mike had already gone back and I returned to India with Andrea in October, having invited my mother out for Christmas. She, aged 72, accepted with alacrity and was very excited at staying in Sunset Cottage with her own personal bearer, my friend Subba Rao. But it was not to be as we were on the move to Guntur. *Great God! That awful place!*

Net fishing on Vadarevu beach

Chapter 26 – Patabipuram 1976

Guntur was the place where I was most unhappy, Mike was too busy to be happy or unhappy, but it was not a place he enjoyed. It was dire, hot, filthy, desperately boring with absolutely nothing to offer. Having grumbled all through my time in Chirala, it was quite the best place we lived after the independence and spaciousness of Hassan. In Guntur there was no occupation, no garden, no transport, no children and, most of the time, no husband. Chirala was not mentally stimulating, but it was incredibly busy.

One of the young wives came from Bombay and found Guntur and its filth almost impossible. She would phone me in tears, "Natalie, how can I live in this place, I cannot stand it, this is not like Bombay, I feel as if I am rotting in hell." I called her over for coffee or tea, and tried to cheer her up without saying the obvious, *and how do you think I feel living in this dump?*

Bujie, Premila and Mariamma buying bangles

All the families in ILTD made adjustments but Mike and I made more, we were the last expatriates in the company, which was going through a difficult changeover. During his time in ILTD, as an Englishman, Mike felt more and more like a fish out of water. Our employment was during a transition from a British to an Indian company and there were many differences. His way of coping was to keep everything at arms length, and mine was to become as much a part of the scenery as possible. Easy to say without having to run a job or have any position of authority, he mixed well with his colleagues and enjoyed a joke with them, but always at a distance.

The children were maturing and were much in need of our company and comfort, they had reached the age where life was all questions, unknowns and indecisions. My role was to stay in Guntur for Mike's sake, he would have found it almost impossible to cope without my company, although his hours in the house were very limited. But all the time I was failing the children, not achieving much as a wife and feeling definitely on the shelf, like a woman with no dowry.

Mariamma realised my unhappiness and was steadfastly cheerful. Once we were settled, we worked together in the tiny garden, we made jams and juices, chutneys and pickles. We learned where we could buy bread, onions and tomatoes, and made friends with the dhobi who was so unreliable, he became the bane of both our lives. I played with her little ones and taught them to read and sing.

Although illiterate Mariamma was mature and had an amazingly perceptive concept on life and we spent many evenings in discussion and became sincere and long lasting friends. High spots were school holidays with all seven children running around the compound and Mariamma's kitchen was a hive of activity. When our children had been home for only a few hours Mariamma cautioned me, "Madams you are already shouting, " and when hers came home I wagged my finger and said, "Mariamma you are already shouting," and we both burst into laughter.

Andrea, my mother and Monica outside the Patabipuram house

The reason for our move to Guntur was Mike's new job of Production, Planning and Marketing in charge of both Anaparti and Chirala factories, as well as being Export Manager. India, then, was the third largest exporter of tobacco in the world, America and Brazil being numbers one and two, and he was expected to do a lot of travelling. Before we moved he visited Guntur and, as usual, struck lucky in finding a good house on an undeveloped estate at Patabipuram, well on the outskirts of ghastly Guntur. The property had a small garden, the boundary marked by coconut palms, planted before the house was built. If there was ever any breeze the large fronds rustled and the shade helped to keep the rooms a little cooler. Coconuts need a lot of water so a well was dug but the water was brackish.

Unattractive from the outside, urban Indian architecture seemed to follow a pattern of making small houses look bigger than they were. This one was designed with parapets, window shades, bits sticking out here and there plus a large breezy partly shaded roof area, a godsend in the hot weather. There were far reaching views to the hills to the west, and a narrow gauge railway line on which chugged a little puff puff train always stuffed with people, some hanging on the roof, and going west into the interior. Although quite small, the house was light with a study, an en-suite guest room and a sitting dining room plus small kitchen on the ground floor. At the rear were well built but tiny servants quarters with bathroom facilities, and a wee patch of garden with enough space to grow strips of coriander and plant a banana tree.

Upstairs were two more bedrooms with bathrooms and we soon developed a roof garden with lots of pot plants, small trees and tempting greenery for the birds to explore. There were veranda chairs and a table, a bar and our precious radiogram. Before we moved into the house it needed plumbing and carpentry work, mosquito netting on windows, carpets, curtains and complete redecoration. We moved in, auspiciously, on 1 November 1976 in heavy monsoon weather and Mariamma and Surinderao came with us, also Nanny now blind, deaf and paralysed down one side. India has a *new neighbour* custom where, as soon as you are moved in, the next door people visit and bring a little *curd* (yoghurt) starter, something it is impossible to carry from the last residence. Our nearest neighbours were a farming family living on the next plot in a round mud house with a palmyra fronded roof. They kept buffaloes and chickens and supplied us with milk. The lady of the house came nervously with a little steel *katori* (pot) with some curds in the bottom. Mariamma and I were delighted to greet her, and to receive her gift. Once you have curds on the go you can start your own forever, or until you move again.

Bujie, Premila and Monica

We were not used to having a telephone that worked, but the one at our house in Guntur did, although the operators found it very difficult to understand us. It took some time to get connected but one day a couple of men appeared and linked us to the line.

"What is the number please?" I asked

They looked blank so I repeated the question in my kitchen Telugu somewhat improved after six years of constant use. They understood, consulted a piece of grubby paper and said, "Rendu, rendu, rendu, rendu, nalugu."

This was going to be tricky; our number was double two, double two four.

Next day I wanted to make a call to Ongole, about fifty miles south. Local calls could be direct dialled; every other call was connected by the operator and described as trunk. International calls were still impossible and, although the business language of India is English, the Guntur telephonists had their own version.

What is your number wanting? enquired the girl abruptly

Wongole mudu, aru, wocatee, yedu, I pronunciated carefully (Ongole 3617)

Sorry Madam, I am not understanding your accent, she was irritated and almost cut me off, *What please is the number you are desiring?*

I repeated my numbers carefully, adding *thank you please* at the end.

"Name?"

"Wheatley."

"Spell."

"W - H - E - A - T - L - E Y"

"I am not understanding. Spell again."

"Double yew - yaitch - yee- yay - tea - yell - yee - why" I said slowly.

"Oh. Vitley," she said, "Ordinary or lightning?"

"I am wanting only ordinary please," I said. Lightning was used in emergency or super frustration, costing four times more.

"Repeat your number," she said, "Are you on the line?"

"I am not knowing which number to repeat," I said, "Are you wanting this telephone number or Wongole number?"

"*Purst* you give me your home number, I am not understanding your accent, isn't it?"

"Double two double two four, OK?" I said slowly and carefully.

"Please speak in English Madam, why are you tricking me?"

"Not tricking, simply saying," I replied, "Two, two, two, two four."

"Now you are making joke, isn't it?" she was not amused, "You are saying double two, double two four, yes? *Wokay.* Now tell me Wongole ordinary."

"Please connect me to Ongole three, six one seven."

"Madam you are thinking Telugu, speaking Telugu, I beg you speak English now, no more joke please."

"Wongole mudu, aru, wocatee, yedu," I said again.

"Ah!" she was happier, "You are wanting Wongole 3617? Now I understand your English," and tapped on the line. There was a pause, "Out of order, Wongole line down," and cut me off.

At the end of November Hebron broke up for the Christmas holidays and I fetched Andrea and enjoyed the carol concert and the end of term play. She was very excited and had stuffed all sorts of secretly wrapped packages into her luggage. In Madras we enjoyed our usual special time with Bulbul and her girls, and managed to do some shopping at the Victoria Technical Institute. This was an arts and crafts emporium specialising in beautiful embroidered items, carved wood, paintings and all sorts of hand-made knick knacks and ornaments. The organisation was archaic, their accounting system tedious with six different hand-written bills, plus four carbons, for each item purchased, but we always came home with little pieces of treasure.

It would soon be Christmas and my mother was looking forward to her visit. I had made meticulous arrangements for her to travel to Hyderabad assisted by the BAT meeting and greeting staff, who put Grannys under their wings as ably as they coped with children. Susina, Simon and David were due to arrive first and my mother to come a day later. Letters between us flew back and forth as everything was firmed up so that she should have an easy passage. However the taxi to take her to her local station did not turn up making a late start, my brother reluctantly kept her overnight and just about got her to the airport but, when the Air India Jumbo took off, it sucked in seagulls and was forced to return making a long delay. Meanwhile I was anxiously awaiting everyone in Hyderabad and staying with Alan and Barbara Rands. The children came on schedule but we had to move to a guest house which was not expected, nor my mother's delay. Without transport and with little cash to pay the guest house, I decided to send the children alone on the six-hour train journey to Vijayawada. Barbara kindly prepared drinks, fried egg sandwiches and fruit and off they went. None of us ever felt unsafe in India and they were left in charge of the guard. Rickshaws took me repeatedly back and forth to the airport and my mother finally arrived, looking as fresh as a daisy. She was so busy chatting up a young, good looking Indian man, that she did not bother to look out for me waving excitedly. Eventually she spotted me but was more anxious to introduce her new friend than to greet me. My heart sank, it always did when we met, somehow she managed to do or say the wrong thing as her priorities were to impress strangers in favour of family or friends. She spent six weeks with us and it opened her eyes to our lifestyle and the hard work involved in just living.

Wooden fishing canoe, Vadarevu

"I never realised that your life was so incredibly difficult," she said after a few days. She was interested in everything and well respected by my lady friends. Any person over the age of about 50 was given the treatment and, at the ripe old age of 72, she was considered almost saintly. She lapped it up and it was probably one of the happiest times of her life as she was bright, witty and the centre of attention. Although I did my best, my best was never good enough although we carried on an amazingly good correspondence, but our relationship together soon wore thin. The company wives were a good lot and we bonded over the next two years, as they came and went, we shared as much fun together as we were able, with all the privations of lack of transport, phones out of order and husbands away. During my mother's stay each and every one of them arranged a tea, coffee or dinner party to welcome her. She expected the weather to be very hot and brought summery clothes, but was soon shivering either in air conditioning or in the cool evening breezes. This brought out all the wives shawls and cardigans, even hot water bottles, and she was soon cosily nurtured by lovely women in shimmering saris, their gold necklaces glinting in the lights from the trees. We spent a happy Christmas at Vadarevu and she loved watching the fish landing in nets on the beach.

She returned to her old love of swimming and disappeared into the waves heading out from the Coromandel coast towards the Andaman Islands, seemingly oblivious of sharks, currents, or massive turtles. This brought back childhood memories of my anxious father running in the shallow waves shouting, "Dorritt, Dorritt" as her little head bobbed into the distance. She was the same with walking, always loving it so much that she forgot, even well into her eighties, that she should leave enough energy to get back again.

One thing she did not enjoy were the field rats which invaded our house. Having already established their own tracks and trails, when a new house was built, they ran *through* it rather than *round* it. Field rats are enormous, like bandicoots, and very relentless. They climb through tiny apertures, shin *up* the insides of drain pipes and waste pipes, and gnaw their way through electric cables, larder doors, and clothes in the wardrobe. We never knew when they were coming, but they were frequent visitors. Our bathrooms had metal covers over the floor level waste pipes, but the rats ran up and knocked them aside, and were soon into all the bedroom cupboards. We put big stones over the metal covers but they soon heaved them away. One night, with my hand dangling over the bed, I was bitten by a (rabid?) rat and nearly hit the ceiling with fear. It took a long time to get rid of the beasts and I still have visions of my mother standing on a chair clutching her skirts.

I took the children back to Hyderabad to fly to England, but Andrea was on her long holidays and not due to return until nearly February. She caught horrible chicken pox and my mother was good in playing games and amusing her with stories. Then it was time for school and we caught the train (first class for a change) to Madras, and travelled with Andrea up into the hills. My mother coped very well with the journey, somewhat different from British Rail, and enjoyed seeing Hebron School and staying in St Margaret's. Our friend Ranee Kuttaiah asked us to Thaishola for lunch and it took hours driving through tea gardens to get there. Ranee enthralled my mother by unlocking all her heavy silk saris and collections of family jewellery and giving her a display of real Indian wealth.

From Ooty we travelled by car down the short cut, the Sigur Ghat, to lunch at Bamboo Banks, a guest complex owned by Siasp Kothavala, a wildlife expert and retired Parsee coffee planter, and his culinary wife, Zerene. They were a jolly, hospitable couple and were one of a few Indian nationals branching out into the tourist business and luring foreign visitors to their dreamy, tropical paradise deep in the Mudumalai hill range. They opened their guest house and cottages in 1974 and were doing a roaring trade, it was a great location for elephant riding, bird watching and stalking elusive tigers. We sat on the veranda surrounded by brilliant tropical flora and fauna, sipping iced lime and watching blue flycatchers, kingfishers near the pond, black headed orioles, sunbirds and blue robins. We did not have time but could have visited the Theppakadu elephant breeding farm; there is nothing better than nudging baby elephants and feeding them bread rolls and bananas whilst their mothers look greedily on.

After coffee we drove down the rest of the mountain until we got to the busy, messy little town of Gudalur and onto the main Mysore road. It was the time of the Maharajah's wedding, His Heaviness – who was a pleasant man – to a very young bride, no doubt arranged by his family. Zohra, by some miracle, managed to get tickets for this great event, so we dressed ourselves up as well as we could, popped small pearls or tiny diamonds into our ears, and off we went to the palace with several thousand other people. The wedding was in the great hall and we sat on carpets on the floor. For once my mother did not try to get the best seat, or even complain, this occasion completely silenced her and she did not even request to be taken to the loo, she sat as quiet as a mouse and loved every magic moment of such a grand affair. Just the surroundings were enough, but when the main players came into view, their rich clothes, huge pieces of jewellery, pearls the size of apricots and diamonds dripping from every visible part of the body, it was a sight indeed. It was a memorable occasion, a taste of old India which was fast disappearing, an atmosphere of wealth that we would never see again, and a classic example of the great divide of the dramatically rich and the pathetically poor. The Hindu ritual was intense and serious; the bride a mere wisp enveloped in red silk, her head almost covered, her eyes ringed with kohl and little hands fluttering nervously.

We returned together to Guntur and straight into the season. Our first Japanese customer moved in with us, giving my mother yet another focus. He was Shegiru Inoue, spotty and keen, he was like another child in the house and arrived with three worn out changes of clothes and the rest of his suitcase stuffed with dried seaweed, noodles, packets of sticky rice and an endless supply of sauces and powders to sprinkle on anything that he could find edible. He was kindly, gauche and twanged *rub songs* (love songs) on his guitar to us in the evenings which was somewhat embarrassing. He, and his counterpart from the Japanese Monopoly, Tamio Iwasaki, stayed with us during the two long seasons they were in Guntur. Tamio was much more difficult because he was chronically homesick and silent, although his English was not too bad. It was difficult having him around the house, and wonderful that Mariamma was able to sense his distress, and make sure that at least he got the food he enjoyed. Both Japanese were very anxious not to eat any Indian meals to the point that any contact could adulterate them forever. Both were experts at hawking, spitting and throat clearing, and the resonations from the bathrooms in the early mornings was enough to wake the dead. Fortunately they disappeared after dinner each evening to join the other Japanese at their big guest house on the Ring Road where they played cards until the early hours, stumbling home somewhat drunk and very weary. Needless to say it was my job to deal with these house guests alone as throughout the week Mike was travelling either to Chirala or Anaparti factories and staying overnight and, soon, my mother flew back to her bungalow in the New Forest. We all had worked overtime to ensure that she was happy, and she was, it went her way.

Shegiru Inoue (Japanese Monopoly) and Natalie

There was still a lot of entertaining to do, but without the back-up of Chirala compound servants it was more difficult. In Patabipuram we were much alone, more so when Surinderao, our strange and lonely *mali,* who had been with us for six years, did his final disappearing act never to be seen again. Mariamma was steady and worked very hard, but also coped with looking after her three children, two of whom went to the local school, and the care of Nanny who had aged and deteriorated. We employed a teenage girl called Jessica, daughter of one of the Chirala cooks, who worked with us until we left. She was cheerful, and could race up and down the two flights of stairs to the roof with beers and sodas, as well as helping with sweeping, kitchen work and running errands.

Guntur was a spread out town so it was necessary to send a begging note to the traffic clerk for a *vee-hay-ikle* (car) and shopping took a whole morning. I went to the bazaar for rice, and soon learned that raw rice must be tossed into the mouth and crunched to test its age, new rice was a waste of money as it did not swell up like the old stuff. The wheat was very dirty and full of tiny stones, it was purchased by the sack and thoroughly washed and laid on sheets on the roof until completely dry, having been turned over and over, then I took it to the mill to be ground into flour. One of our favourite breakfasts was fresh chapatis, home-made buffalo butter and black grape jam, which we made and kept in the fridge.

We had brought our granite grinding stones on the lorry, they were very heavy but an important part of our cooking tools. One was like a massive pestle and mortar and the other was a flat chunky piece of granite with a matching rolling pin. Often the bangle man called with his trolley and Mariamma and the children ran out to buy a few jingly pieces. Less often we heard the bells of the stone sharpener coming up the road, we called him in and, with a chisel, he sharpened up the granite so that the onions and tomatoes were pulverised quickly. We ate a lot of idlis, made from fermented rice and lentils and steamed. They were very healthy and delicious with hot spicy rasam, and coconut chutney ground on the stone with lime juice, salt, curds and green chillis. Once the chutney was ready it was garnished with fried *mennapoppu* (mustard seed). Curries were made with wet masalas and dry masalas. The first composed of onion, ginger, garlic and chillis, the second comprising dried coriander, cumin, black pepper, fennugreek, black gram dall, channa dall, poppy seed, cloves, cinnamon sticks, cardamoms, ginger, peppercorns and turmeric. I was more familiar with the Telugu names and purchased them as danya, zeera, mirialu, avalu, mentelu and so on. The more I became involved with the nitty gritty of living away from the company compound, surviving on my new found skills and improved language confidence, the happier my mood. Mariamma's Indian cookery was no better than mine, so we learned together to make drumstick and *channa pindi* curry, *mutter panir* (peas and cheese), *upma* (savoury semolina), *brinjal* (aubergine) *masala and sweet and sour bhindikayalu* (okra). She also made murkoos and Bombay mixture and these were a sure fire necessity for school tuck along with peanut brittle.

We hired a neighbourhood *chowkidar* (watchman), a wily Gurkha, and we paid him a retainer to keep an eye on us and our house at night. He wandered about, blowing his whistle but, after some time, he was not often seen or heard until he came for his money. He was not around when a robbery occurred at night during the school holidays. Mike was in Anaparti and I was fast asleep, but Simon aged 12, was jet-lagged and restless. He was in the boys' room downstairs and suddenly heard a strange noise, whilst David slept on. He got up and quietly opened the door into the sitting room and saw two men in the house. Although absolutely terrified he shouted, scaring them so badly that they dropped their haul, a cigar box full of marbles, and legged it. Shaking like a leaf, Simon braved the dark stairway up to our room, not knowing if the thieves were hiding in any recess, and told me what he witnessed, hardly able to speak he was so frightened. We went downstairs together and found that the intruders had hacksawed the heavy padlock off the kitchen door, leaving the servants nearby still in the depths of their slumbers. In the morning we called the police, they came curiously and lethargically and were more concerned about what valuables we *had* in the house, rather than what had been dropped on the ground.

Susina, Simon and David came home for the dreadfully hot Easter holidays, but Andrea was at Hebron until May. They missed the sea breezes of Chirala and we did not get to the beach much. The boys were off on their bikes catching six inch fish in the water mains and generally exploring, but came home soon after ten in the morning as the sun beat down on them unbearably, whilst Susina was bored and always desperate for something to read. There was no radio or television, often no power to run the radiogram and, worse, nowhere to go. Sometimes we went to Vijayawada for a vegetarian lunch and a film, sometimes to Chicpet to visit the Zimbabwean gang and swim in their pool, but there was not much else on offer, hampered by lack of transport. David was given an autograph book and was collecting as many signatures as he could. One day KS Rao, a colleague of Mike's came to visit and the book was thrust into his hand. "What do you want me write?" he asked David.

"I want your name," said David, "And what you think."

So KS, one of the sloggers in the company wrote, *Work is Worship - I am a donkey and I work like a bloody donkey.*

At Goodwill Stores, Guntur

It was a struggle to have clothes made for them. I was totally unaware of fashion trends, and could not refer to *Jackie*, the teenage girls magazine, and I did not have a clue what was available in English shops. Our children hated going to the tailor, did not want to be measured or fitted in a wayside stall with a hundred lookers-on, and have to wear the offending outfit back at their expensive schools where everyone else was top notch on the fashion scale. Denim was becoming popular, as were bomber jackets and bell bottoms. Guntur was still in the world of sweaty nylon shirts for men and orthodox shrouded clothing for women. Little girls ran around in highly decorated satins, and boys were conventionally dressed in checked shirts and shorts with a multitude of buttons, which melted when ironed. Getting our teenage message over to an oily haired tailor with a treadle sewing machine was impossible.

Going back was upsetting. We travelled to Madras by Circars and stayed at the Chola. For once there was water in the pool, and we ate some nice food. They were all so upset at the airport that a large policeman took pity, accompanied me to the plane and allowed me to strap them in before reluctantly leaving them. They always insisted that I wait until the plane disappeared into the black night sky. And this I did, with tears rolling down my face, and then travelled by rusty auto-rick the several miles down town to the railway station to board the disgusting train back to Guntur. Soon it was May and there was no rain since the previous November, the level of water in our well dropped three feet and it was 116°F (47°C).

Chapter 27 – Books and Medals

My need for books was becoming intense, the weather was hotter and there was nothing to do but read. But what? The British Council in Madras had a library, so I visited hopefully to become an out of town member.

"We can put your name on waiting list," they said unsympathetically, "You will be number 342." The library was not specifically for British people, but for everyone who wanted to borrow books in the Madras postal area. To be 342 meant that I would be a zombie by the time they got to me. Mike wrote to the High Commission to see if they could help. Written on posh paper came a letter, *Since you are the British Representative in the Andhra Pradesh West Godavri region, we can put your wife at the top of the list and she can receive books as soon as she has made a selection.* Gosh! Here was a lifeline indeed. I sent for the catalogue of books which brought back swift memories of Mysore library. Each volume was numbered and titled, but no author. Hardened to these peculiar indexing methods and scanning the titles carefully, I made a choice of six; my first package promised to be a surprise. The British Council sent me a letter that my books *would be despatched shortly* and allotted me a personal number – 13948.

For the next two years regular supplies of books were delivered. It did not matter what they were, they were manna from heaven and stopped me from going stark, staring mad with boredom. They came by train, a big package all wrapped up in toughened brown paper and tied up with hairy jute string. A *peon* went to the station to get them and, if Mike was not in town (most of the time), it was a question of waiting patiently until he got back and collected them from his office. Book day was joy day, my choices were often weird and choosing by title meant that my reading was eclectic and adventurous. Nothing was abandoned, everything was absorbed and it was a journey of learning from Aldous Huxley to Pearl Buck. To be able to read without interruption for hours on end was a privilege, and the opportunity has never occurred again. The experience also pointed to my complete loneliness, but the books brought hope. On a later visit to Madras I called in to meet the librarians at the British Council and explained myself as number 13948. They clustered around me, interested to put a face to a number.

"You choose a wide variety," said one earnest woman, her eyes looking at me curiously through her heavy framed spectacles.

"I am never knowing what you are wanting," a young man chipped in, puzzlement on his thin boned face, "Now I am seeing your face 13948, now I am getting an idea."

"I *thought* you were a woman," a bold lady in an emerald sari came closer, "But your name *Natalie,* I was not knowing if you were male or female. You choose interesting books, but I cannot understand your particular interest."

Explaining that choosing by number and title gave no indication of the content of the book confused them, they were so stuck with their system that their faces became blank, they could not understand the problem. Never mind, we made friends and, if in the future they could not provide a requested book, they substituted one they thought would please, *Dear 13948, I am sending my respects and wishing to inform that your title Native Stranger is out of station, so I am despatching to you a book Strange Natives which I hope will suffice. With God's blessing, Savitri Sharma.*

In Guntur we were surprised by a flying visit, 24 hours early, from the Deputy High

Commissioner, Alfred Hall, who could not have travelled from Madras in worse heat. He was nearly dead when he arrived, well after dark and dreadfully dehydrated, as he came by jeep and did not carry sufficient water. We made him comfortable with cool drinks and a decent meal, he sloshed in a bucket of water and slept in a clean bed. He was a delightful man and very good, if quiet, company. Mike had to go to work but, next day with Andrea, we went round the whole area where any British passport holder was living. It was stinking hot and the dirt roads were swirled in thick dust, it was an enlightening trip for Alfred and he was stoic. We visited many poor Anglo-Indians, old nuns, Indian nationals and retired, worn-out missionaries. We went to the Leprosy Hospital at Bapatla and Edna Rowley was in residence, but Brigadier Plummer was away visiting her daughter and grandchildren. That evening at home we gave a party and invited the few British tobacco merchants who were still braving the hot weather.

May 1976 Guntur Station – Mike, Andrea, Martyn Bougourd, Alfred Hall with onlookers

Next morning at breakfast Alfred said casually, "I have an OBE to give away."

"An OBE?" we queried, "Is that how you distribute them?"

He smiled, and said no, but after only a short time in India, he had not been able to find a suitable candidate who would deserve such an award, did we know of anybody? We immediately thought of Hilda and told him about her 50 years of devotion to leprosy patients. He said he would let us know, and we saw him off at the railway station, back to Madras.

Several weeks later it was my job to visit Hilda and find out if she would accept the medal. It was a strange mission, she was pleased to see me and, as usual, she was wearing her Salvation Army uniform with her white hair tidied into a bun. She was a big woman with a quiet, slightly northern, lilt to her voice and an amiable friendly smile. She made coffee and we drank out of chipped but china cups. Once we finished with bits of news I said, "I've got something to ask you." She was interested.

"The Queen has heard about you," I said.

"The Queen! How can the Queen have heard about me?" she was so surprised.

"I am not sure," which was a white lie, "But she wants to give you something."

"How can she possibly?" Hilda faltered, her lips quivering, "How can the Queen know about me?"

"Maybe she's heard about your leprosy work," I suggested as, outside, the villagers clattered and shouted and the crows cawed. "She wants to award you the Order of the British Empire."

Hilda nearly fell off her uncomfortable wooden chair, and put her cup on the floor.

"The Order of the British Empire, how can she?"

"Will you accept it," persisting, "She really wants you to have it.!

"I couldn't possibly refuse the Queen," she said very worriedly, "I couldn't refuse."

"Good," I said and then tried to calm her down, she was looking pale and shocked.

Leprosy Hospital – Alfred Hall, DHC and Hilda Plummer with her little family

Hilda suffered from bad knees and, when it was ventured later, that she could fly home and have her investiture at Buckingham Palace, she refused point blank, "I can't kneel down," she said, "The Queen would be ashamed of me." There was no persuading her so, instead her preferred choice was to have a huge party, invite all the beggars and all the leprosy patients and hold it at the hospital. Alfred Hall travelled up from Madras and pinned the award on her uniform and she stood as proud as punch with her little Indian family surrounding her. It was a tear jerking experience and perhaps one of the more unusual ceremonies. All the Salvation Army big brass from Madras came and suddenly the leprosy hospital was full of visitors and the beggars enjoyed the best day of their lives.

Hilda's life was enhanced when we lived in Chirala, we took her to the beach to dabble her old toes in the waves, and we also fetched her to stay with us in Guntur for the odd weekend. These little trips away from her village life were a real holiday and she enjoyed English food like shepherd's pie and sausages. She did not want to return to England, instead she ended her days in her little house and died there peacefully in 1980.

Andrea returned to school for her last term. She missed her brothers and sister and the shared holidays, and was anxious to leave and join them in England. This particular journey was one of the worst as a train derailed down the line and we were forced into a 12-hour, boiling hot detour to Vellore, across the dry, brittle plains, to join another broad gauge line to Madras. Our water ran out, forcing me and dozens of others to scramble out of the train when it stopped, and fill our bottles from barrels, cooled by wet ropes wrapped around them. God knows where the water came from, all the passengers were frantically thirsty, and it was a scary business queuing to collect it and boarding the train before it steamed off without any warning. The woman opposite, dressed in a yellow crumpled sari, bought a meal off a vendor, it was wrapped in a leaf and, as she unfurled it, a large curry-covered cockroach crawled out. "Amma! Amma!" she cried, pushing the creature off her knees, it was so bloated it could not move. Everyone was looking and shouting, "Cockroach, cockroach" she cried in Telugu, and shook her sari whilst someone threw the half-wrapped meal through the metal bars and out of the window, on to the embankment. It was a horrid journey, but Andrea was uncomplaining and sat there in the filthy train, her blonde hair shining in the sun, dressed in a pretty pink top and cotton shorts. My stamina for such journeys was wearing thin, or maybe we were becoming hardened as we sat there on the dreadfully hot slatted benches patiently awaiting our arrival in Madras. We were so late that we raced for the Nilgiri Express and continued onwards without a shower or food.

On my return Mike had left for Bangladesh routing himself through Calcutta where he stayed with his brother, Gerald, now working there with ITC. I started thinking of how to help Mariamma should we suddenly leave India without much warning. She was a hard worker and cheerful, but had difficulty in keeping her children in order and looking after Nanny who was weak and ill. Nanny had been a faithful, shadowy, servant, willing to put her hands to anything, and she deserved better than being abandoned by her rotten son, Richard. After making enquiries I discovered, near the Catholic church, a Home for the Aged run by Hindu charities and the Rotarians, and went to have a look and then talked to Mariamma about putting Nanny there; she was reluctant, but saw the the sense of it. Indian people have great respect for their elderly relatives and their prime purpose is to look after them until the end. Mariamma thought about it for a few days, during which time Bujie suddenly became ill with septicaemia caused by treading on a piece of metal and cutting his foot. He was feverish and I noticed little pustules on his chubby arms and quickly took him to Dr Sambasiva Rao, our Guntur company physician.

"Septicaemia," he said wisely, and prescribed strong anti-biotics which did the trick and Bujie was soon running around.

Dr Sambasiva Rao, or Dr Sam as we knew him, was a delightful cheerful man and, in his way, a talented doctor but rather casual. He was also a professional Bridge player and a master spitter. The noises he made when walking up the garden path discharging phlegm from his mouth into the flower beds was quite ear splitting. Once he was playing snooker in the club, clad in pristine white dhoti, looped up between his legs and tucked behind his back, and a starched *kurta* (long shirt) fresh from a bath. He leaned on his snooker cue, cleared his throat ominously working out where to aim the spit, and managed to fire it right over the snooker table and through the open window onto the dusty cannas outside. Another time he was not so fortunate, he visited one manager in the ILTD, who kept an immaculately clean office and a clear desk. The Doc walked in, cleared his throat and aimed at the open window, which wasn't open and the gob landed and dribbled down the pane. Not embarrassed, he was just surprised that anyone could have such polished windows and took the end of his shirt and wiped it off as best he could.

One evening we were in the Guntur club watching the men's tennis doubles, one of the players being an 80-year old Indian, much revered in the community. Imagine our horror when he literally dropped dead like a stone in his white cotton shirt and dhoti which splayed across the *murram* (sand) court. Dr Sam was playing snooker and ran out and declared him *thoroughly dead - instantaneous heart attack* and the body was carted away almost immediately. Death was so final, and next day there was a long procession through town and a cremation.

Bujie

Nanny was seriously ill in her home with heart disease. She was a Catholic and I always promised her the Last Rites and felt that this must be the time so, one Sunday, Mike, Mariamma and I trailed round a wet monsoony town looking for a priest. We located a pleasant, elderly man who willingly got into the car bringing his bag complete with candles and a lacy cassock. Nanny presented a harrowing picture of human degradation after only a few weeks, and we were suspicious that she had not been properly looked after, having left sufficient money and provided all the things she needed. We washed her and made her comfortable but she was just a collection of bones. The priest started his prayers, she knew exactly what was happening and wailed and wailed and all the inmates joined in. Mariamma cried, I cried and Mike was swallowing hard. Next day she died and Mariamma, who was very upset, made funeral arrangements. It was beyond me to know what to do and it seemed sensible to stay in the background. Mariamma hired a rickshaw, went to a material shop and purchased a piece of white cloth, collected the body and wrapped it and made her way out of town. On the way she was mugged and the sheet was stripped off Nanny and stolen. Mariamma was devastated, human life is so expendable amongst the poor, there seemed no respect for the dead.

Soon after this awful event, we started looking for an orphanage for Monica and Bujie, one where they would receive an education. Mariamma was struggling and the children got under her feet all the time, so she was open to this idea. The children were described as semi-orphans as their father had deserted them.

We often passed the AMG Home in Chilakaluripet (Chicpet) on our way to Chirala so, one day, we called in and met the superintendent, a dark skinned man from Kerala called John David who I did not immediately trust. He thought we were coming to help him and provide financial aid, whereas we wanted him to help us. After lengthy explanations he agreed in principle to take Monica and Bujie and ensure that they were educated up to the tenth standard. The home was run on the *adopt a child* method of getting people abroad to fund the children and they received money from USA, UK, West Germany and Australia. The buildings were modern, spartan but clean and the 520 girls and boys looked tidy and seemed relatively cheerful. Mike, who had a better sense of Indian men than me, seemed fairly confident that it was a good choice, he was fond of Mariamma's little lot and wanted them to have a secure place and a good education. On the next visit Mariamma came with us and quite liked the idea of her children being looked after and educated at no cost. We were given tea and photographed with lots of children, destitute women, old crones and converted prostitutes and we handed over sacks of of rice and lentils and donated a generous amount of money, hoping it would not go astray. Then we started getting their clothes ready, and Mike organised that two wooden trunks were made for them in the factory, whilst I made patchwork quilts for their little beds.

AMG Home, Chilakaluripet

There was a company leaf conference in Guntur, Eric Chaube came over from Mysore and Gerald, Mike's twin, came from Calcutta. The emphasis was on a five year plan, but as every year was different from the last, this was a little ambitious. Soon afterwards, with Andrea, I went to England to attend end-of-term functions for the other three children and also to prepare her to start at the junior school of St Felix in Southwold. Mike was not able to get away until much later, missing most of the children's holiday.

In his new position, Mike made a trip to Portugal and won a big order, only to discover there was not enough tobacco to fulfil it, a frustrating business. We returned to India together leaving all the children in their different English schools and feeling like rats jumping off a sinking ship. We came back to severe cyclonic weather causing a great deal of damage to infrastructure and crops, the rice had been harvested and left to dry but there was so much rain that it floated and fermented. All night long the people sat on the side of the road turning their little wet piles of grain, trying to dry it, about 75% of the crop was lost and tobacco was badly hit.

In December the children all flew in to Madras on two separate days and we enjoyed a lovely reunion using the Chola Hotel and its amenities before boarding the train. When we got to Patabipuram, Monica and Bujie came home also and there was great jollifications as the children ran all over the roads and fields and played together. The disparity of their ages, culture, educational levels and language, caused no difficulty, they were all good friends.

Christmas was difficult, it was the first in the house and there was no one to share it with, Guntur was devoid of like minds and fellow revellers. Some of the local tobacco merchants delivered huge cakes smothered in margarine cream icing swamped with jam. It was a kind gesture but soon the cakes ended up in the quarters and were gobbled up eagerly by the inmates and whoever was visiting. We laid the lunch table with some particularly beautiful table mats which my cousin, Jen, brought from Hong Kong. They were fine and white and embroidered in the shadow style. The candles were of the dribbly variety and when we had finished, I blew them out. The hot wax landed on the mats and burnt them all in several places, it was a horrid end to an imperfect day, not helped by an unsuccessful game of Monopoly when *someone* bought all the red hotels and left the rest of us in debt and homeless.

Bujie, Mariamma, Premila and Monica

Chapter 28 – Travelling 1977

In late January Mike had a week's business in Bangladesh, and suggested I travel to Calcutta so we could meet up for a weekend with his brother and wife. The children had returned to UK to school and the house was empty. Little Premila often came to see me providing comfort, and she sang her nursery rhymes in a funny little Guntur voice.

Mariamma encouraged me, "You are missing children Ma, too much missing, you go and have nice holiday with Master's brother. When children get bigger missing is more, children wanting now. Sujeena now 14, needing Mummy, isn't it?."

A couple of days after Mike left, I travelled 1500 miles north on the Howrah Mail, a 24-hour journey along the eastern seaboard from the Coromandel Coast to the Bay of Bengal, ending up at the grand Howrah station, Calcutta. I was so used to diabolical train journeys in India, but had always enjoyed travelling overland on my own. I went by second class three tier and the compartments, accommodating six people, were compact and constructed from hard materials with wooden slatted benches, each one opening on to a corridor. Every carriage was independent, and locked between stations. It was necessary to adopt a certain mindset, or the journey became tedious and frustrating. A driver took me to Vijayawada and a coolie carried my bedroll and baggage and waited with me until the train arrived from Madras; it was early morning, coughing and hawking time. The diesel engine roared in, black and threatening. The coolie pushed his way into the compartment and bagged my reserved place, I gave him a tip and, with luck, he picked up another passenger or two before the train chugged out. There were no refreshment facilities on board, but vendors clambered around at each stop. The usual hot drink provided in the south was coffee - hot, milky and steaming in a little (washed?) glass. Further north the drink became tea, and was offered in tiny handmade throwaway earthenware cups and, I was told, 10,000 potters were employed making these vessels. I did not trust platform food so took a supply of home-made Indian eats, plenty of fruit and water and relied on the tea, which I disliked, but it was hot and sweet and revived my energy levels. I also chewed betel nuts, a very local habit which I had adopted on journeys. They came in little packets, I found the taste refreshing and the residue was easy to dispose of, rather like bits of bark. I did not like paan, the triangular green pouches made of betel plant leaves fixed with a clove. They came with a mixture of fillings, including gold leaf for the wealthy, and ranged in price. Paan wallahs parked themselves outside restaurants making up the little green pillows and stuffing them with sugar, dried fruit, coconut, lime and all manner of pungent spices. Traditional in the olden days, they were perfect mouth fresheners, later to be discovered as highly carcinogenic.

There was always a tap and a squat loo at the end of each carriage, and at large stations these were sluiced out, but not always. I took a few wet flannels in my wash bag, toilet roll and a toothbrush. Soft sticky drinks were available en route, lots of local fruit and greasy snacks, but no bottled water.

Normally I had travelled through the night and heard only staccato vernacular voices at stations and saw nothing but the odd stream of light as we passed through somewhere, so this was a new adventure to travel many miles during the day. The countryside on the eastern seaboard is flat and uninteresting, but not uninteresting to me because it was new. Luckily it was the dry season, otherwise the vast deltas of the Krishna and Godavri rivers could have flooded causing diversions, also the weather was cool, I had a blanket in my bedroll and a jacket in my luggage and a couple of books to read. We passed through Rajahmundry, Samalkot and Vizakhapatnam and then onwards to Vizianagaram, Brahmapur and across the border to Orissa and Bhubaneshwar, known as *temple town.* It was so named because it was once covered with many ancient temples dating from the 8th to the 13th century. As we waited at the station waving away persistent fruit sellers, an old man sitting opposite caught my eye and nodded towards the town, *Wover seven thousand temples,* he said, *Wery famous place,* and then snoozed off. Someone else muttered, "Five hundred, nothing like seven thousand," and a controversial conversation continued in whatever colloquialism was understood by all. Doors opened and slammed and, immediately, a new language caught my ear which I could not understand, it was Oriya and I felt as if in a foreign land. Embarking passengers stared at me, it was not common to meet a lone European woman in three tier, and I was unable to exchange pleasantries apart from folding my hands into the simple greeting, with a respectful nod and a mumbled *namaste.* The train stopped and started, every station was interesting, bubbling with humanity, animals, food vendors, hawkers, dogs, women begging, crawling lepers and little boys running alongside the moving train trying to sell the last orange flung through the bars of the window. Trains in India are a different experience, quite apart from any other. They are a way of travelling over vast distances and being at one with the people locked together inside the carriage.

My first journey on the Circars Express was painful, this one was comforting, I felt almost at home and quite peaceful, jogging along dozing, dreaming until eventually, after a night roaring across the plains under a star filled sky our destination was reached. This journey was a catalyst of my personal time in India. We had arrived when I was 26 at the start of married life with only the experience of a rather wealthy West Africa behind us. I had read in a book that when foreigners arrived in India they followed a particular cycle; stage one was *everything marvellous,* stage two was *everything not so marvellous* and stage three *everything Indian abominable.* Our reactions had been totally the reverse. India was a huge shock and difficult to manage in a rural situation, to run a house and servants and bring up children. In Ghana our expatriate life had been limited but in India it was almost non-existent and, apart from Chirala, we had not sheltered under the company umbrella. It was very different in the old Imperial Tobacco days when all the staff lived on compounds with clubs, established domestic staff and a life organised round work and play in a very disciplined manner. Our experience had been quite the opposite and made us the people we are today. Over the years we integrated ourselves, in our own way, into whichever society we happened to land; it was a question of constant adjustment and adaptation, most it was a question of tolerance and acceptance. As we were probably nearing the end of our time on the sub-continent it seemed that both of us had come to terms, assimilated and were no longer bucking the reins.

After Cuttack and Kharagpur, reached in the dead of night, our destination was not too far away and my fellow passengers were stirring and stretching, yawning and belching, above and below me. We were now in West Bengal and heading for the shifting delta of the great Hooghly river and the city of Calcutta, and we slid through the shanty towns into Howrah station at 5am. Gerald had sent a message that he would meet me, it was Saturday morning and barely light, an awkward hour to expect someone, but no contact details were given so I was unable to get a taxi. The platform was seething, coolies shouting at me in Bengali, but I waved them away. Eventually Gerald turned up and we drove through the expected squalid slums and over the great Hooghly bridge into the city. Calcutta has a reputation of filth and dirt and it certainly manifests that in a big way, but it also has a tradition of friendship, humour and Bengali hospitality. All our expatriate friends had much enjoyed their time there, having a great social life and joining one of the two famous clubs, either the Tollygunge or the Ballygunge, as well as playing on an excellent golf course. Calcutta had hotels, interesting shops, fantastic markets full of fruit, vegetables, cheese, beef and well fed chickens plus, my passion, baskets of fresh lychee fruits brought down from Bangladesh. It also suffered horrendous traffic and buses which looked as if they would collapse with all the passengers hanging on to the outsides.

Calcutta with Iti Misra, Veena Khanna and Bitty Malik

Anthea was up and about by the time we got to their flat, and little Charlie was crawling around, whilst his two older sisters were at boarding school in England. It was a busy American Tournament tennis weekend and all-day matches were planned so, without recovering from my journey, I nearly went cross-eyed watching, from the side, three tennis matches at the same time, feeling totally out of my element. Several of my girl friends were now living in Calcutta and I was soon on the phone to Iti, Bitty and Veena arranging to meet, as well as dear Bulbul, as she and Benji had been transferred from Madras. Next day we all had a hilarious lunch and reminisced about our difficult times together in the heat and dust of Guntur, a place none of us had enjoyed. They were all north Indians and had found the town as difficult as I still did. I had more in common with these women than with any of the expatriates I met in Calcutta.

Afterwards and alone I visited the Victoria Memorial, probably the most solid reminder of the British Raj, a rather Taj Mahalish museum in strong contrast to some of the towering colonial buildings on Chowringhee, flanking the great Maidan. Previously I had read of Emily Eden, spinster sister of George, Lord Auckland who was Governor General from 1836-1842. Emily joined him in India when she was 39 and they travelled extensively for more than two years. She was a novelist and developed into an excellent water colourist, painting an entire cross-section of Indian characters from servants to street people, and Maharajahs and their families. There was a lovely exhibition of her flower and plant paintings and of her illustrated diaries. It was an unusual and uplifting experience and made me realise that we were all kin in this land of great hardship.

Her travelling was by barge, foot, and by pony. In the Himalayas they went by sedan chair and travelled as far afield as Allahabad, Fatehpur Sikri, Mussoorie and Lahore. It made my little journey on the Howrah Mail seem quite tame. It was a poignant visit, seeing her beautiful art so tastefully portrayed by the people of the land that she obviously loved.

Calcutta – Bulbul, Mike, Natalie, Gerald and Anthea

Mike returned from Bangladesh, and we had an enjoyable weekend seeing friends and then it was time to return to Guntur, Mike going his way by air and me going my way. Gerald and Anthea took me to catch the 8pm train, the station was dim and crowded, we waited surrounded by a bunch of highly made-up transvestites or eunuchs. They were men with shaven chests, elaborate hairstyles, pulling bright shiny saris round bony bodies, their voices squeaking above the chatter of the crowds, their ear and nose rings twinkling in the lamplight. They were an eccentric lot and not in the least curious about other passengers. It was probably Anthea's first visit to Howrah and the culture shock for anybody new to the country was obvious, railway stations are like human anthills with just about everything possible going on all around you. Feeling perfectly safe I waved out of the window until they were out of sight, which happened in seconds as they were swallowed up by the crowds. My journey back was as peaceful as the one up, and it was good to get home to Guntur only to find that our first Japanese house guest was already in residence, well settled in the spare room strumming Susina's guitar. Luckily Mariamma, with all her good sense, was looking after him like a mother hen, clucking to me, "Why he bring no clothes, only packets of food and three shirts? Lucky we have no monsoon, how to dry, isn't it?" His arrival ensured that we were immediately back into the hectic life of *the season* which overcame us once again.

It was March 1977 and election time. Indira Gandhi was campaigning like a woman bewitched and the whole country was in uproar. She was coming to Guntur! I couldn't believe it and rang all the girls and said that we must go and see her. They were flabbergasted, "What for?" they asked, "Why do we want to see her?".

"She's the most prominent woman in India," I urged, "We must go." So it was almost like another movie outing and we arranged to picnic at the Club as she was attending a rally of 7,000 people in the adjacent park. She addressed the wholly Telugu crowd in English, looking old and drawn, wearing a dreary white sari with a grey border. There was no visual reminder of the striking woman with a white flash in her dark hair, aquiline nose and firm eyes, but she was dynamic, quick moving and forceful and arrived, standing in an open car, waving and smiling. By that time she had travelled thousands of miles showing amazing stamina. Only a few days later someone attempted to assassinate her son, Sanjay, in the north but there was little in our local papers. Indira lost her seat in her Uttar Pradesh constituency, *and* the election despite the strong Congress following in the south. Returning to Delhi she formally ended the State of Emergency imposed in 1974 and resigned. It was a crushing defeat and, at the age of 59, she was unemployed and homeless. Although unsympathetic, I had followed the fortunes of this strong, troubled woman now to be replaced by Moraji Desai, 81, a thin determined freedom fighter and staunch follower of Mahatma Gandhi's ideals.

Back – Kalyani and Prabha
Front - Geetha, Mangala, -, Shireen, Shaila, -

Waiting for Indira Gandhi in Guntur

The following month the children flew out for their holidays and it was difficult to know what to do with them. The kindly Martyn let us use his pool whenever we could get transport, otherwise it was languid living at home. Ever since we returned to Guntur I had resorted to an afternoon siesta. All of us women succumbed because of heat and boredom. Ostensibly it was *to read* but we admitted that we fell asleep despite the noise outside. The habit became unbeatable because it alleviated the boredom. It was difficult for young lively children just out for the holidays to understand how their mothers could wilt in the midday sun but, every day, I was up at 5am seeing Mike off, and somehow managed to get through an intensely lonely day until I could hear his Ambassador car engine rounding the curve, often well after 10pm. Only then would we have dinner together. When they were at home, the children waited long past their bedtime to *see Daddy* but often could not stay awake so late. The habit of an afternoon zizz was well instilled, and the children were very irritated with me as afternoons were such a fallow time and they were at their most bored. There was no answer except that I was a lousy mother who was *always in bed.*

We put up with four windy days at Vadarevu with a lot of customers to look after, and with very little help from the servants. Valerie and Chris Yewdall from Chicpet came down one weekend, scooped us up and we all drove four miles down the beach, cooked a barbecue and played silly games. The sea was incredibly rough but we were careful. One Sunday was very exciting. The night before, Hari Babu, a local landowner, came over with a bottle of Scotch. He often did this, he sought our company and that of other expatriates who might be visiting. He was a mild mannered gentleman, always wearing a dhoti and shirt, often bringing goodies and sitting quietly sharing our conversation. He was a man we all respected and had a great deal of affection for him. The children were jumping around and his eyes sparkled. "Tomorrow," he said wisely, "I will bring you a surprise."

"What surprise? What will you bring?" they were intrigued as not much happened in the surprise line those days.

"Wait and see, I will come at eleven in the morning."

And he did, with an elephant! The animal was so relaxed, having walked ten miles from Chirala and was enjoying all the fuss and attention. We, and all our guests, were flabbergasted, we never expected an elephant. The huge beast went through its paces, taking everyone for rides on its back, garlanding Mike and feasting on all the bananas we could find. Later Hari Babu told us there was a little circus in town and he had persuaded, and paid, the circus master to lend us his elephant for the morning.

On another weekend we arranged a big party on our roof garden and managed to entertain 22 people to dinner, drinks and dancing ending at four in the morning. The children loved it. After a few days they all went back to school and then the heavens opened with unprecedented rains and very high humidity.

Mike was busy with demanding foreign customers who were arriving at the same time but from different directions, and needing to be accompanied to both factories as well as having a few days rest on the beach. Mr I was being his difficult self which added to the stress, and there was a conspiracy erupting but nothing came of it, although company politics were on a big wobble. It was obvious that everyone was feeling nervous and the weather was unusually hot and the season unusually drawn out. We were beginning to feel that our days in India were numbered and, an added complication for Mike, was that three British nurses working at the Kugler Hospital had been employed under false pretences, and were not provided with return tickets to the UK. I did my best for them over the weeks, writing lots of letters to the High Commission. They were decent girls – two from Wales and one from Glasgow – and did not deserve such shabby treatment. Eventually they were repatriated and very grateful for our help and intervention.

Alfred Hall, the Deputy British High Commissioner in Madras, always firmly supported us once he had witnessed the way we existed. He wanted some recognition for Mike and wrote to the Chief Secretary of Andhra Pradesh in Hyderabad in June 1977, suggesting that an award come from the Indian side. An extract of the letter states: *It is that of Mr M T Wheatley who is Manager Production Planning and Marketing of the India Tobacco Co Ltd, ILTD Division at*

Guntur. This company earns for India, foreign exchange at the rate of about 25 crores (ten million) *of rupees a year. Mr Wheatley is totally in charge of all export of leaf tobacco and, in addition, a million kilos of exportable tobacco as well as very large amounts of tobacco for domestic use. ITC-ILTD exports tobacco to all countries of the world except China and South America and are responsible for the development of tobacco and tobacco cultivation, the purchasing and processing of tobacco, and its sale for industrial use in both export and domestic markets.*

Apart from the factory and field aspects, Mr Wheatley, most ably supported by his wife, make it their business to entertain a stream of foreign buyers of all nationalities who come to Andhra to inspect the crop and verify their purchases. In itself this is, I would suggest, a valuable contribution to relations between the State of Andhra Pradesh and the outside world, as well as of significance for the tobacco and industry. The Wheatleys have been doing this for many years.

It was a wonderful gesture on Alfred's part but, literally the day after he wrote the letter, Central Government announced that they were suspending all Indian awards.

Bujie became very ill at the AMG orphanage in Chicpet and we fetched him home. Previously they refused to allow him out but now I insisted having heard from Monica that they did not have much to eat, "We only get three bowls of rice a day," she said in her little voice, "No milk or curds, no banana or vegetables" The doctor confirmed that Bujie was suffering severe anaemia, so bad he almost needed blood transfusions. We put him on a gentle high protein diet and administered the medicine the doctor prescribed. He was so weak he could hardly walk but, gradually, he became well and strong again. Bujie enjoyed the most happy-go-lucky attitude and was always a cheerful smiley boy, it was more than distressing for all of us to see him so sickly. I was angry with Mr John David who was creaming off the cash and made him aware that we were not pleased.

I was getting fed up, we had two Japanese staying in the house, Mike was shortly off to Thailand and we had just coped with an invasion of directors from Calcutta. Mike wrote to David at school in Suffolk from Chiang Mai, *I am in Northern Thailand where I am buying tobacco. It is a lovely place on the borders of Laos and Burma. The countryside is very pretty as they have just planted the rice crop and all the fields are a beautiful emerald green. The hills are rather like the ones in Ooty and they cut teak trees and have elephants to load the logs onto lorries. The people are very nice and live in little houses that stand on sticks. In one village they make parasols with bamboo covered with painted silk. All my love Daddy.*

We were having constant power cuts and water shortages and intense heat. I had reached my limit coping with ILTD politics, heat, servants, bazaar shopping and, above all, my own company. Mike was not companionable, his mind was too engaged, and I was beginning to doubt my sense of survivalism, I was bored, angry, and losing my grip in this alien environment. Even Mariamma was flagging.

"Too hot," she tried to smile, "Last year not so hot, no? This year bad," she was chopping onions and tears streamed, "Sorry Ma, only onions," and laughed a little. I wanted to hug her.

Lightness and brightness for me was the gaggle of Indian women in the company who included me in their movie outings. Mike hated me going off to the sweaty flea pits with the flasks of tea and sandwiches, but what else did I have to do when not eternally entertaining? Someone would phone in the morning, either Geetha, Shaila, Kalyani, Mangala or one of the others. "Natalie are you ready for the movies? We're going to see *Siddartha* today." A car collected me and my little snack basket, and we drove into town to sit in the best (very dirty) seats and giggle our way through whichever Tamil, Telugu or Hindi movie was on. They were full of colour, dash, drama, intrigue and passion, each scene enhanced by amazing sequences of singing and dancing. I was privileged to be included in their girlie outings and it helped my sanity. Mike was hardly at home and worked and travelled endlessly, it was a terribly hard time and could have broken a lot of men - and women.

He was due a trip to Japan and *finally* sensed that I was running out of steam, so suggested I may like to go some of the way with him and stay with friends, Doreen and Mike Teale, who were with BAT Hong Kong. Having put up with so many disappointments in the last two years, I was not prepared to even think about it until the ticket was in my hand. Justifiably, as a planned trip to Madras to firm up details was cancelled at the last minute for a Russian inspection, but Mike sent a telegram to Hong Kong and then went to Anaparti for several days. I was on tenterhooks as the reply was to be delivered to the office, the phone didn't work and I was reliant on a messenger on a bike to bring me the news. At 11am on a Saturday morning the khaki-uniformed *peon* arrived and knocked on the front door, "Telegram Ma," he saluted.

Hakka people in the New Territories

Opening it slowly, my heart was beating. The words *Most Welcome* hit my eyes. I literally screamed with joy, screamed and screamed. The *peon* was embarrassed, "Yes Ma," hesitantly, "Bad news Ma?"

"Good news! Good news!" I screamed and jumped up and down.

"I am going Ma," said the *peon* shaking his head in confusion.

Mariamma came out of the kitchen wiping her hands, "Madams! Madams! Wokay? Why you making this noise?" I calmed down and explained to her that I was going away with *Ayagaru* in an aeroplane to China, "Just for a few days."

"Good Ma," she said, "You need a holiday, but I shall be lonely, never mind Ma I'll take the 28 bus and we'll all go cinema," and went back to her chores. I was so excited and there were only three days to get my clothes together and arrange for the house to function, the Japanese to be looked after and everything to tick along as it always did."

We flew into Hong Kong, swooping through the high rise buildings, peeking at people through their windows eating breakfast, and landing dramatically at Kai Tak airport on a runway that seemed to disappear into the sea. I couldn't believe that it was me being whisked away from such misery by a husband with a magic wand. The Teales were most welcoming and Doreen went out of her way to show us around that first day, before Mike flew on to Tokyo.

It was ten days of joy, Hong Kong was such a modern and slick surprise, at least on the surface, and a huge cultural change from Guntur. Doreen was such a good listener having lived and coped with children in various parts of Africa, she understood, sympathised and made me feel a great deal happier. We did all sorts of exciting things like going up the Peak on the steep railway, shopping at Aberdeen, taking the Star Ferry to Kowloon hunting for hand painted china, visiting the New Territories, buying pirate cassettes in the night markets, riding on a junk and sailing out in the harbour with friends for lunch. It was all new, exciting and very restorative. Mike and I travelled back to India via Bangkok and Dacca in Bangladesh and I felt, for the first time for years, that it was a real holiday.

As soon as we got back to Guntur, I was busy settling up bills organising to go on leave, and flew to UK in July to see my mother and attend speech and sports days at the four different schools in Suffolk. Mike, having fought off company conspiracies, arrived back exhausted in August, and we spent a busy time with the children, friends and relations. Realising that a new posting may be imminent, we purchased a mansion flat in Chiswick, London with the intention that the children should eventually use it and continue their further education in London when the time was right.

1977 David and Andrea

Simon

Susina

Chapter 29 – Cyclone

Mike returned to Guntur and I joined him in November, a cooler time of the year; when we were more relaxed as it was the slack season. He met me at Hyderabad, my journey was hampered by delay and I caught a connection from Bombay by cajoling everyone to help. The usual cockroaches greeted me in the hotel bathroom, on the plane there was a dead fly in my coffee and, at Patabipuram, the rats were back causing dreadful damage inside our cupboards. On the first morning, a rat crawled over the toilet seat, and I was upset by a monstrous house which had been built behind ours, obscuring all views and deflating our breeze. It was time to go, by then we knew this was our last tour, Mike had been requested by BAT Head Office in London and we would depart the following May.

Mariamma was totally upset and shocked, "But my children are too small," she sobbed.

Guntur Bazaar

Then, on 19 November, the Andhra coastline was struck by one of the worst cyclones in memory. All India Radio failed to alert the population of this impending deterioration of weather, so the majority of fishermen were lost. Lack of weather forecasting and warnings caused more death than was justified and, on land, people were just *swept away* in their hundreds. Estimated mortality was between 6,000 and 10,000 people. It was midday on a Saturday and Mike was unusually at home. The storm began mid-morning and was getting worse and we were in for 12 hours of winds up to 150 mph and 16 inches of rain. Our experience was frightening but for the thousands of hut dwellers living by the river it was the end of their world.

We moved carpets and furniture into an upstairs room and soon the ground floor was flooded. The house was flimsily built with cheap windows and doors and lots of glass. The folding veranda doors opening on to an outside patio were quite unsafe and, had they gone, the whole house would have been trashed. Mike and I spent four solid hours holding them together with our hands and feet which were made more secure by our rubber flip flops. The pressure and sound of the wind was overwhelming. The buffalo man's house next door collapsed and we accommodated nine wet, shivering people in our sitting room overnight providing blankets, food and hot coffee. For poor people like this the situation was dreadful. Next day, everywhere was wrecked and damaged with people sitting on boxes or buckets holding a baby or a chicken, cold, hungry and homeless. All around there were dead bodies and animals putrefying in the humid sunshine. Three days after the event I wrote to my mother, *The rain just lashed and damage to buildings is unbelievable, 75% of all trees are uprooted and steel electric poles bent to the ground, wires hanging everywhere, roads blocked, railway lines buckled and all communications severed. To begin with we could only be reached by army helicopter but now a few trains are running, but all phone lines are still down.*

Mike's priorities were toward company personnel and property, and any British citizens. We set off in a jeep to Chirala and visited all the depots, the factory and also Brigadier Plummer. Her house was completely flooded and her cat had drowned, much worse was that the local church collapsed, killing over a hundred people sheltered inside. Devastation was everywhere, whole villages immersed in water, all the paddy crop flooded, dead buffaloes, cows and sheep were rotting all over the place. The stink was awful and the journey difficult as we drove round wrecked bridges, fallen trees and turned over vehicles. There was nothing that was untouched, not a single thing left intact, it was as if every building and field been methodically smashed. We toured the whole area apart from the impassable villages in the delta area, which were obliterated by a tidal wave, and we were totally speechless at the extent of death and destruction. On 29 November we prepared a report for the British High Commission which was sent off to the Foreign Office in London and acknowledged with gratitude.

The Indian Express on Tuesday 22 November highlighted the death toll of the low lying districts of Krishna and Guntur which took the brunt of the cyclone and, without warning, an 18 foot tidal wave forced itself through the coast line and roared ten miles inshore swallowing everyone and everything in its path. People understandably forget that tidal waves rush in but, several hours later, suck back out again with equal force, this wave was phenomenal taking its share of life inwards and collecting the rest clinging on to trees or a few flimsy grass roofs on its return to the sea.

A reporter, Abu Abraham, visited a place called Pamarru, 20 miles from Vijayawada, *We stopped the car to buy naphthalene balls and I put several in my shirt pocket and then lit a cigar.*

The stench of decay hit our nostrils, a charred buffalo lay on the left and a mangled cow, dead for days, to our right. The removal of carcasses and dead bodies is no easy job. There are thousands of them, some have been partially burnt with petrol, but don't burn easily when covered in wet mud. The land is flat like a billiard table, this is the rice bowl of Andhra, the paddy fields stretch out to the horizon, dotted by clusters of broken down mud huts and lined criss cross by palm trees. The telegraph poles, battered bent and twisted, stand in various postures of submission, their wires broken and curled up in confused patterns across the beaten fields. Banana plantations and orchards are totally wrecked and tobacco fields and buildings have gone without trace. There are no vultures – have they had their fill? There was no water, the wells filled with corpses. Survivors were gathered at Avanigadda, the taluk headquarters, ambulances, army jeeps, VIP cars, CARE workers, volunteers, Congressmen and foreign journalists were all gathered to help these, the most wretched people I have ever seen anywhere in the country, cyclone apart they are the poorest of the poor, ill-fed, ill-clad and down trodden. Why is it that so rich a region has such wretched poverty? What is this system that we have been tolerating for so long that these peasants and fishermen should live in their miserable mud huts with palm leaf thatching that can be wrecked by any monsoon storm, never mind a cyclone? How is it that these people who fill our granaries and earn foreign exchange from exported fish, are the most neglected and starved, driven like slaves?

The Andhra government set up rescue services using the army and navy and a Cyclone Relief Fund to which the ILTD donated one lakh of rupees. The media were alerted; Billy Graham, promising US$100,000 aid, flew in from America and Mother Teresa came down from Calcutta and was reported in the Indian Express, *Andhra Pradesh has suffered a natural calamity in which thousands of people have perished. In all these human tragedies God is trying to teach us something. We are not able to understand Him.* She, and her Sisters of Charity, said they would help to rehabilitate people. The Hindu of 22 November relayed, *Fear and insecurity prevails in the slums of Guntur, where the poor people have borne the brunt of Saturday's cyclone that hit the coastal districts. Slum after slum, the people go about salvaging what all they can with a fatalist look on their faces. Asked how many people were killed in the slum, a man pointed to a hut on his left and said four people were killed there. Then he pointed to another hut and said six people were killed there. Finally he pointed to a third hut in front and said he did not know how many people were killed there, because nobody yet attempted to clear the débris.*

We were completely cut off for over a week with no power or kerosene for lamps. Fortunately our well coped with washing and cooking but was risky for drinking. Many of the leaf storages lost their roofs and much of the packed tobacco became rain damaged. Both Chirala and Anaparti factories were closed for seasonal overhaul but were reopened to re-dry the damage. This took three months, management and workers forfeiting their annual leave and the factories running non-stop triple shift through both seasons.

Captain and Mrs Dartnall-Smith were then managing the badly damaged Bapatla leprosy hospital, their daughter aged 16 was coming home by train from Coonoor, but the service was severely disrupted and they did not know where she was. On a long shot I made the 20 mile journey to Vijayawada, people had spotted a young expatriate female and, after two hours searching, she was found in a shop trying to phone her parents. Miriam was exhausted and desperately worried so I was able to set her mind at rest. She travelled third class *alone* due to some mix up of travel plans, and was constantly bothered by young men. In Guntur she cried with relief and we kept her overnight, setting out next morning to find her mother in the middle of a crowd with a cholera vaccine team. Once she and Miriam greeted each other with relieved tears, she continued to vaccinate about ten people a minute with the same needle.

In England Susina was having breakfast at school listening to the BBC news and heard that Guntur was severely battered by a cyclone. The school contacted BAT and she eventually heard that we were safe, as did our other children. Over the weeks we received some wonderful letters from friends who sympathised with the terrible situation the people of Andhra were suffering. Susina sobbed with relief when she saw us at Madras airport. Christmas was spent in Patabipuram with six young English cyclone relief volunteers we discovered, it was a jolly time. The buildings at the beach were all badly damaged, but we spent a day there and enjoyed an incredibly calm sea and a beautifully clean beach as well as lovely weather.

1978 – Taj Mahal

On New Year's Day an Air India 747 crashed on take off from Bombay with all 230 lives lost. This terrified us, as the children were flying home shortly after, but we kept the news from them. Leaving Mike in Guntur, we flew from Hyderabad to Delhi and Simon picked up the newspaper on his seat. "Mum! Mum!" he called from several rows behind, "There's been a terrible Air India crash, did you know? Everyone was killed."

"Yes we did know," I called, "It will be all right."

"*All right*?" questioned a gruff woman in a maroon sari across the aisle, "Do you call complete air crash *all right?* We should all be fearing for our lives, what do we know about this pilot we have today, is he *all right?"*

I did not know what to say except "I'm sorry, I had hoped my children would not hear about the crash, they are flying alone to London on an Air India 747," and she touched her forehead with three little taps of the tops of her fingers, a sign of distress, and we continued the journey in silence.

We were en route to the Taj Mahal which I was insistent we all see before we left India, having always clung to some strange idea that it towered over the whole city of Agra. When we rolled into the station I implored them to "Look up! Look up!"

"Where is it Mummy?" Andrea was excited after all this anticipation.

"It's here! Look up!" But there was no Taj and no Mahal. We took a taxi for a couple of miles before Susina said, "There it is."

"Where? Where?" I was excitable, scared of missing my promised treat. And there it was, in its beautifully laid out gardens, a mere shadow of my imagination. The children giggled at my foolishness.

We stayed at a wonderful ITC hotel in a suite and enjoyed every minute of the luxury. The marble palace set with precious and semi-precious stones was exquisitely beautiful and was built in memory of the third wife of Shah Jehan, Mumtaz, a Persian princess who died giving birth to their 14th child. It took 22 years to construct by 20,000 workers with the help of 1,000 elephants heaving materials to the site where Shah Jehan also lies. We loved north India, the tall stately Sikhs with their colourful turbans, the tasty meals and delicious snacks, the grand buildings and the cold weather – it was actually freezing. In Delhi we saw the British Prime Minister, James Callaghan and his wife Audrey, meeting with Moraji Desai at the Red Fort. We also visited the silver bazaars and the arts and crafts stalls and took a taxi to Fatehpur Sikri, an abandoned Moghul city, driving through rugged countryside where we passed two black bears on leads. The children terrified me at the deserted city when they climbed to the top of the palace and ran around the flat roof which had no retaining walls, and they had no vertigo.

Next evening, two by two, the children boarded their separate flights, quivering with fear since the crash, and I returned to Vijayawada by air feeling more of a traitor than ever. The flights were severely delayed due to heightened security, and they all returned to school absolutely and utterly exhausted.

1978 - Hassan Mission House and dilapidated quarters

Visitors were constant for the next few months, plus our usual Japanese house guests, and Mike was away most of the time, so it was decided that I make a farewell tour of all our south Indian friends who lived on tea and coffee estates in the hills. Travelling by my usual second class to Bangalore I caught a very bumpy bus to Hassan and went to look at the Mission House. It was in a very bad state of repair and had become a large office selling tractors, there were ugly garages on one side, piles of tiles on the front lawn and the mango orchard had been cut down. For us it was such a happy home full of tumbling children with a garden bright with flowers. *Going back* was not a good idea. I continued up to the Foster's stud farm and enjoyed a happy and relaxing time and also contributed my skills as vintner and grape jam maker before departing. The Byerly Stud holds very special memories for all of us, a unique part of English India. I took another bus to Mysore City to stay with Zohra and enjoyed the scenery and flowering trees after the barrenness of Andhra. I was beginning to realise how much we would miss India and our dear friends, the food, colour and warmth. When in Delhi I purchased yards and yards of natural cotton curtaining at a factory called FabIndia, and arranged to have it made up by Spencer's furnishing department in Madras. They did a first class job complete with linings, rufflette tape, even brass hooks, and we had curtains ready to hang on arrival at our new flat in London. Having sold quite a lot of second hand goods in Guntur I was able to buy brass lamps, silk lampshades and a glorious rust red Kashmiri woven mat.

I made a side trip to the Annamalai hills, a place I visited before, travelling up from Coimbatore by bus to Pollachi round 40 hairpin bends. The driver was a show-off and spent more time with his head turned towards his friends in the back, rather than on the road ahead. I had often done this journey and it was always scary but just wonderful to reach its termination into a valley 22 miles long and 12 miles wide, thick with green tea bushes. I stayed with the Rawlleys earlier at Thay Mudi, but this time they were living on Iyerpadi Estate in a house made completely from wood. Meena was lonely but her usual sweet and welcoming self, I would miss her generous company. Nickoo was in a state of mid-life crisis and trying to find himself, but hospitable and gracious

Meena Rawlley at Thay Mudi Estate, Annamallais

I returned to Guntur absolutely exhausted and Mike was still away. Mr Iwasaki became ill with infective hepatitis and flew to Delhi and on to Tokyo thinking he may die, but he didn't. His homesickness made him a morose guest, but Shegiru Inoue, his Japanese Monopoly counterpart, always cheered things up.

On 26 April 1978 Mike received a letter from the British Deputy High Commissioner in Madras, Neville French, *I should like to record here the gratitude of the High Commission for the sterling services you have rendered to British interests throughout your 14 years, of which I have some small personal experience after the cyclone and storm wave of last November when you acted so promptly to keep me informed about UK residents and the general situation in your area. As I think I have told you, your report on the aftermath of the disaster was first class, and the copies I sent to London and Delhi were received with genuine appreciation.*

We were definitely now on the downward slope to departure and, in no time, the children were out for the Easter holidays. This would be their last and we were delighted that, as we were to leave in May, we could all enjoy the last few weeks in ILTD as a family together. The children were now 15, 13 and the twins, 11, and were all able to enjoy the plethora of parties given in our honour. The weather was very hot and the seats in the Ambassador car were covered in towels to stop us sticking to them. With our driver, Sesh Giri Rao, we all squashed in and travelled several times from Guntur to Chirala, to the depots and for a couple of nights to Anaparti factory. Despite all the problems with living and adjusting particularly to Andhra, we were always aware of the kindness and affection that our Indian counterparts had for us, sometimes difficult for them to express, it was very evident that they were particularly fond of Mike, the last expatriate in the company and also his lively family. We gave a large party for 60 people on our roof, decorating the whole area with twinkly coloured lights. Mariamma and I cooked the food, and super music was provided by the Chicpet tobacco buyers who brought a powerful stereo system and all the newest cassettes. It was exhausting, and afterwards we packed up all our stuff as there were no professional packers available, it was even harder for the children clinging on to their few belongings, but they finally let go.

1978 - Sesh Giri Rao, Simon, Susina and Mariamma on the way to the airport

Monica, Bujie and Premila were sad little figures peeping round doorways watching the break up of what had been an extension to their home for several years. They were sweet, quiet children and we loved them all. I spent several weeks making patchwork quilts for everyone, and one or two left over, the thick cotton being just right for the winter months. Mariamma was very uneasy, like a dog that was to be left behind, her whole world was falling apart. I had worked so hard to make her independent, and she was strong and determined, but so sad. Whenever it was necessary to *sign* for money from her post office book, she was finger printed because she was illiterate, rolling her fingers and thumb on a purple inked pad. I was determined before we left that she would learn to write her name, but first I had to learn how to write her name and then teach her. It took several weeks to get the twirly bits right but, finally, we went to the post office to withdraw money and she wrote *Mariamma* in Telugu - it was thrilling for both of us as the man stamped her book and handed out the money.

Although she did not want to continue with domestic work, preferring a 9-5 job, she realised her qualifications were limited, so we arranged for her to be taken on by Maddi Lakshmaiah in Chicpet, and work in his company guest house. She and her children were a very special part of all our lives, their ups and downs, their sickness and health, we were very bonded together, and we still are. We did everything possible to set Mariamma up with some security, she had a savings account and a job, all the children were being educated in the improved AMG Home, and she had the commitment to settle in Chicpet and to save up enough money to build a simple dwelling with a strong roof. The last thing we gave her was a brand new radio.

When the children went back to school she accompanied the driver and saw them off at Gannavaram airport, weeping her heart out, but steadfast in her farewells.

Mr I, always aware that Mike had kept him at arms length, and always aware that he never once received an invitation to our home, gave us a farewell party and, to the end, the relationship remained dignified. We had all had a rough ride under such tyrannical management and he was unrelenting, but gave a courteous respectful speech. We smiled and shook hands and left the ILTD on a good footing.

Mariamma wailed when we left, completely heartbroken. It was the hardest thing to cope with, even Mike hugged her with tears in his eyes and she, and the weeping children waved pathetically from the gate.

We flew to Calcutta and there stayed with the Sparrows, themselves shortly posted to London – it was strange that the first company expatriates we stayed with in India in May 1964 were the last we stayed with in May 1978. Having all done our best, we survived and had a good innings.

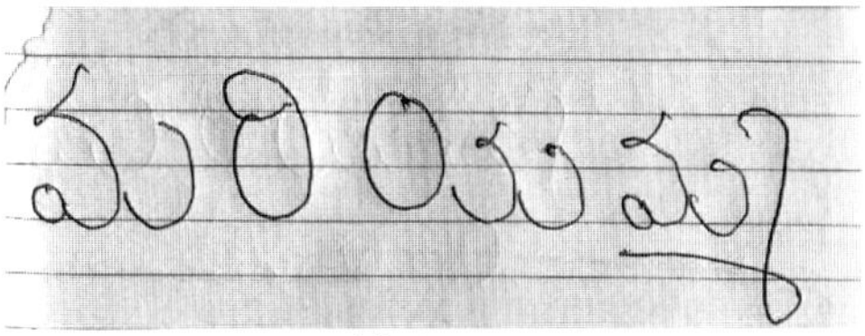

Mariamma

Chapter 30 – London and Sierra Leone

London was difficult, we had not lived in such a noisy city nor amongst so many of our own kind. We were more at home amongst the sari shops of Southall, eating dosais and bumping into brown men in wool jackets and Astrakhan hats. Our large flat was a godsend, we all fitted in until our Woodbridge home was tenant free. The children continued at their East Anglian schools, taking important exams and going through their own paces of teenage drama, it was good to be on hand but the fees stretched us. Mike worked out of BAT Head Office in Millbank and travelled to Canada, Korea, America, Japan, Thailand and India. Clothes were a problem, on the same trip he was often in temperatures of minus 40°C, and the next week in plus 40°C.

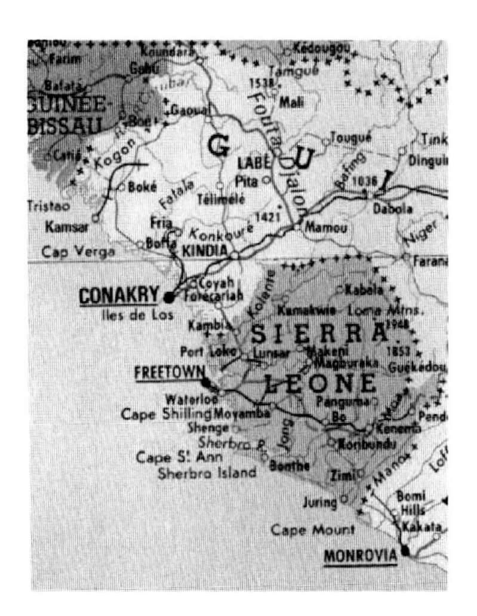

Qualified only for testing the suppleness of okra or how to remove weevils from flour, it was decided that I should return to work and, as I retired at 22, this was formidable. I joined a government secretarial re-training course and, after struggling through exams, enrolled at Key Employment Agency in Shepherds Bush and worked through them as a temp for the next two years. Companies do not like temps or paying for temps and I met a lot of unfriendliness. However I worked my way up to the top floors of large civil engineering and construction companies, and the big bosses thought I knew what I was doing – my years abroad seemed to have given me a certain aura of internationalism, rather than an intense familiarity with Guntur smells. I loved it all; good clothes, properly cut hair, make-up that did not slide off my face, and learning, just learning all the time. It was hard work managing the kids, two homes, two jobs and lots of travelling and jet lag for Mike. We often left Woodbridge late on a Sunday night and our adrenalin reached high levels as we beat the 17 sets of traffic lights on the Marylebone Road. The whole performance had to be timed exactly right and it didn't matter who was driving, it was like the start of the Grand National. We hovered gently until the first lights turned green and, from then on, it was the acute knowledge of exactly when the next ones had been programmed to change. Most Sundays we won the race, and howled and hooted with joy as we sped over the Paddington flyover and got back to our lofty and freezing flat.

Mike phoned from Millbank one day, "We've been posted to Sierra Leone." My heart stopped, I was on the crest of a career and the children had become so used to us being *at home*. He was up for a new challenge and pleased to return to leaf growing, but what was I going to do in Freetown – coffee parties and sewing sessions? I hardly had time to think, the flat was rented out, my current job completed, the children kitted out for beaches, parties and a teenage paradise. It was December, no summer clothes in the shops and we were going to White Man's Grave with intense heat and humidity. So I bought a Barbra Streisand record of *Guilty*, packed my bags and travelled out with a Sierra Leonean lady who had seven hats on her head, *You no go bring any hat?*" she asked me, *Why for no one tell you dat in Freetown you can never go for church unless you have a good hat and dress.* She was right, we were soon summoned to church by our Aureol Tobacco Chairman in Waterloo village, and I had to borrow a hat for the occasion and sat beside a man called Mr Crowther-Nicol, a Krio, who wore a wool pin-striped suit with waistcoat, a gold watch chain stretched across his tummy, shiny black shoes and carried a Homburg hat. These people were formal and proper.

Brimah

Sierra Leone has a deep history, and Freetown was the place freed slaves were repatriated in the 18th century. In 1787 a party of 400, including 70 white prostitutes, arrived and set up their own Province of Freedom and were later joined by 500 Maroons from Jamaica. Over the next 60 years some 500,000 liberated slaves settled in Sierra Leone, mostly Christian Creoles or Krios. The rickety wooden houses teetering along Pademba Road are of creole design, constructed from clapboard with little balconies and bougainvillea climbing over the corrugated iron roofs. Hill Station is another area, cooler and forested and, once, a little train chugged up and down from the city. Many of the houses, and the club, were wooden and were said to have been pre-fabricated and shipped out from Harrods department store in London, and were known as *Harrods* houses. This was the residential preserve of colonial government officers who also had their own Hill Station hospital and took the train daily to the city to work. The stations had English names like Regent, Hastings and Wellington. We enjoyed the company of many Krio families. They were tall and handsome, rather academic and elegant, always good company sharing a lot of mirth. Many of them had double-barrelled names like Taylor-Morgan and Sho-Sawyer and followed careers in law or medicine rather than entrepreneurial pursuits, leaving those to the Lebanese who lusted for diamonds.

When we arrived in 1980, Sierra Leone was on the brink of economic collapse and civil war, due to corruption and diamond smuggling, sliding away from the comfort zone of adequate food, education and jobs for everybody. With a backdrop of lush mountains, Freetown steamed with a poverty stricken richness which only survives in tropical surroundings. Ancient old buses and *poda podas* (collective taxis filled to bursting point) plied the pot holed streets, hooting ceaselessly as they teetered round the 500 year old Cotton Tree and through the crowds of traders, market mammies with picans clinging to their backs, labourers, a few safari suited foreigners and ragged children darting everywhere.

The cost of living was high and there were shortages, I met a Dutch woman in the cold store who gave me the best advice, "If you look at the price of everything you will starve." We inherited a wily old cook, Conteh, whose previous employer was on a bachelor footing, so Conteh had a flourishing ice cream business operating from our kitchen freezer. He introduced us to Brimah, a tall, friendly lad, "He can be our *small boy* Missis, too much work for me." Conteh got smarter and lazier and we parted company. Brimah was our faithful, friendly servant for the next six years, he was a Muslim and illiterate, but an honest and hard worker. He loved to talk and, after a little while, I understood his pidgin English. In the dusky evenings we leaned out of the kitchen window together, watching the people climbing up the steep Signal Hill, weary after a day in the city below. "How de body," they would call to Brimah and he, always laughing, would reply "De body fine, thank God."

Soon after I arrived, our neighbours invited us to dinner, it was a large gathering and a buffet meal. A diminutive French woman wearing a boob tube and lots of lipstick introduced herself because I was new. After a high powered job in London, I was trying to adjust to hopping drains and searching for anything that looked like a vegetable.

"What are you going to do here?" she was curious, "Can you play Bridge?"

"No," was my reply."

"Or golf?"

"No," I smiled.

She sighed in desperation, "What about tennis?"

"I'm no good at tennis, can't hit the ball."

"What are you going to do then?"

"I shall be all right," I said, and she clicked off in her high heels to find someone more amusing.

Freetown was our first overseas *city* experience within a gated compound of four houses called Millbank. After the privations of India it was wonderful to be supplied with two large fridges, a freezer, a proper gas stove, hot water in the kitchen and *three* air conditioners. We lived upstairs and slept downstairs and the view from our balcony was stunning, stretching over the length of a lagoon and then Lumley Beach, and far across the Atlantic to the invisible coastline of Brazil. During the day we watched humming birds playing in the acacia tree, and bigger birds in the other trees. For the children on holidays, it was paradise, they made friends, had parties and it was a treat to see them enjoying themselves so much. We bought a Datsun station wagon, and Simon was soon driving and taking everyone down to Lumley Beach in the afternoons. I did my own shopping and went deep into the markets looking for curtain materials and carpets. Freetown had a burgeoning cloth business on Little East Street, mainly cut pieces from Liberty's and out-of-date Marks and Spencer fashion. There were piles of second hand clothing from Europe, known as *dead white man's clothes.*

Mike worked at Aureol Tobacco Company, a small cigarette making factory in Wellington, and also at Rokel Leaf, a company based in the town of Makeni 100 miles away over unspeakably rough roads, turning right at the decrepit Bond Street hotel. The leaf growing areas were further north in Kamakwie, Kamalu and Kabala. If I accompanied him, he left me in Makeni in a filthy company rest house crawling with insects and constructed from packing cases and mosquito netting. I felt like a chicken put in to roast slowly ready for the evening meal, and preferred the uncomfortable journeys and bush whacking. Instead I got a tin of Vim and a reluctant *I haven't cleaned this place for years* caretaker-cum-cook called Alimammy. The station manager lived next door and had a chimpanzee called Janet who, some feared, was an instigator of *juju* or black magic.

Simon and Janet

We experienced frightening electrical storms in Makeni, the thunder and lightning so fierce it sparked right through the circuits of the flimsy building. The climate was generally hot and humid and, in the summer months, the rain deluged and was deafening on the corrugated iron roofs. There was no mains electricity so it was back to candles and kerosene lamps when the generator failed, and water was supplied by lorry in drums. Away from a deteriorating Freetown, it was obvious that the countryside was undeveloped and uncultivated. On one trip we drove through the mangrove swamps and rain forested coastal plains to inspect tobacco fields, and Mike and his team went far into the bush. It was hot and there was a lot of walking, so I sat on a tree trunk for a couple of hours and waited until they returned. It was one of my nicest times, the villagers did not expect to see a white woman sitting on a tree trunk, they did not ignore me, but stopped with a quiet greeting, "How de body? "they asked politely. “Thank God,” I smiled, knowing it was the correct reply and they walked on with their machetes under their arms and baskets on their heads. Many people passed and not one threatened me, they were peaceful and desperately poor. The villages had mud huts and grass roofs, naked children waved at the roadside and old men sat under trees and dozed. Village life revolved around the church or mosque, the market and the school, that is if they were lucky enough to have any of those facilities. Sometimes there was not even a well.

Mr and Mrs Chief Alimammy Mansaray of Bafodia

We made a trip to Kabala, a hilly region 200 miles north east of Freetown over unmaintained laterite roads, the rivers bridged by tall trees, the trunks set length-wise not crosswise. In wet weather they were impossible to walk on and hazardous to drive over. Kabala was known as Little Switzerland, peopled by the Mandingo and Limba tribes and we were taken to meet a friendly old chief who entertained us in his circular hut settlement.

Afterwards we visited with some American Baptist missionaries who had sons called Jordan, Moses and Gabriel. As we drank tea, the preacher arrived with his shotgun and two dead baboons. His wife jumped up with joy, "The kids will enjoy these, I've got cassava and leaves to make a stew," and she scurried off to skin and butcher them before they stank. There was no fish in that area, so they existed on animals, rice, palm oil, yams, pineapples, pawpaws and whatever tinned food they could carry from Freetown.

Freetown has the third largest deep water natural harbour in the world, and in 1982 it was well used for supplying ships en route from Britain to the south Atlantic, after the Argentinians invaded and occupied the Falkland Islands. Emotions ran high, both countries adopted an air of fierce patriotism and Prime Minister, Margaret Thatcher, became the ruler of the waves. A naval task force was launched, the air force mustered and Britain was at war. The children were out for their Easter holidays and we heard, through the High Commission, that the P&O liner, Canberra, carrying troops would be re-fuelling next day at dawn. We had a collection of Union Jacks and dragged them out of the cupboards and, very early, drove to the Oil Refinery on the other side of town. We could see the liner out at sea, and could not understand why lights or glass were glinting in the sunshine, realising suddenly that the men on board were observing us waving our flags through their gun sights. The boat eased into the dock, almost at a list, as the men eyed our voluptuous blonde daughters, "Fancy a trip to the Falklands?" was the general jeer, with various other rude remarks meant to flatter rather than insult. It was our *five minutes of fame* for that evening we were on ITV's News at Ten and lots of people saw us. We felt rather proud being described by Brent Sadler, as *the only British family who came to cheer our brave troops.* We were the first to greet them, but other families provided a bank of support from the walls of the Bintumani Hotel as the ship sailed out re-fuelled, loaded with fresh water and replenished with vegetables and fruit.

Susina, Simon and Canberra

The following year a book was published called *Don't Cry for me Sergeant Major* giving a slightly different account of our greeting the Canberra, *The family had come in a spirit of goodwill and patriotism, with words of cheer and comfort for the troops. They soon wished they hadn't bothered. Mother was fat, and told so many times by the men at the rail. Father was offered everything from light tanks to cases of small arms for the loan of his buxom daughters. Young son was ignored, except when he shouted out 'Rule Britannia' in an attempt to boost morale. The troops replied loudly with such replies as 'Piss off you, little queer' or 'Here's a fiver, go and fetch your other sisters.*

A tender moment of Royal Marine courtship followed, as a member of 40 Commandos leaned over the rail and politely invited the young lady to 'Get your kit off and show us your tits.'

In Freetown, the Diplomatic Wives, *Dippy Wives*, were well organised into their lunches, coffee mornings and Bridge sessions which had no appeal, so I was reluctantly persuaded to join the British Women's Association, *Bitches and Witches,* and was soon busy compiling a monthly newsletter. I joined Keep Fit and helped with charitable work, the women were friendly and I took up golf which I enjoyed. My best hole was a par 5 dog leg which took me 23 shots before I got the ball in the hole. The course was close to the beach and we ricked our ankles in holes avoiding crabs as they scuttled out to grab our golf balls. I became Hon Sec of the Golf Club, a neglected position which became almost a full-time job. When not away, Mike worked a five day week which meant we actually had weekends, and Sundays were spent at various beach parties and evening occasions became more frequent.

Entertaining Freetown orphans at ATC's Baw Baw beach

The expatriate population of Freetown was a mixed bunch mostly international aid workers, a melting pot of senior management verging on retirement, a few young bloods starting out on careers abroad, and consultants who turned up with a couple of suitcases and stayed in hotels for a month or two. Many of them had not lived abroad before and found the conditions difficult. There were the usual volunteer organisations, Peace Corps, CUSO from Canada, VSO from Britain and Médecins Sans Frontières operating all over the country. We had our own company sponsored VSO, Rob Stevens, known as Rob the Pot, who lived in Mambolo and worked as a potter. He often stayed with us and house-sat when we were on leave, he shared our riotous Christmas's, and was a good friend to Brimah as he spoke pidgin so well. Bert and Lissa Kinsey were retired when they joined VSO, and worked as teachers, having been with the Navy in Mombasa and Gibraltar. Their life was difficult, with no water, proper food or accommodation, but they integrated well into the community of Port Loko, particularly with the Catholic church. We met them in Suffolk and discovered we were nearly related by marriage, and told them they were welcome to stay with us in Freetown. Confidently they said "We won't come without warning, we'll ring you from Port Loko."

We laughed, "You won't, you'll come unannounced from Port Loko by poda poda or lorry, find our house on Signal Hill and ask the guards to let you in." They spent many weekends with us, resting and rejuvenating, eating poached eggs on our veranda and drinking gin and tonics in the moonlight.

Elaine Lund and Ruth Hartley

Wheatley Family

Andrea, Jenni Comley and Kerri Doble

We were members of the Aqua Club and had a small sailing boat called Twinkle so were able to join in some of the water sports. There was always plenty to do, plenty going on and we made many good and long lasting friends in Freetown. We acquired our first dog, a fluffy mongrel with sweet brown eyes and the ridiculous name of Hearthrug. Brimah could not get his tongue round this and called her Alfred. We all adored her, she was a gentle, delightfully clean animal. We were told that when we went on leave our servants would pinch the *dog's chop,* but as we fed them too, there was no fear of that. For fun, I asked Brimah to lift the dog and stand on the bathroom scales, then I weighed him on his own and took one from the other and had 22 lbs of dog. When we returned they popped on the scales and we had 26 lbs of dog!

Mike also worked a week each month for the Monrovian Tobacco Company in Liberia. The country was known as *cops and robbers*, the cops being as bad as the robbers. In 1980 there was a military coup led by Master Sergeant Samuel Doe who deposed and murdered the President, and from 1989 to 2003 the country was wracked by civil wars with an estimated 200,000 loss of life. Mike started working in the country after the first coup, and the atmosphere was threatening and restless. He flew to Monrovia, was picked up by a jeep, the name *RENEGADE* splashed in orange across its doors, and driven by Amos. They went through the Firestone Rubber Plantation Concession established in 1926, said to be the world's largest, then way up into the bush to Ganta, where he stayed in a grotty little bar called Annie's Paradise on the Guinea border, until he got better accommodation. Early in 1981, having finished a week's work up-country, he returned to Monrovia to catch a flight back to Freetown. At that time the ground floors of all buildings on the streets of the city had been looted and stripped bare and, at night, there was a curfew and shooting on sight by rebels and para-military. Amos dropped him at the hotel entrance and he climbed the stairs and was violently mugged, but managed to beat off four thugs somehow protecting his wallet and watch. His trousers were in shreds and his legs covered in deep finger-nail scratches.

"Are you all right sah, you still got your wallet?" asked the receptionist on the first floor, who had a big torch on his desk. Mike nodded and went into his room making sure he was securely locked in. In the middle of the night he was attacked again by two men, a large metal torch was stuck into his face and the other cut into his throat with a knife. He pleaded that they leave his passport and air ticket but they took his wallet and watch, having forced their way through the glass louvres and disappeared the same way. He recognised the torch on the receptionist's desk next morning. Mike escaped murder, it was a nerve shattering experience and he flew out lucky to be on his way home to Freetown.

He continued his monthly visits and established himself in a small house in Ganta avoiding any overnights in Monrovia. Liberia, *Land of the Free,* was formed by freed African American slaves between 1821-1842 and was supported by the US Government. The slaves, known as Americo-Liberians, never assimilated with the 85% indigenous tribal population. From then on I accompanied him fairly regularly, Liberia was a very unsettled country and their style the worst of the Wild West, which seemed to emanate from anyone who had a smattering of authority, or wore a uniform. Our journeys up-country were hazardous as we had to pass through many road blocks manned by armed drunken soldiers who could have been government or rebels, gathered in mobs and very threatening. Amos was a calm driver and was usually arrested and accused of being a spy. He and Mike had a system that never failed. Whilst Amos was locked up, Mike played poker, always losing enough to set Amos free and amusing the soldiers, whose mood could change in an instant. I sat in the jeep and waited, it was stomach churning stuff.

Ganta was a nothing town in a nowhere place. There was one shop selling the usual corned beef, tomato purée and sardines, and a few women with baskets on the side of road hawking yams, plantains, leaves and perhaps a few oranges. Mike spent his days in the bush, and I was left with a short wave radio and a deafening generator in the so-called bathroom. There was a big empty space opposite our house and I watched endless games of village football. It made me realise what a universal game it is, which can be played anywhere with any number of people and have all sorts of rules. A football can be the key to a young lad's enjoyment and pleasure for the whole of his childhood, creating enormous fun and exercise. We were there one week in June, and I spent the time glued to the radio listening to Wimbledon, but mostly I took books to read, there was nothing else to do and it was always hot. I had no fear, as is usual in villages away from big towns, the people were pleasant, friendly and left me alone, but they knew I was there. We had a friendly caretaker, he cooked up bath water and made the inevitable chicken and rice in the evenings. We mostly sat in candlelight as we could not bear the noise of the generator.

Our final visit to Liberia was at a time when it was tumbling again towards anarchy and civil war. Incidents of violence and murder were common and everywhere, and we were sitting ducks on the lonely road, it was just us and Amos. The tobacco extension work had gone well, the crop had been harvested and it was the time to buy the tobacco and pay the farmers for their hard work. From the airport we had gone into Monrovia to collect the necessary dollars. Mike had worked out how much was required.

"This is not enough," he said.

"Don't worry," he was told, "We'll send up more later today."

Mike was insistent, "I cannot pay one farmer and not the other farmer, they will not understand and will become violent."

"We'll make sure you get the balance," and with that we left with the inadequate money tucked under the driver's seat.

"Not good," said Amos, "Farmers get angry, very angry." By 10pm no money had arrived, the farmers were agitating and Mike had to postpone the payout until the next day, they were not happy. By 3-00 next afternoon nothing had happened apart from rising discontent. Mike decided to face the farmers whilst Amos and I sat in the jeep near where they were meeting, still with the inadequate amount of dollars under the seat. I asked Amos if he was frightened, "Too much fear Missy, why no money come?"

I felt as if Mike had thrown himself to the gladiators and was almost physically sick and Amos was shaking. We sat tight, it got dark and, finally, Mike came back and got into the vehicle, "I've told them they will get it tomorrow," he said exhausted, "I have given them my word."

We had a flight to catch and set off for Monrovia in pitch dark, not a good time to travel with frequent road blocks. Half way there Amos spotted a company car coming towards us and stopped it, inside with the driver was a lone Liberian woman, one of the secretaries from the office. She was loaded with a huge amount of cash and should never had been sent on her own. The soldiers at the road blocks would definitely have been suspicious and, if they had found the money it is doubtful if the money, the car or the woman would have been seen again. Both could have been killed, the money and the car disappearing across the border to Guinea. Mike persuaded her to return to Monrovia and, next day, the cash was sent up under armed guard and distributed as he had promised.

It was a disappointing way to leave Liberia for the last time. Mike had worked hard with the farmers and knew they had been let down. It was obvious, at least, they trusted him and were prepared to let him go and wait yet another day, he would have liked to have rewarded them himself.

Leading the way to Black Johnson Beach

Sierra Leone's beaches are fabulous with white sand, backed by the tropical jungle of the *Lion Mountains*, some close to Freetown, but the most beautiful are further round the peninsula accessible only by forest pathways and breaks in the cliffs. There wasn't a single footprint on Black Johnson Beach which we discovered one Sunday after a few nearly naked villagers helped us locate the place. Another beach, Lakka, was steeply shelved, Essex was busy with fishermen and Number Two River changed with the tides, always different, and a place to shoot duck and hunt crocodiles in the deep inlets.

We took advantage of all the places and had an enjoyable group of friends, but I was becoming bored and needed a job. Striking lucky, I was employed as PA to the Delegate of the EEC (now European Union) which had diplomatic status. Mr Koedderitzch was my boss, an elderly, amusing Bavarian, ill-fitted for living in such a crumbling country but clever and knowledgeable about Non-Governmental Organisations, and the inside of a beer tankard. We got along fine because I organised him and he liked that. It was another *sorting out the filing* jobs, a succession of disinterested secretaries had taken up the post for a few months here and there, and no one had come to grips with the horrendously bureaucratic system hatched up by DGVIII – a floor in the vast EEC headquarters in Brussels. With difficulty I got my head round it, but sorting through decades of muddle was daunting, however I was encouraged by the engineering, economic and agricultural experts – Tony Kirk, Björn Gerslov and Johannes Sode – and the excitable Mr Koedderitzch. Wrestling with the clacking telex machine was another matter and the electronic typewriter, a new invention, as typing has never been my *thing*. I loved being back at work again, more so as I was paid in sterling, plus a local salary, and my National Insurance contributions were made in the UK. There were two Sierra Leonean women working in the office, Beatrice in charge of accounts and Tita the typist. We made friends and had a laugh but, in the end, it was really my clothes they were interested in when we left.

At times Mike was travelling 22 days a month, and I was one of few wives who were left alone so it was good to have a job. He went to Nairobi and flew to the leaf area, Malakisi, some distance from the capital. Four of them made a return flight in a twin-engined Cessna without navigational aids, except the pilot's compass and maps used by the passengers. They landed on the mud airstrip and, in the late afternoon, and took off for Nairobi encountering a fierce electrical storm. The pilot dived underneath the storm in order to keep track of his location, and the squawk box warned of constant danger as they flew terrifyingly at less than 100 feet altitude. The lightning was cracking and sparking and the windscreen obliterated by pelting rain, its wipers uselessly banging backwards and forwards. It was getting dark and the ground was uneven and bumpy and they flew between lines of eucalyptus trees absolutely sure they would crash land. Suddenly they came out of the storm, flew on to Nairobi, got out and shook hands, and nothing was said.

While he was away Brimah came one morning with a tiny sickly baby in his arms, "Me son," he said, without explanation, "He name Momoh".

"Your son?" having no idea he was married or had a son.

"Not well," he said worriedly, "Me missis she come down from Port Loko, baby sick"

"How old is the baby?"

"Ten months, not reached one year."

"Ten months!" the child did not look as if it had reached ten weeks and was chronically ill.

Brimah brought his wife into the house, she smelt strongly of *plassas* the local chop made of fish, palm oil and leaves and had an expressionless face. She was young and dim and had an enormous pair of pendulous breasts. There was a British paediatrician in town married to a Lebanese, so I bundled them all into the car and drove down Hillcot Road into the heat of the city. Dr Mary examined the baby, questioned the mother who seemed unable to feed it, and wrote a note to admit them into the Military Hospital. There they stayed for several weeks, the baby on the brink of death and the mother so ignorant that she had totally neglected it, Momoh did not have the strength to cry. He also had worms. I visited twice daily, irritating the nurses as death to them was part of the pattern.

"How is Brimah's baby," I enquired politely

"Not Brimah's baby, *your* baby," they shrieked with mirth.

While I was there I could hear the raucous sounds of a Mother and Baby clinic, the women Army officers teaching health, hygiene and good sense to the Wilberforce village women. The best song, delivered with force was, *When you got a pican on your back, you no want a pican in your belly,* repeated time after time with much dancing and loud laughter.

A recovered Momoh with his mother

Gradually Momoh got stronger and put on a bit of weight and the wife, nagged by the nurses, started to take an interest in him and feed him carefully and regularly. For Dr Mary, fairly new to the country, it was a learning curve, "The first thing I should do with every patient," she said, "is check them for worms." After we had left we heard that Momoh had reached his fifth birthday which is the turning point for infant survival.

The expatriate population was dwindling and, daily, Freetown was becoming more and more run down, post and telephones had ceased functioning, power was more off than on and we were totally reliant on deliveries of water by bowser. It was also becoming more dangerous, burglaries and mugging were common and road blocks appeared at night, manned by armed criminals demanding money, one of whom shot dead the Norwegian ambassador. High Commission friends were mugged by rebels with machetes, and I nearly got cut up on the beach road by a furious poda poda driver determined to ram my car.

There was a severe shortage of fuel and I spent many hours in queues along with the taxis and lorries waiting for my ration. Often fuel was adulterated and caused engine failure, which happened to us way out in the bush north of Makeni. Mike and the driver had to drop the fuel tank, drain off the diesel and filter out the water through his shirt. Several hours later the pump was cleaned and we were on our way as darkness fell. Spare parts were hard to get and, on another occasion, his Land Rover's fuel pump stopped pumping, then the wire accelerator or cable broke. Not short of ideas, his driver ended up sitting on the bonnet with one hand feeding the fuel into the engine from an oil can through a plastic pipe, and the other hand pulling a string operating the accelerator.

It was during this time that a party of us, with a lot of children, decided to visit the Banana Islands and a canopied canoe was hired from a Mr Bangura. We gathered with picnics on the beach at Number Two River without realising that it was a special religious Sunday and the sea was seething with people. Although early in the morning they had been drinking palm wine and were pretty wild. Mr Bangura's hand hewn canoe looked seaworthy if leaky, but more impressive was his very expensive brief case with a coded lock. I was confident that Mr Bangura would never allow that *fine fine* object to land at the bottom of the ocean, it had cost him far too much money.

We set off and were almost immediately surrounded by swarms of naked swimmers trying to sink us, and we had to beat them off. Some of our teenage boys became Captain Hookish and behaved rather violently, but it did the trick and the swimmers backed off. Then the little engine chugged out into the sea for the fairly short ride to the three islands either named for their shape, or for their production of bananas. We landed in a rocky inlet and were again almost immediately surrounded by unfriendly islanders. One island was completely uninhabited, the rest had a small population, there were no roads but several churches, originally the islands had been settled by freed slaves.

Off to the Banana Islands with Mr Bangura

We staked our claim on a small beach to eat our lunch, whilst the children paddled and fished around the rock pools. The islanders were restless, old women and men shouted and waved their fists yelling *Fokof! Fokof!* They made menacing moves towards us and were joined by nasty lads with sticks and machetes. Mr Bangura, and his briefcase, sensibly decided that we should embark and retreat to the peninsula. A few of our boys had already picked up useful words in *pidgin English* or *Krio* and practised their newly acquired language by yelling *Fokof! Fokof!* in return. This was not a medical term used *For Cough* and the offer of linctus, but the common term for *Go Away* in Krio. The teenage public school Captain Hooks, by now excited and angry, responded angrily with *Eff-Off* in Krio using the appropriate hand signs in English.

Mr Bangura was too nervous to land at Number Two River as the hordes were still in the sea, so he made a diversion, which necessitated baling out the canoe with bent saucepans, to land off our private beach at Baw Baw. This presented a problem as the tide was high, there was no jetty and we had to swim ashore. Some were understandably nervous, the sea was deep and choppy and they were not strong swimmers. With sense and team work the strong helped the weak and we all got ashore safely, and Mr Bangura deposited our belongings on the rocks. Night settles early in Africa, we were a long distance from our cars and the men, some not as brave as they pretended, climbed through the jungle to retrieve them while the rest of us waited. Someone had a short wave radio and was quietly listening to the football results, and another pronounced that "This has to be the time for Chocolate Bath Olivers," and offered us all a biscuit from her soggy basket.

Mike's retirement was imminent and the children flew back, Susina worked abroad with

Thomson Holidays, Simon was at Chelsea School of Art and Andrea and David were following college courses in London. Our posting in Freetown had given them the best holidays ever, and long lasting friends.

We sold our stuff, packed our boxes, enjoyed the farewell parties, made sure Brimah had a secure job and boarded a looted Russian helicopter to hop over to the airport. Next day the same helicopter crashed into the sea losing all on board.

Not long after we left, Sierra Leone and Liberia were ranked the lowest for human development and poverty, both suffering from endemic corruption, suppression of the press and the HIV/AIDS pandemic. We had clearly seen the signs on our arrival in 1980 and by 1991 the country was over-run by the Revolutionary United Front backed by Charles Taylor from Liberia, and more than 20,000 civilians died or suffered amputation by machete. Years of violent cross border civil war continued with loss of life and displacement of people reaching staggering figures. Sierra Leone had provided freedom for its settlers in the 18th century, but had become a hell hole of political corruption and violence, caused mainly by avariciousness and greed on account of diamonds. This beautiful country with delightful people is only now beginning to find its feet again, thanks to British military intervention, and maybe now there is more than one tourist footprint on Black Johnson beach.

1986 Simon at Number Two River

Postscript

Suffolk 1986 – Simon, Natalie, Andrea, Mike, Susina and David

Once settled in Suffolk we travelled independently and extensively to Europe and the Far East. Mike undertook consultancy work for BAT and I set up a secretarial business at home, then became an established freelance Business and Travel Writer doing my own marketing, as well as receiving commissions from an agent for ten years. I edited The Suffolk Sage, a nostalgia magazine, and wrote a regular column for Suffolk Norfolk Life, broadcast on BBC local radio and was a salaried secretary with the Post and Telecommunications Advisory Committee for 12 years, rewarded by an invitation to a Queen's Birthday Party at Buckingham Palace when Mike had to shake out his grey morning suit for the occasion.

We both joined British Executives Services Overseas, a quasi-government volunteer agency (a geriatric VSO), working under the auspices of the Department of Trade and Industry. Through them we travelled several times to Manchuria and Yunnan Province in China and lived and worked in tobacco factories running various projects, also a leaf extension programme in Zambia. These assignments continued our interest of being *with* people rather than viewing them from the window of a tourist bus. There is still a lot of world we want to visit.

We keep busy helping with our six grandchildren, they are great characters. Susina, the true traveller, studied Travel and Tourism at college and worked in Portugal, then London (Wincanton) before moving to Hong Kong and Australia, working in both places. She climbed Ayers Rock and bungee-jumped at Milford Sound in New Zealand and we later met up with her, Andrea and Stewart, in Madras, re-visiting old haunts, before touring Sri Lanka. She married David Sutton (HSBC) in 1993 and they have two boys. She has become today's expatriate wife and has managed moves to Korea, Hong Kong, Philippines (twice), Israel, Panama, UK (twice) and has turned full circle, ironically, setting up home in Hyderabad, Andhra Pradesh enduring power cuts and bureaucracy.

At school Simon gained the Duke of Edinburgh Gold Award. He studied graphic design, worked as a motorcycle courier in London desperately saving money to travel the world, some of the time with Amy Bradshaw, and they married in 1996. They met as teenagers in Freetown, now have two boys and are settled in Cumbria. He has worked in public relations and was marketing manager with Majestic Wine Warehouses, before joining a dynamic people development company (Impact) and continues to travel extensively. One week he can be eating kimchi in South Korea, and another he and a team will be in the Swiss Alps building igloos in which they sleep and freeze. He facilitates thought-provoking team and leadership courses, that include personal challenge activities such as sump diving, waterfall jumping and leaping out of cable cars attached to a bungee rope.

Andrea studied and worked in London before travelling to India, Kashmir and Ladakh with Stewart Rippon, and then onwards to Australia and New Zealand. They married in 1996 and have settled in Norwich with a son and daughter. Whilst coping with a newborn baby, Andrea studied and gained a First Class Honours degree in Professional Development; she now juggles with kids and teaches at the University of East Anglia, as well as freelancing as a trainer and facilitator.

David has had a varied career and, like all our children, is particularly good with people. Both he and Andrea completed tough Outward Bound Courses and David worked in retailing before moving to Saab, where he was awarded Best High Achiever for Warranty and then head hunted by H R Owen. He moved to Norfolk and joined Centurion who manufacture health and safety equipment. David married Rebecca Sutton in 2005 and they live in Norwich, where he runs his own decorating business and has completed a plumbing course at City College.

Mariamma is settled in Chilakaluripet (Chicpet) and has built a sturdy house for her family. She is now a great-grandmother and matriarch, a good woman, honest and sincere. We have returned to India many times and have arranged for her to be pensioned annually. After the hovels of Hassan she now owns a gas stove, TV and a telephone, and she calls us regularly on her mobile, "When are you coming Madams," she persuades, "My children want to see their English Mummy."

Monica became an auxiliary nurse and had a son called Lewis. He is now married to Renuka and they have a baby son. Bujie is a trained carpenter and lives with his wife Eswari and their two children, Rakesh (Raki) and Mrudula (Sonia). Premila qualified as a State Registered Nurse, works at a big hospital outside Guntur and is a theatre nurse assisting with cranial surgery. She is married to Raju, has a son called Mahendra and is expecting another baby.

Brimah Tarawally continued working with Aureol Tobacco Company. We have had no direct contact with him, but understand he escaped the horrors of the civil war. Brimah always assured us he would not join people in revolt, "Life is too sweet," he said.

Glossary

AFM	Assistant Factory Manager, Chirala
ATC	Aureol Tobacco Co Ltd, Sierra Leone
BAT	British American Tobacco Company, London
BSA	Birmingham Small Arms Company, UK (motor bikes)
BESO	British Executives Services Overseas, UK
CFAO	Compagnie Français Afrique Oriental, Ghana
CMC	Christian Medical College, Vellore, India
CSI	Church of South India
CUSO	Canadian University Service Overseas
EEC	European Economic Community
EOKA	Ethniki Organosis Kyprion Agoniston (Greek) – Greek National Organisation for Cypriot Fighters
FM	Factory Manager, Chirala
HAL	Hindustan Aeronautics Ltd, Bangalore
ILTD	Indian Leaf Tobacco Development Company *or* In Liquor 'Til Dawn
ITC	India Tobacco Company previously Imperial Tobacco Company, India
MGM	Metro Goldwyn Mayer
NAAFI	Navy, Army and Air Force Institutes, UK
PTC	Pioneer Tobacco Company, Ghana
RN	Royal Navy
TVS	Transport Vehicles Services (freight), India
UAC	United Africa Company, Ghana (Unilever)
UDI	Unilateral Declaration of Independence, Rhodesia
UTC	United Trading Company, Ghana (Swiss)
VRO	Village Reconstruction Organisation, Guntur
VSO	Voluntary Services Overseas, UK
VW	Volkswagen, Germany
WACRI	West African Cocoa Research Institute, Ghana

Bibliography, Photographs and Visuals

Bibliography

A Million Mutinies Now by VS Naipaul pub Vintage 1990
Challenge and Change - The ITC Story 1910-1985 - Champaka Basu pub Orient Longman 1988
Curries and Bugles by Jennifer Brennan pub Viking 1990
Diplomatic Baggage by Brigid Keenan pub John Murray 2005
Don't Cry for Me Sergeant Major by Robert McGowan and Jeremy Hands pub Futura 1983
Google and Wikipedia
India pub Lonely Planet 1993
Indira by Katherine Frank pub Harper Collins 2001
Kannada Made Easy by H T Rao - *By the Natural Method in Roman Characters with a Copious English-Kannada Vocabulary* 1st Ed pub D B Taraporevala Sons & Co Pvt Ltd (no date)
Leaf Tobacco pub The Economist Intelligence Unit Ltd 1980
Learn Telugu in 30 Days by K Srinivasachari pub Balaji Publications 3rd Ed 1971
Off the Beaten Track – A Traveller's Anthology by Laura Stoddart pub Orion Books 2002
Out of India by Ruth Prawer Jhabvala pub John Murray 1989
Personal correspondence 1960 onwards
Practical Key to the Kanarese Language by F Biegler, Missionary, 4th Ed pub The Kanarese Mission Book & Tract Depository, Mangalore 1920
Rhino Link - The Journal of the Kings African Rifles - various volumes.
The Chambers Dictionary 1998
The Timetables of History - Bernard Grun - Simon & Schuster/Touchstone 1991
Under the Old School Topee by Hazel Innes Craig pub1990 BACSA

Photographs and Visuals

Majority by the author, friends and family
Lobi Girl – Frank Guard
Tipu Sultan – Kesar Singh 1982
The Pioneering Years – ITC archive
The Retreat, Vadarevu – ITC archive
and Old Postcards